Assessment Policy Reform

This book highlights the impact of policy and politics on assessment across the globe. With contributions from England, the Irish Republic, Northern Ireland, Norway, Sweden, Switzerland, and Wales, it explores state-led assessment policies and practices that have been the subject of much debate.

We are experiencing a shift from using assessments—especially national tests—as measurement instruments designed to produce information, to a reliance on tests to influence policy and instruction. Once tests become high stakes—for students, teachers, and schools—even those that might have been reasonable monitors of educational success can lose dependability and credibility. However, not all countries' assessment policies follow the same model and the contributors explore and analyse a range of different national (and supra-national) assessment policy approaches and perspectives. The chapters identify the impetus behind changing assessment policies and practices and analyse ways forward and innovative approaches. Readers can draw their own conclusions about which model(s) can provide the best outcomes for learners—surely the most important part of the equation.

This book was originally published as a special issue of *Assessment in Education: Principles, Policy & Practice*.

Tina Isaacs is an Honorary Associate Professor of Educational Assessment at the UCL Institute of Education, UK. She specialises in assessment policy and politics and has written extensively about assessment policy in England and the US, as well as about culture and controversy in international examinations standards and comparative curriculum and assessment.

Iasonas Lamprianou is an Assistant Professor of Quantitative Methods at the Department of Social and Political Sciences at the University of Cyprus, Nicosia, Cyprus. In addition to his methodological interests, he specialises in high-stakes, large-scale assessments and investigates their footprint on the social and political fabric of local societies.

Assessment Policy Reform

Edited by
Tina Isaacs and Iasonas Lamprianou

Routledge
Taylor & Francis Group

LONDON AND NEW YORK

First published 2020
by Routledge
2 Park Square, Milton Park, Abingdon, Oxon, OX14 4RN

and by Routledge
52 Vanderbilt Avenue, New York, NY 10017

Routledge is an imprint of the Taylor & Francis Group, an informa business

Chapters 1–6 © 2020 Taylor & Francis
Introduction © 2018 Tina Isaacs and Iasonas Lamprianou

British Library Cataloguing-in-Publication Data
A catalogue record for this book is available from the British Library

ISBN13: 978-0-367-34522-8

Typeset in Minion Pro
by codeMantra

Publisher's Note
The publisher accepts responsibility for any inconsistencies that may have arisen during the conversion of this book from journal articles to book chapters, namely the inclusion of journal terminology.

Disclaimer
Every effort has been made to contact copyright holders for their permission to reprint material in this book. The publishers would be grateful to hear from any copyright holder who is not here acknowledged and will undertake to rectify any errors or omissions in future editions of this book.

MIX
Paper from
responsible sources
FSC™ C013985

Printed in the United Kingdom
by Henry Ling Limited

Contents

Citation Information

The chapters in this book were originally published in *Assessment in Education: Principles, Policy & Practice*, volume 25, issue 3 (June 2018). When citing this material, please use the original page numbering for each article, as follows:

For any permission-related enquiries please visit:
http://www.tandfonline.com/page/help/permissions

Notes on Contributors

Emma Armitage is a Lead Researcher in the Research & Development Division of AQA (Assessment and Qualifications Alliance), UK. She has cultivated an interest in the theoretical and methodological aspects of standard setting, as well as education policy.

Rhian Barrance is a Researcher in Education and Social Sciences at the Wales Institute for Social and Economic Research Data and Methods (WISERD), a research institute at Cardiff University, UK. Prior to joining WISERD, she completed her PhD in Education at Queen's University Belfast, UK.

Eyvind Elstad is a Full Professor at the University of Oslo, Norway. His research interests are professional development, school leadership, school reform issues, teacher evaluation, teacher education, and teachers' work.

Jannette Elwood is a Professor of Education at the School of Social Sciences, Education and Social Work, and the Dean of Graduate Studies at Queen's University Belfast, UK. She is an Executive Editor of the journal *Assessment in Education* and a Visiting Senior Research Fellow at the University of Oxford Centre for Educational Assessment, UK.

Susanne Ender is an Academic Associate at the Institute for Educational Evaluation, an Associated Institute of the University of Zurich, Switzerland. Her work focuses on the development of assessment instruments and educational reporting. She is also a PhD Candidate at the Institute of Education of the University of Zurich, Switzerland, where she analyses the impact of international standardisation and student assessment on the Swiss educational system.

John Halbert is an Acting Deputy Chief Executive of the National Council for Curriculum and Assessment, Ireland.

Flavian Imlig was a Research and Teaching Assistant in Educational Science at the University of Zurich, Switzerland. In 2017, he began working at the Zurich State Department of Education, Switzerland. His research focuses on the history of education and educational policy. He has been working on the history of teacher training in Switzerland, school reform processes, and contemporary initiatives in monitoring educational performance.

Tina Isaacs is an Honorary Associate Professor of Educational Assessment at the UCL Institute of Education, UK. She specialises in assessment policy and politics and has written extensively about assessment policy in England and the US, as well as about culture and controversy in international examinations standards and comparative curriculum and assessment.

Håkon Kavli has a Cand.Polit. in Political Science from the University of Oslo, Norway. His research interests are in teacher education, induction programmes/mentoring in schools, and education research in general. He is a director in the Department of Administration and Strategic Priorities, at the Norwegian Ministry of Education and Research.

Iasonas Lamprianou is an Assistant Professor of Quantitative Methods at the Department of Social and Political Sciences at the University of Cyprus, Nicosia, Cyprus. In addition to his methodological interests, he specialises in high-stakes, large-scale assessments and investigates their footprint on the social and political fabric of local societies.

Caroline Lau is a Data Analyst and Developer in the Centre for Education Research and Practice (CERP) at AQA, UK. Her knowledge of processing and analysing large datasets, along with her background in programming and mathematical modelling, is used to improve the way CERP approaches data and computing tasks.

Sølvi Lillejord is a Full Professor in Education, the Director for the Teacher Education program at the University of Bergen, Norway, and a Honorary Research Fellow in the Department of Education at the University of Oxford, UK. Her research interests are educational policy, research use, school leadership, teacher education, and evaluation and professional learning.

Ann MacPhail is a Professor in the Department of Physical Education and Sport Sciences at the University of Limerick, Ireland. Her main teaching and research interests revolve around instructional alignment, curriculum development, and teacher education.

Hal O'Neill retired in 2014 as the Director of Curriculum and Assessment with the National Council for Curriculum and Assessment, Ireland.

Sverre Tveit is a Lecturer at the University of Agder, Kristiansand, Norway. His research interests are primarily in the areas of educational assessment, policymaking, policy borrowing, and teacher education.

International assessment policy reform: nothing new under the sun

Tina Isaacs and Iasonas Lamprianou

For the first editorial for *Assessment in Education: Principles, Policy & Practice* in 1994 Patricia Broadfoot wrote, 'Politicians around the world are looking to changes in assessment practice to effect policy decisions concerning the conduct and desired outcomes of education. They have realised that if the stakes are high enough with individual life chances depending on the outcome of such assessments, any changes in the form or content of what is to be measured will bring about equivalent changes in curriculum emphasis' (Broadfoot, 1994, p. 1). In the almost 25 years since she penned those words, nothing much seems to have changed. If anything, politicians are increasingly using assessment policy changes in the hopes of strengthening their country's social and economic standing in the global marketplace.

Governments set assessment standards policy in the belief that learners' assessment outcomes are a good measure of national educational achievement, and that a well educated citizenry ensures that the country will be internationally competitive. They desire both to influence and to gauge reliably how well the various components of the system – including individual students and teachers, localities, regions and the nation itself – are performing against education policy objectives. Quite commonly the measure used is derived from assessment results, resulting in a shift from using assessments, especially tests and examinations, as measurement instruments designed to produce information to a reliance on testing to influence policy and instruction. Once assessment systems become high stake, even those that might be reasonable monitors of educational success can lose dependability and credibility (Koretz 2008).

State-led assessment policies and practices have been the subject of much debate. As Stephen Ball has written, 'policies are contested, interpreted and enacted in a variety of arenas of practice and the rhetorics, texts and meanings of policymakers do not always translate directly and obviously into institutional practices. ... They are inflected, mediated, resisted and misunderstood, or in some cases simply prove unworkable' (Ball, 2017, p. 10). While Ball is writing about England, we can clearly see these debates manifesting themselves in many countries. The role of national assessments can become dominated by a culture of delivery – in particular, the fast delivery of government policies as politicians look for quick wins between elections. However, not all countries' assessment policies mirror the English model and the articles in this special issue explore and analyse a range of different national (and supra-national) assessment policy approaches and perspectives. They examine the implications of high stakes testing in the relationship between assessment policy and practice, evaluating both major assessment policy reforms and particular assessment policies, as well as the relationship between assessment and governance.

Not surprisingly for a government that has an official 'nudge' unit (the Behavioural Insights Team, http://www.behaviouralinsights.co.uk/), England's policymakers have, through accountability measures, provided incentives for schools to increase student take up of the English Baccalaureate (EBacc). Armitage and Lau explore the repercussions of a policy that would see the vast majority of 14 to 16 year olds taking at least five GCSE qualifications in academic subjects, which the Government purports will give students better life chances, not least in further education and employment. Finding that increased numbers accessing the EBacc does not necessarily mean increased numbers achieving it, Armitage and Lau ask whether the policy goal of having the vast majority of students taking the EBacc is a move in the right direction. By showing clearly that 'the EBacc precipitated a dramatic rise in the number and percentage of students studying the relevant subjects, which testifies to the power of accountability measures to steer school behaviour' (p. 241), Armitage and Lau have added to the debate around assessment policy-driven curriculum change.

While ostensibly putting in assessment policy changes in the best interest of learners, policymakers rarely involve the learners themselves in policy decisions. Barrance and Elwood look at the changes that Northern Ireland and Wales have made to their GCSEs – both countries going in a different direction from England, while retaining the qualification's name – and interrogate them from students' perspectives. Using an innovative approach that included young people in framing and carrying out their mixed-method research, the authors found that young people are concerned about the loss of three country regulation – something rarely touched on in the academic literature – which undermines portability and comparability. Tellingly, they found that 'students were sceptical, not so much about what the actual changes were to GCSEs, but about their governments' *reasons* for introducing the latest reforms' (p. 265). This questioning of governmental motives is a theme that runs throughout this special issue.

Similarly, Imlig and Ender discuss the different expectations of groups of stakeholders regarding educational assessment and the use of assessment instruments. The authors identify and describe three emerging areas of conflict in the use of assessment instruments in compulsory education in Switzerland: a conceptual, an evaluation and a teaching perspective. Throughout the article it becomes evident that the complex historical and political context of the country may affect and shape both the expectations and the beliefs of stakeholders. As one might expect, research in such a complex and dynamic environment is challenging; as the authors rightfully suggest, 'the wide variety of policy and practice levels, the multiple relevant stakeholder groups or the different linguistic regions in Switzerland offer possible starting points [for further research]' (p. 285).

The different and conflicting expectations of different groups of stakeholders are also the main focus of the paper by MacPhail, Halbert and O'Neill. The Republic of Ireland has set in train education policies reforming the Junior Cycle (lower secondary) that emphasise assessment for learning and teacher-driven assessment. MacPhail, Halbert and O'Neill analyse the policies' somewhat rocky journey away from the primacy of external assessment. When in 2012 the Government proposed fundamental assessment policy reforms that essentially shifted the balance away from examinations at the end of the cycle, teachers objected, and by 2015 a compromise was reached that featured both internal and external (end of cycle) assessment. 'While a level of stability might well have returned to the school environment, the cost in reform terms was very significant (p. 322).'

Similarly to the Republic of Ireland, Norway and Sweden have seen changes to their national systems of large-scale educational assessment. Tveit reveals the 'over-(ambitious)' agenda of policymakers in the two countries, pushing towards the integration of multiple purposes of assessments into one testing programme. The study analyses both policy documents and expert interviews with politicians to suggest a conceptual framework for researching the various roles of educational assessment as they are often emphasised in governments' policies. Although there were political aspirations in both countries to have a formative assessment dimension in their national testing programmes, the official political rhetoric was shifting emphases towards the use of national tests to (a) certify, (b) govern and/or (c) support learning and instruction.

The complexities and conflicts discussed in the other papers in this issue are also evident in the teacher evaluation study by Lillejord, Elstad and Kavli. The authors present the establishment of a successful teacher evaluation system as a problem with three dimensions: the political, the administrative and the professional. The authors propose to approach it as a 'wicked problem', as it is 'difficult to solve because contradictory intentions ... are embedded in the problem' (p. 294). Teachers' evaluation, however, is closely related to professional development; achieving the 'professionalisation' of teachers needs leadership, as well as 'a collective effort within the profession to establish a joint research- and experience-based knowledge base' (p. 305).

The common thread joining all the articles of this issue is that there is often a big gap between the ambitious aspirations of policymakers and politicians and the realities on the ground. This discrepancy may sometimes seem to be too wide to bridge, making this a 'wicked problem'. In other cases, however, it is a matter of political consensus or compromise. As Ball (1990) said three decades ago, '(e)ducation policy is infused with economic, political and ideological contradictions...' (p. 211).

References

Ball, S. J. (1990). *Politics and policy-making in education: Explorations in policy sociology*. London: Routledge.

Ball, S. J. (2017). *The education policy debate* (3rd ed.). Bristol: Policy Press.

Broadfoot, P. (1994). Editorial. *Assessment in Education: Principles, Policy & Practice*, 1(1), 3–10.

Koretz, D. (2008). *Measuring up: What educational testing really tells us*. Cambridge, MA: Harvard University Press.

Is the English Baccalaureate a passport to future success?

Emma Armitage 🆔 and Caroline Lau

ABSTRACT

In England accountability measures have often been used to steer school behaviour in pursuit of policy goals. In 2010, the English Baccalaureate (EBacc) was introduced to increase uptake of traditional academic subjects at GCSE. These subjects, it was argued, would enhance students' future prospects, in part because they are favoured at A-level by high-ranking universities. However, such prospects are only likely to be accessible for students who achieve at least a grade C in these subjects since it is good grades that act as the primary gatekeepers for entry into higher education and employment. Hence, this paper seeks to problematise this claim using multilevel regression models to investigate the relationship between EBacc uptake and attainment. The findings are used to frame a discussion about the merits of encouraging more students to take the EBacc given the growing tension between the need to achieve good grades and the government-held view that all students should be studying this academic core.

Curriculum in England is tightly regulated by government both explicitly through the National Curriculum and indirectly through a dominant accountability framework; the latter of which has led to claims that the 'accountability tail wags the educational dog' (O'Neill, 2013, p. 9). Since 1988, state schools[1] have had to follow a National Curriculum, which outlines the subjects that students must be taught and the assessments they must sit across four compulsory key stages (Isaacs, 2010). The two most relevant stages for this paper are Key Stage 2 (KS2) and Key Stage 4 (KS4). At the end of KS2, when they are 11 years old and about to transition from primary to secondary school, students sit English and mathematics assessments on which their performance is categorised as 'beyond expectations', 'at level expected' or 'below expectations' (Department for Education [DfE], 2010a). At the end of KS4 when they are 16 years old most students sit high-stakes GCSE assessments in, on average, eight subjects, which must include English, mathematics and science. Their performance is graded on an eight-point scale ranging from A* to G.[2] In stark contrast to the high degree of centralisation in the earlier curriculum, and the subject prescription in other countries (DfE, 2015g), when choosing their remaining GCSE subjects students have traditionally been given a reasonable degree of freedom (DfE, 2015a; Hodgson & Spours,

ⓑ Supplemental data for this article can be accessed at https://doi.org/10.1080/0969594X.2017.1396203.

2011). In 2010, the creation of a new accountability measure changed that, and it is with this policy change that the current paper is concerned

In 2010, the then Secretary of State for Education Michael Gove, introduced the English Baccalaureate (EBacc), a school performance measure which reports the percentage of students who enter, and achieve A* to C grades in a specific suite of GCSE[3] subjects: English,[4] mathematics, science,[5] either geography or history, and a modern or ancient foreign language (DfE, n.d, 2010a, 2015g). This was followed in 2015 by the announcement that in future cohorts 90% of students will be required to enter the EBacc (DfE, 2015a, 2017c), and in 2016 the introduction of Attainment and Progress 8, new headline performance measures which also afford privileged status to the EBacc subjects[6] (DfE, 2017a). Together these changes represent a shift in England's accountability system from a focus on the number of A* to C grades students achieve – the primary school performance metric until 2015 – to increased emphasis on the subjects being studied, thus, signifying a new interest from the state in the specific knowledge students acquire during their secondary education rather than just the standard of qualification they achieve. Since English, mathematics and science were already compulsory in effect the EBacc served to elevate the status of humanities and languages.

Accountability measures in England are used to rank schools in performance tables and as such have considerable power to drive curriculum provision and assessment in schools (Hutchings, 2015; O'Neill, 2013; Taylor, 2016). Indeed, one of the rationales for introducing the EBacc was to combat schools' attempts to improve their A* to C pass rate by entering students for less rigorous GCSEs or equivalent qualifications in which they might be more likely to attain a grade C (DfE, 2010b, 2013b; Wolf, 2011). Instead the government wanted to incentivise the uptake of rigorous academic subjects argued to be most likely to enhance students' future educational and occupational prospects (DfE, 2010b, 2015b; Long & Bolton, 2017), in part, because they are favoured at A-level by high-ranking universities (Russell Group, 2011). However, arguably such prospects are only accessible for students who achieve good grades in these subjects. Grades A* to C are considered 'good GCSE passes' and therefore, grade C typically acts as the primary gatekeeper for entry into higher education (Russell Group, 2011; Which, 2016) and employment, rather than the subjects studied. Hence, this paper seeks to investigate the impact of the EBacc as a new performance measure and to problematise the assumption that studying the EBacc will enhance students' future prospects, by analysing the relationship between EBacc uptake and attainment between 2010 and 2014. It should be noted at this point that the EBacc is not a qualification for students. Students enter and achieve GCSEs in *EBacc eligible subjects* that are later packaged as *the EBacc* in school performance tables. However, hereafter the phrases 'entered the EBacc' and 'achieved the EBacc' are used as shorthand.

The case that was made for introducing an academic core identifies some clear benefits for students, yet it has also ignited debates about the merits of a prescribed versus self-selected curriculum and which subjects constitute the most appropriate core (House of Commons Education Select Committee, 2011). England has traditionally given students more freedom than many other countries (DfE, 2015a; Hodgson & Spours, 2011) to choose the subjects they study, meaning that in any given GCSE cohort students can be studying a number of different subject groupings. Hence, on one hand, and consistent with government rhetoric, providing students with clear parameters on subject choice might mitigate against the risk of them choosing subjects which prematurely narrow their future options or prove incompatible with their career aspirations (McCrone, Morris, & Walker, 2005). However, such prescription reduces students' freedom to choose GCSE subjects that align with their interests and perceived ability, factors that are known to influence their decision-making (Stables & Wikeley, 1999; Wilkins & Meeran, 2011). Moreover, it has been reported that pressure on schools to increase the size of their EBacc entry has resulted in students being channelled into particular subjects based on ability, in some cases via the use of tailored GCSE option booklets, which direct students who are seen as academically able towards the EBacc subjects and those seen as less able towards a less academic subject combination (Robertson, 2016). These attempts to influence subject choice could prove detrimental to students' motivation and level of engagement in their chosen subjects (Neumann, Towers, Gewirtz, & Maguire, 2016), which in turn may negatively impact upon the GCSE grades they achieve.

Equally divisive is the subject composition of the EBacc, which focuses on a 'rigorous academic core' of subjects (DfE, 2010b, 2015a, 2015b). Opposed parties argue that it lacks an evidence-based rationale (House of Commons Education Select Committee, 2011), and that Religious Studies (National Association of Teachers of Religious Education, 2012), the arts (Expressive Arts Subjects, 2016; Royal Society for the encouragement of Arts, Manufactures & Commerce, 2016) and more technical disciplines (Baker, 2016) are equally rigorous. Rigour has played an important role in defining the EBacc, yet the concept of rigour remains curiously undefined in this context.

Perhaps, the most obvious assumption is that rigour means difficulty and therefore, it is the challenge posed by the EBacc subjects that makes them especially worthwhile. This argument finds indirect support from elite universities who explicitly prioritise these subjects (Russell Group, 2011), and the fact that traditionally they have been studied by high ability students (Cadwallader, 2012; Iannelli, 2013; Jin, Muriel, & Sibieta, 2011). A related interpretation is that rigour refers to the perceived importance of the knowledge contained within the EBacc subjects (DfE, 2015c). Education ministers have described them as providing 'intellectual and cultural capital' (DfE, 2016c) and 'the foundations of a good education' (DfE, 2015e). This perspective is aligned with the historically high status position these subjects have occupied in the curriculum hierarchy, which in turn is rooted in the idea that the theoretical focus of traditional academic subjects is more valuable than the practical focus of other subjects (Bleazby, 2015). However, Bleazby (2015) argues that such assertions are 'embedded in a dubious epistemological framework that equates knowledge with certainty' (p. 672). Another possibility is that labelling the EBacc subjects as rigorous simply reflects the government's desire to draw a clear distinction between them and poor quality GCSE equivalent or vocational qualifications (DfE, 2015a, 2015d; Muir, 2013; Wolf, 2011). The lack of clarity regarding the meaning of the term rigour in relation to the EBacc, and indeed the justification for the subjects included in it, are two of the reasons it is important to investigate the impact of incentivising its uptake.

Success in the EBacc subjects rests, in part, on students' ability to perform well at GCSE (Cook, 2013). School leaders, while recognising the merits of a core curriculum, have consistently argued that the EBacc subjects are unsuitable for students who are not academically inclined and whose path to success might reside in the study of other subjects or vocational qualifications (Greevey, Knox, Nunney, & Pye, 2012; SSAT, 2015; Vaughan, 2015). Such claims are countered by the DfE (2015e; 2016a), who argue that low expectations of any student are unacceptable and serve to further entrench educational inequalities. However, historically, clear biases are evident in the EBacc candidature.

Retrospective analyses of pre-EBacc cohorts reveal that prior to its formalisation as a performance measure, the EBacc subjects were more likely to be offered by selective schools and less likely to be offered by schools with a high proportion of students eligible for free-school meals (Jin et al., 2011). Furthermore, in 2009 the EBacc (had it existed) would have been achieved by fewer, but more academically able, students than the five A* to C metric (Cadwallader, 2012). This evidence of an association between high prior attainment and EBacc uptake was not taken into account by a DfE statistical bulletin (2011), which reported that students who would have achieved the EBacc in 2006 were more likely to remain in education at age 19 and less likely to be 'not in education or employment' (NEET), than those who achieved 5 A* to C grades in a wider selection of subjects. Since this analysis did not control for prior or concurrent attainment it may be that the students who achieved the EBacc (which requires six or seven[7] A* to C grades) were a higher ability cohort with better overall GCSE performance than students who achieved five A* to C grades, and therefore, more likely to succeed regardless of the subjects studied.

Beyond the methodological issues with this analysis, it is interesting to note that it highlights the benefits reaped by those who *achieved* the EBacc, rather than merely *studied* it. This is an important distinction given that entry onto A level courses and into employment typically depends on a certain level of attainment, rather than programme of study (DfE, 2015d, 2015f; Which, 2016). Thus, while students who achieve the EBacc may well benefit from a broader range of A level subject choices, including those prioritised by top universities (Russell Group, 2011), than students who take other subject combinations, what is gained by students who fail to achieve the EBacc remains an open question. The answer to this question hinges on where the EBacc's value lies – in the grades achieved or the subject combination itself. If the former is true this lends support to the critics' argument: students who are less academically able or whose interests lie elsewhere might be better served aiming high in non-EBacc subjects. Conversely, if there is some inherent value in studying this combination of subjects irrespective (within reason) of the grades achieved, then entering the majority of students might be advisable.

While the evidence reviewed thus far supports the former view, support for the latter perspective can be found in Cadwallader's (2012) retrospective analysis of the 2009 GCSE cohort. After accounting for the influence of prior attainment, gender and school type he found that students *studying* the EBacc achieved a higher average GCSE grade than those who did not study it. Speculating about the reasons for this, Cadwallader suggested that these subjects might foster transferable skills. For instance, studying mathematics might improve physics performance and the literacy skills developed in English may be beneficial in history. However, it should be noted that the final regression model only accounted for 55% of the variance in average GCSE grade, weakening the claims that can be made about the benefits of the EBacc. Moreover, if the EBacc entrants in this cohort were high-attaining students any advantage conferred by the EBacc may be specific to this type of entry. Hence, the possibility that this collection of subjects somehow boosts overall performance warrants further study. Accordingly, one of the main aims of the current study is to investigate the presence and extent of this 'EBacc effect' in more recent post-EBacc cohorts, which evidence suggests have diversified.

The introduction of the EBacc triggered a rise in entries, which increased by 17% between 2010 and 2015 (DfE, 2015g) as schools made rapid adjustments. In 2011, a survey of 1500 maintained secondary schools revealed that the EBacc had influenced the curriculum offer in 52% of them (Centre for Analysis of Youth Transitions, 2011). Many schools reported facilitating the EBacc without enforcing it by ensuring classes were scheduled to allow all students the option to take it (Greevey et al., 2012). Running counter to this, they also reported that several schools were continuing to recommend it for only the more academically able students, perhaps, reflecting the perception that taking this subject combination is only beneficial if it results in good GCSE grades, typically grade C or above. In line with this, recent work comparing EBacc uptake between 2012 and 2015 has shown that a larger percentage of high-attaining students are entered for every EBacc subject pillar, and that these students are largely responsible for the rise in entries to humanities and languages (Allen, 2015). Nonetheless, entries to science have increased for middle ability students and more low ability students are entering English literature.

Focusing on schools that made especially rapid adjustments to their KS4 curriculum between 2010 and 2013, Allen and Thompson (2016) found that middle ability students were those most affected by efforts to improve EBacc uptake. In these schools although the percentage (of all students) attaining the EBacc improved from 4% to 20%, the average grade in all EBacc subjects fell, most likely reflecting the change in candidature. It is clear then that the EBacc has had a significant impact on the proportion of students studying what is argued to be a rigorous academic core, and that as a result of changes in school entry behaviour (Allen, 2015; Allen & Thompson, 2016; Greevey et al., 2012) more recent EBacc cohorts may have had a more mixed academic profile than previous cohorts (Cadwallader, 2012; Jin et al., 2011). However, to date little research has attempted to link changing entries to attainment in order to evaluate the claim that studying the EBacc will enhance students' future prospects. This therefore constitutes the main focus of the current study, for which the principal research questions are:

(1) How has EBacc uptake changed between 2010 and 2014, and does uptake differ according to prior attainment and school type?
(2) How has EBacc achievement changed between 2010 and 2014, and does achievement differ according to prior attainment and school type?
(3) Do those students who study the EBacc achieve better grades at GCSE than those who do not, regardless of whether they achieve the EBacc or not?

Method

The analysis included 3,078,999 Year 11 candidates from the National Pupil Database (NPD) who had taken at least one full course GCSE in England between June 2010 and June 2014. Students were matched to their prior KS2 attainment, where possible.[8] To ensure a representative sample only Year 11 students, who are typically aged 16 when they sit the majority of their GCSEs, were included in the analysis since they constitute the main cohort of GCSE candidates and thus, exemplify a 'typical' path through education. However, where these students had sat one or more GCSEs early these results were included in the analysis. To ensure consistency with performance tables, where students had sat the same GCSE specification multiple times their best grade was included in the years 2010–2013, while their first grade was included in 2014.[9]

In order to analyse EBacc uptake and attainment in relation to prior and concurrent attainment and school type, average KS2 level, average GCSE grade and school type variables were created. Average KS2 levels were determined by first calculating a student's levels for English, mathematics and science, using their individual test marks and the associated threshold marks, and second averaging these three levels. Average GCSE scores were calculated by converting letter grades into numeric values (e.g. A* = 8, A = 7 ..., U = 0) and taking the mean across all full course GCSE subjects taken. Students who took fewer than three GCSEs were considered atypical, since three subjects is the minimum number of GCSEs usually taken (in English, mathematics and science), and thus, were not given an average GCSE score.[10] As such these students were included in the descriptive statistics regarding EBacc entries and attainment, but were excluded from the multilevel regression analysis. The averaging method used gave equal weight to all subjects such that, for example, an A grade in dance was worth the same as an A grade in chemistry. While there has been considerable debate in England about aligning grade standards in different subjects no action has been taken to ensure inter-subject comparability (Ofqual, 2017), hence our method is consistent with the way GCSE grades are awarded and used. Schools were classified into six categories: comprehensive, selective, secondary modern, independent, academy and free schools.

EBacc eligibility was calculated by first, identifying the eligible GCSE qualifications in each subject for each year using qualification accreditation numbers (QAN), and second identifying those students who had taken eligible qualifications in all of the necessary EBacc pillars – English, mathematics, science, humanities and languages. EBacc attainment was then calculated by determining whether students' grades in each subject pillar met the conditions needed to 'pass'. These are subject-specific but generally demand that students attain a grade C or higher. It was therefore possible to distinguish between three groups of students: (1) students who took EBacc eligible qualifications and achieved the grades needed to 'pass' the EBacc, (2) students who took EBacc eligible qualifications and did not get the grades necessary to achieve the EBacc and (3) students who did not take the full suite of EBacc eligible qualifications.

The EBacc variables were computed using slightly different criteria for each year between 2010 and 2014 as a result of changes in the qualifications deemed EBacc-eligible. This ensured that our EBacc entry and attainment figures accurately reflected schools' efforts to enter students for the EBacc, and the percentage of students who achieved it. A small number of AS level qualifications are eligible for the EBacc but are not included in the calculations here because they are higher level qualifications than GCSEs so taking them at age 16 is atypical of the GCSE population. This is unlikely to have affected the correct classification of EBacc students since it would be very unusual for a student to take an AS qualification in a subject that they were not also taking, or had previously taken, at GCSE. For instance, if a student were taking AS History we would also expect them to have taken GCSE History, meaning the student would be classified as entering the EBacc regardless of whether AS qualifications were included in the calculations.

Results

EBacc uptake and success between 2010 and 2014

Between 2010 and 2012, the percentage of students entered for the EBacc remained stable but in 2013 and 2014 a large increase in entries occurred; the 2013 GCSE cohort were the first group of students to have made their subject choices (in 2011) after the introduction of the EBacc (in 2010). The marked increase in the number and percentage of students entering the EBacc was accompanied by a decrease in the percentage of *entrants* achieving the EBacc (see Table 1). Although a greater *number* of students achieved the EBacc in 2013 and 2014, these students represented a smaller *proportion* of the entry cohort than in previous years.

The highest *proportion* of EBacc entries consistently came from selective schools, in which between 73 and 83% of students entered the EBacc. Similarly, selective schools had the highest *proportion* of students achieving the EBacc, closely followed by independent schools. The lowest proportion of EBacc entries came from secondary modern schools, in which between 11 and 23% of students entered. They also had the lowest proportion of students achieving the EBacc.

EBacc uptake and success according to prior attainment categories and school type

In order to examine whether the *nature* as well as the *size* of the EBacc entry had changed between 2010 and 2014 students were grouped into three prior attainment categories used by the DfE (2010b; 2016b; 2017b): 'low-attainers' (students who attained an average KS2 score lower than a level 4), 'middle-attainers' (students who attained an average KS2 score of a level 4) and 'high-attainers' (students who attained an average KS2 score above a level 4). The entry and success rates of these groups across different school types were then explored (see Supplementary Appendices A, B and C for a breakdown of the raw figures).

Differing entry and attainment patterns and differences in the conversion rate from entries to attainment emerged for each prior attainment category (see Figures 1(a) and (b)). Very few low-attaining students were entered for the EBacc, and only a small proportion of those entered went on to achieve it between 2010 and 2014. By comparison more middle-attaining students were entered for the EBacc and a larger proportion of entrants in

Table 1. Percentage of students who entered and achieved the EBacc between 2010 and 2014.

Year	Entered for EBacc	Achieved EBacc (as a % of those entered)
2010	140,429 (22.5%)	99,365 (70.8%)
2011	135,671 (22.1%)	97,881 (72.2%)
2012	135,536 (22.2%)	96,003 (70.8%)
2013	211,665 (34%)	137,872 (65.1%)
2014	227,651 (37.4%)	139,669 (61.4%)

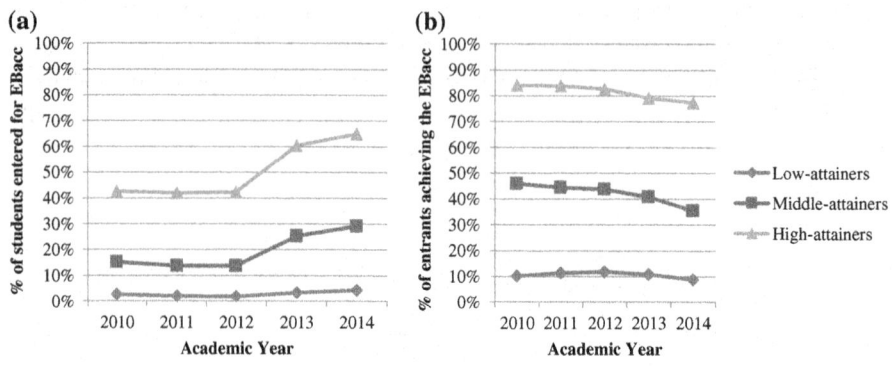

Figure 1. (a) Percentage of low-, middle- and high-attainers entering the EBacc between 2010 and 2014. (b) Percentage of low-, middle- and high-attaining entrants achieving the EBacc between 2010 and 2014.

this group achieved it. However, high-attaining students were the most likely to enter and achieve the EBacc. These patterns did not differ substantially across different school types.

Strikingly, similar *changes* occurred over time for all three prior attainment categories. In each group an increase in the number and percentage of entries in 2013 and 2014 was accompanied by a decrease in the percentage of entrants achieving the EBacc. Again, although a greater *number* of students in each group achieved the EBacc, these students represented a smaller proportion of their respective entry cohorts than in previous years. This effect was most pronounced for the middle-attaining group; between 2012 and 2014 the proportion of students being entered rose from 13.8 to 25.4%, while the proportion of entrants achieving the EBacc fell from 43.8 to 35.4%, suggesting that the chances of EBacc success for students in this group are the most uncertain. These patterns held across school types with the exception of independent and selective schools. In the former, percentage entries and attainment remained stable, and in the latter the percentage of middle- and high-attaining students achieving the EBacc remained stable.

Failure to achieve the EBacc

Between 2010 and 2014, the percentage of students who were entered for the EBacc but did not achieve it rose from 29 to 39%. The majority of these students failed to achieve a grade C in a language (see Figure 2); this pattern held for middle- and high-attaining students across all school types. By contrast, low-attaining students more often failed science or humanities subjects. However, this pattern was less striking and inconsistent across school type, since there was a smaller disparity between individual subject failure rates in this group.

The majority of students who entered but did not achieve the EBacc failed to get a grade C or above in only one EBacc eligible subject, although the percentage failing to get a grade C or above in multiple eligible subjects has been rising since 2012 (see Figure 3).

These patterns did not hold for students in every prior attainment category. Students in the low prior attainment category who entered but did not achieve the EBacc had an average GCSE score on the grade D/E borderline (see Table 2), and a larger percentage of these

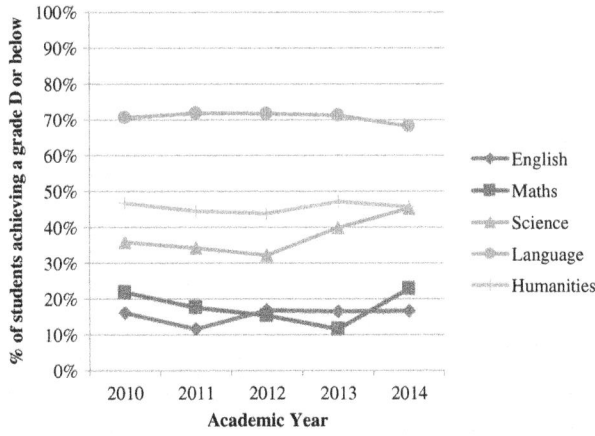

Figure 2. Percentage of students (who did not achieve the EBacc) attaining a grade D or lower in each EBacc eligible subject between 2010 and 2014.

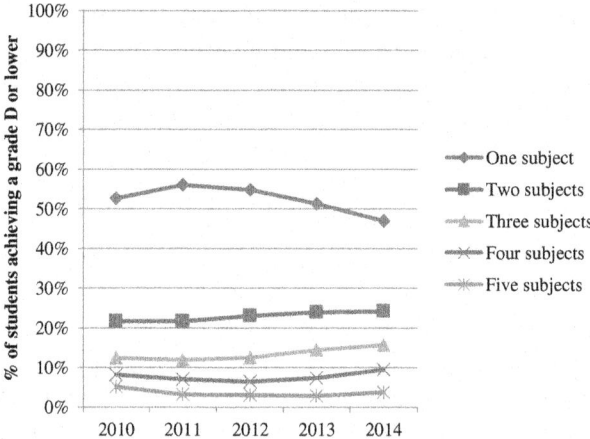

Figure 3. Percentage of students attaining a grade D or lower in one, two, three, four or all five EBacc eligible subjects.

students failed multiple EBacc eligible subjects than failed a single eligible subject. Students categorised as middle-attainers who entered but did not achieve the EBacc had an average GCSE score on the grade C/D borderline, confirming that their chances of obtaining the EBacc are the most uncertain. Approximately, 45% of these students failed to get a grade C in a single subject – most often a language – while the remaining 55% failed multiple subjects. Finally, high-attaining students who entered but did not achieve the EBacc had an average GCSE score equal to a grade C, and the majority failed a single subject – most often a language. However, it is important to note that the percentage of middle- and high-attaining students failing to achieve a grade C in multiple subjects has been rising since 2012. These distinct patterns held across all school types.

The EBacc and average GCSE attainment

Linear multilevel regression models with random intercepts were used to explore the relationship between entering the EBacc and average GCSE attainment, given claims that studying this collection of subjects will improve students' future prospects. The models have two-levels, individual student at level 1 and school at level 2. The data met all necessary assumptions for multilevel modelling. The two most important variables – average GCSE score and average KS2 score – were normally distributed. Average KS2 score exhibited a slight negative skew since the majority of students achieve scores between 3 and 6 on a scale that ranges from 0 to 6, but no ceiling effects. There was some evidence of ceiling effects in

Table 2. Average GCSE grade of students who did not achieve the EBacc, according to prior attainment category (grade B = 6, grade C = 5, grade D = 4).

	Academic year				
	2010	2011	2012	2013	2014
High-attaining students	5.37	5.38	5.36	5.24	5.22
Middle-attaining students	4.82	4.84	4.83	4.75	4.74
Low-attaining students	3.91	4.00	4.05	4.04	4.02

average GCSE score with approximately 0.5% of students achieving the maximum score of 8. The effect this had on the analysis is discussed.

The model of average GCSE score – the outcome variable – y_{ij} for student i who attended school j is:

$$y_{ij} = \beta_0 + \beta_1 x_{ij} + \beta_2 x_{ij} + \beta_3 x_{ij} + \ldots, + u_j + e_{ij}$$

where the explanatory variables are x_{ij} (student level) or x_j (school level). The student level explanatory variables were *prior attainment* measured by average KS2 score (centred), *gender*,[11] a series of dummy variables denoting *academic year*,[12] and *EBacc eligibility*: whether or not a student took GCSE subjects that made them eligible for the EBacc (irrespective of whether they achieved the grades necessary to secure it). The only school level explanatory variable included was *school type*, denoted by a series of dummy variables.[13] The fixed part of the model is represented by the n regression coefficients $\beta_1, \ldots, \beta_n$, while the random part of the model is represented by the error terms – $u_j + e_{ij}$, where u_j is the school (level 2) residual and e_{ij} is the student (level 1) residual. Both residuals are assumed to be normally distributed and independent. Incorporating fixed and random effects into the model accounts for the hierarchical structure of our data, in which students are clustered within schools. Using a multilevel model to explicitly model this dependency ensures accurate standard errors.

Four models were built and are summarised in Tables 3 and 4. Model 1 confirmed the existence of between-school variance in average GCSE score and thus, validated the use

Table 3. Multilevel model fixed effect coefficients for average GCSE score.

Fixed effects	Model 1 (null) B	SE	Model 2 B	SE	Model 3 B	SE	Model 4 B	SE
Intercept	4.84	0.01*	4.67	0.010*	4.56	0.010*	4.56	0.009*
Prior attainment			1.60	0.001*	1.46	0.001*	1.43	0.001*
Gender			0.32	0.001*	0.30	0.001*	0.30	0.001*
School type: Ref Comp								
Selective			0.85	0.044*	0.64	0.041*	0.83	0.042*
Secondary modern			0.02	0.033	0.01	0.032	0.02	0.032
Independent			0.67	0.020*	0.69	0.019*	0.81	0.019*
Academy			0.23	0.016*	0.19	0.015*	0.21	0.015*
Academic year: Ref 2010								
2011			−0.03	0.002*	−0.02	0.002*	−0.02	0.002*
2012			−0.08	0.002*	−0.07	0.002*	−0.07	0.002*
2013			−0.10	0.002*	−0.16	0.002*	−0.02	0.002*
2014			−0.14	0.002*	−0.22	0.002*	−0.26	0.002*
EBacc					0.55	0.001*	0.50	0.013*
EBacc*Prior attainment							0.17	0.003*
*EBacc*School type*								
EBacc*Selective							−0.27	0.009*
EBacc*Secondary modern							−0.09	0.010*
EBacc*Independent							−0.43	0.007*
EBacc*Academy							−0.06	0.003*
*EBacc*Academic year*								
EBacc*2011							−0.03	0.004*
EBacc*2012							−0.00	0.004
EBacc*2013							0.07	0.004*
EBacc*2014							0.12	0.004*

*Denotes *B* coefficients more than twice their SE.

Table 4. Multilevel model random effect coefficients for average GCSE score.

	Model 1		Model 2		Model 3		Model 4	
	Variance	SD	Variance	SD	Variance	SD	Variance	SD
Random effects								
School residual	1.106	1.052	0.2951	0.5432	0.2590	0.5089	0.2608	0.5107
Student residual	1.608	1.268	0.7455	0.8634	0.7019	0.8378	0.6993	0.8363
Variance partition coefficient (VPC)	41%	–	28%	–	27%	–	27%	
Log-likelihood	−4,347,184		−3,340,465		−3,261,515		−3,256,686	–
Deviance (−2*log likelihood)	711,248		2,013,438		157,901		9656.6	
Marginal R^2	–		52%		55%		55%	
Conditional R^2	41%		65%		67%		67%	

of a multilevel modelling approach. Model 2 revealed that including prior attainment, gender, school type and academic year as fixed effects reduced the between-school variance by 13% and explained 65% (R^2C) of the total variance in average GCSE score, 52% of which was explained by the fixed effects (R^2M). Model 3 showed that adding the EBacc as a fixed effect results in a small decrease in between-school variance, and increases the total amount of variance explained to 67%. On average, students who took the EBacc achieved an average GCSE score that was approximately half a grade higher than their non-EBacc peers. Finally, including interactions between the EBacc and other fixed effects in model 4 did not reduce the between-school variance or explain any additional variance in average GCSE score; however, due to their direct relevance to the question of how taking the EBacc affects average GCSE score, they were retained. Thus, the final model explained 67% of the variance in average GCSE score. Of the remaining unexplained variance 27% was due to unmeasured differences between schools.

Model 4 showed that EBacc students with average prior attainment who attended a comprehensive school in 2010 achieved average GCSE scores that were approximately half a grade higher (.50) than their non-EBacc peers. However, the *EBacc* School Type* interactions revealed that compared to comprehensive schools this effect was smaller in every other school type, although only markedly so in independent[14] (−.43) and selective schools (−.27), as indicated by their much flatter slopes. The *EBacc* Academic* Year interaction demonstrated that the EBacc effect has changed over time; compared to 2010, the effect was smaller in 2011 and 2012 but larger in 2013 and 2014. The *EBacc* Prior Attainment* interaction showed that the slope of prior attainment was steeper for EBacc (1.43 + .17) than non-EBacc students (1.43), indicating that the gap between the average GCSE scores of these two groups widens as prior attainment increases. On this basis, the answer to the question of whether students who study the EBacc achieve better grades at GCSE than those who do not, would appear to be yes. However, since causality cannot be inferred, *why* this is the case, particularly given that the magnitude of the effect is dependent upon prior attainment, school type and academic year, remains open to debate; an issue which is returned to in the discussion.

After fitting the final model, inspection of the standardised residuals revealed that approximately 0.3% of observations fell outside ±3 standard deviations, the majority of which fell outside −3 standard deviations.[15] This suggests that the model does not adequately predict average GCSE score of students at the extremes of the distribution, which may, at the top end, be the result of ceiling effects caused by the restricted range on which GCSEs are graded.

Excluding students with large residuals did not significantly improve the model or have a large impact on the coefficients and therefore they remain in the final model.

Discussion

The purpose of this paper was to bring together analysis of EBacc uptake and attainment between 2010 and 2014 to investigate the impact of this new performance metric, and evaluate the policy assumption that studying the EBacc will enhance students' future prospects. The findings reveal that the EBacc precipitated a dramatic rise in the number and percentage of students studying the relevant subjects, which testifies to the power of accountability measures to steer school behaviour (Hutchings, 2015; O'Neill, 2013; Taylor, 2016). Consistent with existing research (Allen, 2015), we found a more pronounced increase in entries from middle- and high-attaining students than from low-attaining students. Thus, at a national level, schools appear to have responded to the EBacc's introduction by entering more academically able students, which resonates with the perceptions of school leaders that these are the students best suited to the academic rigour of the EBacc subjects (Greevey et al., 2012; SSAT, 2015; Vaughan, 2015). This belief is borne out to some extent by the finding that students with high prior attainment were the most likely to enter and achieve the EBacc, followed by middle-attaining students. By contrast, students with low prior attainment were the least likely to enter or achieve the EBacc, and when they did not achieve it tended to fail (i.e. achieve lower than a grade C) multiple subjects. However, in 2013 when EBacc entries rose middle-attaining students experienced the second largest rise in entries (after high-attainers) but the sharpest fall in attainment. The success rate of high-attaining students also fell. This suggests that entering more students of a similar academic profile to those entered previously may be insufficient to improve EBacc attainment. Examining EBacc failure rates provided more insight.

Failure to achieve the EBacc

The majority of low-attaining students who entered but did not achieve the EBacc failed to achieve a grade C in multiple EBacc subjects and had an average GCSE score one grade lower than is considered to be a 'good pass'. Similarly, half of the middle-attaining students who entered but did not achieve the EBacc also failed to achieve a grade C in multiple subjects. This could be construed as support for the argument that for some students a general lack of academic aptitude, which could stem from a number of sources such as poor school experiences, teachers with low expectations, or a deprived background, acts as a barrier to EBacc success (SSAT, 2015). On the other hand, these barriers would be expected to be equally detrimental to success in non-EBacc GCSE subjects. That is, unless reaching the grade C benchmark in the EBacc subjects is more challenging for these students than it is in other subject combinations, which is one interpretation of the government's claim that they are rigorous. The latter is plausible given the historically low EBacc entry rates of, in particular, the low-attainers, and school leaders' objections to increasing those entry rates on the basis that these students are unlikely to achieve grade Cs in one or more of them (Greevey et al., 2012). Alternatively, such perceptions may mean that these students are not well catered for in EBacc subject lessons (Francis et al., 2017; Hodgson & Spours, 2011); the tendency for schools to focus on students on the grade C/D borderline is well-documented (Ball, Maguire, Braun, Perryman, & Hoskins, 2012; Hutchings, 2015).

The remaining middle-attainers and the majority of high-attainers who entered but did not achieve the EBacc failed to achieve a grade C in only a single EBacc subject, most commonly a language. Hence, for them EBacc failure may be attributable to subject-specific weaknesses, or in the case of languages, could be indicative of systemic issues in the discipline (Teaching Schools Council, 2016). An in-depth discussion of these issues is beyond the scope of this paper but they include insufficient teachers (Allen, 2016; TES, 2017), a lack of student engagement (Ofsted, 2015; Stables & Wikeley, 1999), the perception that languages are difficult (Greevey et al., 2012; Ofsted, 2015) and severely graded (Coe, 2008; Coe, Searle, Barmby, Jones, & Higgins, 2008; Ofqual, 2014, 2015), and that they are devoted less curriculum time than English, mathematics and science (Schmidt, Burroughs, Zoido, & Houang, 2015; Sousa & Armor, 2010; Worth & De Lazzari, 2017).

Regardless of the reason(s) for their failure, the growing number of entrants not achieving the EBacc serves to caution against entering 90% of future cohorts (DfE, 2015a, 2017). Coupled with previous research (Allen, 2015; Allen & Thompson, 2016; Greevey et al., 2012), our findings indicate that this target would have the largest and most detrimental impact on low-attaining students who currently comprise the smallest proportion of the EBacc entry and have the lowest pass rate. However, it may also see the attainment rate of higher attaining students fall, as was the case between 2012 and 2014, when entries rose and the percentage attainment rate fell. This is especially likely if the barriers to achievement in the languages are not addressed.

If the value in studying this academic core lies solely in the grades achieved then students who do not achieve the EBacc may not benefit, primarily because the English education system typically prioritises grades over subjects studied. Most post-16 institutions require GCSE grades of a C or above in the subjects a student wishes to take at A-level (Which, 2016), and some universities require a grade C or above in GCSE English, mathematics and science. Hence, if a student who achieved grade Ds in history and French would have achieved two grade Cs in non-EBacc subjects, rather than keeping students' options open, the EBacc might inadvertently limit access to pathways where the entry requirements are grade C or above (Russell Group, 2011, p. 27). This could exacerbate rather than remedy existing educational inequalities because high-attaining students and students from independent and selective schools are still more likely to achieve the grade Cs needed to secure the EBacc than their lower attaining counterparts and peers in different school types. Hence, as entries continue to rise the grades achieved and opportunities available to different groups of students would diverge further, particularly if, as seems likely, more students from the groups with poorer attainment rates are entered for the EBacc in future. Conversely, if a student were likely to achieve grade Ds in both subject combinations, the EBacc might offer more opportunities if concessions were made on the basis of the EBacc subjects being more academically rigorous or facilitative, at least in terms of A level subject options and university entry (Russell Group, 2011).

The EBacc effect

The current analysis cannot speak to the possibility that EBacc students would have achieved better grades in other subjects However, in line with existing work (Cadwallader, 2012) our multilevel regression models, which accounted for 67% of the variance in average GCSE score, identified a positive association between the EBacc and average GCSE score, after controlling for the influence of prior attainment, gender, school type and academic year. Students who studied the EBacc subjects achieved average GCSE grades that were approximately half a grade higher than non-EBacc students. Intuitively this finding seems to suggest that there is something valuable about studying the EBacc subject combination, which has a facilitative effect on attainment akin to the Gestalt principle – the whole is more than the sum of its parts (Cadwallader, 2012). Perhaps the EBacc subjects are especially concept-based in nature (Young, 2011) and as a result, students studying them experience repeated cross-discipline exposure to new ways of understanding the world that facilitate knowledge acquisition, and the higher order thinking skills that are required to access higher GCSE grades. Equally, it may be that the content and skills required by EBacc subjects overlap such that gains in one transfer to the others. This could inflate the average GCSE scores of EBacc students relative to students who study more disparate subjects that perhaps encourage a more siloed style of learning. For instance, the critical thinking skills required to interpret an English text might be equally useful in evaluating the utility of an historical source.

The possibility that studying the EBacc facilitates GCSE performance serves to balance the arguments against encouraging EBacc uptake for the majority of students. However, the grade advantage associated with it is small and therefore unlikely to offset generally poor performance, except for students whose gains lift them over the grade C threshold. If this boost is genuinely attributable to studying the EBacc subjects, from a pragmatic viewpoint how advisable it would be to enter the majority of students depends on whether employers and higher education institutions are willing to make concessions for students who study the EBacc, in recognition of their value, but do not achieve at least grade Cs. However, it is pertinent to consider equally plausible non-causal explanations for the EBacc effect. Although the relationship between the EBacc and higher average GCSE scores identified by multilevel modelling is robust – it persists when controlling for a variety of factors and the models explain a large proportion of the variance in average GCSE score – causality cannot be inferred. Furthermore, the final model revealed that the magnitude of the effect depends upon prior attainment, school type and academic year, which suggest that the effect does not stem, at least solely, from value inherent in the subject combination itself.

One such explanation is that it is linked to student level traits that are difficult to quantify, such as their perceived potential to achieve at GCSE. Students are not allocated to the EBacc randomly; prior attainment is important in the selection process but it is also likely that teachers make independent judgements about a student's potential to achieve at GCSE based on their secondary school performance prior to GCSE subject selection. It follows that students perceived as having high potential are the most likely to be encouraged to take the EBacc, and this, not the subject combination studied, might explain their higher average GCSE scores. However, the *EBacc* Prior Attainment* interaction revealed that the size of the attainment gap between EBacc and non-EBacc students widens as prior attainment increases, indicating that entrants with higher prior attainment are in some way better placed to take advantage of the benefits offered by the EBacc. They might be better able to cope with the demands of a heavily academic curriculum or schools may focus attention on them as the students most likely to achieve the EBacc (Greevey et al., 2012; Hodgson & Spours, 2011).

Based on the varying impact the EBacc has on students in different school types *(EBacc* School Type interaction)*, another explanation for the EBacc effect is that it is a product of how different curriculums are resourced. The effect is largest in comprehensive schools, secondary modern schools and academies. This may be because the pressure of performance tables coupled with limited funding means they prioritise the EBacc over other GCSE subject combinations thereby advantaging EBacc students over non-EBacc students. By contrast, the almost complete absence of the EBacc effect in independent schools may reflect their ability to facilitate attainment in any collection of GCSE subjects since resources are plentiful and there is no pressure from performance tables in which they are not included. Additionally, the high socio-economic status backgrounds of many independent school students might exert more influence over attainment than the specific GCSE subjects studied. Finally, in selective schools, which admit students based on ability, the EBacc effect may be smaller because generally high GCSE performance leaves less scope for a gap to emerge between EBacc and non-EBacc students.

Also related to the issue of resources is the growth in the size of the EBacc effect in 2013 and 2014 *(EBacc*Academic Year interaction)*. This likely reflects schools growing efforts to reorganise their curriculum to accommodate the EBacc following its inclusion in performance tables, and the concomitant rise in entries. For instance it could be the result of extra timetabled hours being allocated to the EBacc subjects, either through a reduction in the total number of GCSEs students study or the number of hours devoted to non-EBacc subjects. A recent survey of 1800 secondary school members of the National Union of Teachers (NUT), coupled with case studies of three London secondary schools, confirmed that the range of GCSE subjects available to students has narrowed as a result of the EBacc, and that lesson time has been redistributed in favour of the EBacc subjects. Teachers also reported that students were being removed from non-EBacc lessons for additional 1:1 catch up provision (64.2%) and exam preparation in the EBacc subjects (75.4%) (Neumann et al., 2016). Similarly, research on teacher retention has found that curriculum hours for geography and history have risen by 17% since 2011 – interestingly, the same has not occurred for languages – while non-EBacc subjects have had their teaching hours reduced (Worth & De Lazzari, 2017).

Establishing the underlying cause of the EBacc effect should be a priority for future research. Multilevel models that take into account a broader range of school and student level factors known to affect attainment, such as socio-economic status, free-school meal eligibility and ethnicity (Clifton & Cook, 2012; Stokes, Rolf, Hudson-Sharp, & Stevens, 2015; Strand, 2015), may explain more of the variance in average GCSE score and expand our understanding of the origins of the EBacc effect. Similarly, it will be important to establish whether there is any merit to the claim that the EBacc subject combination is valuable in and of itself because of the knowledge and skills acquisition that it facilitates. To this end, it would be worthwhile to gather teachers' and students' perceptions of the extent to which the EBacc subjects complement one another.

Limitations and future directions

The emphasis in this study was on identifying and tracking associations between factors that have historically been linked with EBacc uptake and attainment, namely prior attainment and school type, the findings do not support causal inferences about these relationships. Including a broader range of explanatory factors in the multilevel models would have allowed stronger conclusions to be drawn about the benefits of the EBacc. However, not all of these factors are amenable to inclusion in a statistical model, most notably those relating to students' motivations in choosing their GCSE subjects, which may indirectly impact upon attainment. This is especially relevant in light of the possibility that the increasing prominence of the EBacc as a performance measure might have resulted in some students being encouraged to study subjects they would not otherwise choose.

Interest in a subject is one of the main drivers of students' GCSE subject choices, and has been linked to motivation, itself a predictor of educational attainment (Adey & Biddulph, 2001; Furnham, Monsen, & Ahmetoglu, 2009). Hence, students who do not choose the EBacc willingly may not demonstrate the same level of engagement or motivation as those who do, and this may manifest itself in performance differences *within* the EBacc cohort. Although the relationship between prior attainment and EBacc success is robust, it is not the case that *all* high-attaining students who enter achieve the EBacc and *all* low-attaining students who enter do not achieve the EBacc. At least some of the gap between entries and attainment may be attributable to the degree to which students choose the EBacc subjects of their own volition. Low levels of interest or motivation amongst high-attaining entrants might mean they underperform in the EBacc, whereas high levels of interest and motivation might propel some low-attaining students to success. It is impossible to distinguish entrants who self-selected from those who did not using the data available. Qualitative research with school leaders and students, therefore, has a key role to play in pinpointing the degree to which students are being encouraged to take GCSE subjects they might not otherwise choose, and exploring the effect of such practices on student motivation.

A more specific criticism of the data used here is that the attainment groupings and school type variables used are somewhat crude. Finer breakdowns of KS2 scores may have allowed more nuanced distinctions to be drawn about the EBacc's impact on students of differing academic ability. However, the aggregated low, middle and high categories used are comparable with those used in school performance tables (DfE, 2010a, 2016b, 2017b) and proved useful in identifying important differences in the EBacc success rates of these three groups, as well as unique areas of weakness, which may have been obscured by more granular KS2 breakdowns.

Conclusion

Like its predecessor, the A* to C metric, the EBacc has galvanised change in the English education system, this time by redirecting schools' attention from the number of particular grades students achieve to which GCSE subjects they study. The five A* to C measure encouraged schools to enter students for GCSE equivalent qualifications in pursuit of 'good pass' GCSE grades, potentially to the detriment of the knowledge and skills they acquired. By contrast, the EBacc has facilitated a rise in the proportion of students studying a core group of subjects, yet attainment has not risen in line with entries. There are an increasing proportion of students across the whole spectrum of attainment who do not achieve sufficient grade Cs to attain the EBacc and for whom it has not been clearly demonstrated that securing lower grades in the EBacc subjects is more advantageous than [potentially] achieving higher grades in alternative subject combinations. This undermines the claim that the EBacc facilitates students' future prospects and highlights a growing tension between the government's desire for students to master particular bodies of knowledge and the need for students to achieve good grades – typically grade C or above – in order to progress to further study or employment. On the other hand, multilevel modelling revealed a positive, although not necessarily causal, association between the EBacc and higher average GCSE scores, which suggests there is some value attached to this constellation of subjects and which may lift a small number of students over the grade C threshold. Nonetheless, while the EBacc is undoubtedly useful to students who can secure good grades in its constituent subjects and therefore, study them at A level in preparation for applying to top UK universities, the 90% entry target will likely see even more students fall short of important grade benchmarks. Even without a 90% entry requirement, EBacc entries look set to rise as Progress 8, which prioritises EBacc subjects, becomes the new headline accountability measure (DfE, 2016b; Schools Week, 2016; Thomson, 2017). The uncertainty of student outcomes in this shifting policy context highlights the importance of continuing efforts to monitor the effects of, and identify the value in, the EBacc.

Notes

1. Academies and free schools do not have to follow the National Curriculum, but the majority choose to Creese and Isaacs (2016).
2. In 2017, a nine-point numerical GCSE grading system will replace the A* to G scale.
3. Some IGCSE and AS levels are also eligible.
4. English Literature *and* English Language.
5. Either double science, core + additional science, or three single sciences (from a choice of biology, chemistry, physics and computer science, two of which students must pass at grade C or above).
6. Attainment 8 measures a student's achievement in 8 qualifications, 5 of which must be EBacc subjects. English and mathematics grades are double weighted in the calculations. Progress 8 measures the progress a student makes between the end of primary school and the end of secondary school in the same group of qualifications, by comparing their Attainment 8 score with the national average Attainment 8 score of students with similar prior attainment.
7. Depending on the science route chosen.
8. Average KS2 scores were only calculated for students who sat all three KS2 tests. KS2 match rates were as follows: 2010: 88%, 2011: 88%, 2012: 86%, 2013: 88% and 2014: 88%.
9. In an effort to reduce the rising number of early GCSE entries, in 2013 the decision was made to allow only a student's first GCSE result in any particular subject to count towards their school's performance table figures (DfE, 2013a).
10. The percentage of students who sat fewer than three GCSEs was as follows: 2010: 3.6%, 2011: 4.2%, 2012: 3.5%, 2013: 4.2% and 2014: 3.4%.
11. Male acted as the reference category.
12. 2010 acted as the reference category.
13. Comprehensive school acted as the reference category. Free schools, which were attended by 2349 students, were excluded since they did not exist in the data-set until 2012.
14. Caution should be exercised when interpreting coefficients for independent schools because they represent only 50% of the independent school cohort. This is because only the students

who had average KS2 scores (those who did not likely went to independent schools where KS2 tests are not typically taken), were included in the multilevel models.

15. The largest negative residuals belonged to students who had high mean KS2 scores but low mean GCSE scores (i.e. low value added rate), while students with large positive residuals had low KS2 scores and high mean GCSE scores (i.e. high value added rate). The final model over predicts the mean GCSE scores of students with low value added and under predicts the mean GCSE scores of students with high value added. As such, caution should be exercised in trying to predict GCSE scores for students outside of these cohorts (for whom value added rates are not known), since it is not possible to know a priori if they will fall into one of these minority subgroups. Nonetheless, since the primary aim of building this model was to assess the amount of variance in mean GCSE score that is associated with taking the EBacc it is adequate for our purposes.

Disclosure statement

No potential conflict of interest was reported by the authors.

ORCID

Emma Armitage (iD) http://orcid.org/0000-0003-1164-4517

References

Adey, K., & Biddulph, M. (2001). The influence of pupil perceptions on subject choice at 14+ in geography and history. *Educational Studies, 27*, 439–450. doi:10.1080/03055690120071894

Allen, R. (2015). Floors, tables and coasters: Shifting the education furniture in England's secondary schools. *Education DataLab, FFT Aspire*. Retrieved from http://educationdatalab.org.uk/wp-content/uploads/2016/02/2015-Educationfurniture-04.pdf

Allen, R. (2016). *Revisiting how many language teachers we need to deliver the EBacc*. Retrieved from http://educationdatalab.org.uk/2016/03/revisiting-how-many-language-teachers-we-need-to-deliver-the-ebacc/

Allen, R., & Thompson, D. (2016). Research brief: Changing the subject. *The Sutton Trust*, 1–8. Retrieved from http://www.suttontrust.com/researcharchive/changing-the-subject/

Baker, K. (2016). *12–19 education: A new baccalaureate*. EDGE Foundation. Retrieved from http://www.edge.co.uk/sites/default/files/documents/14-19_education_-_a_new_baccalaureate.pdf

Ball, S., Maguire, M., Braun, A., Perryman, J., & Hoskins, K. (2012). Assessment technologies in schools: 'Deliverology' and the 'play of dominations'. *Research Papers in Education, 27*(5), 513–533. doi:10.1080/02671522.2010.550012

Bleazby, J. (2015). Why some school subjects have a higher status than others: The epistemology of the traditional curriculum hierarchy. *Oxford Review of Education, 41*(5), 671–689. doi:10.1080/03054985.2015.1090966

Cadwallader, S. (2012). Is the English Baccalaureate the most appropriate academic core? Subject choice and attainment at GCSE and A-level. *Centre for Education Research and Practice, AQA.*

Centre for Analysis of Youth Transitions. (2011). *The English Baccalaureate and GCSE choices*. Sheffield: Department for Education research brief (No. DFE-RB150).

Clifton, J., & Cook, W. (2012). *A long division: Closing the attainment gap in England's secondary schools.* London: IPPR. Retrieved from http://www.ippr.org/files/images/media/files/publication/2012/09/long%20division%20FINAL%20version_9585.pdf?noredirect=1

Coe, R. (2008). Comparability of GCSE examinations in different subjects: An application of the Rasch model. *Oxford Review of Education, 34*(5), 609–636.

Coe, R., Searle, J., Barmby, P., Jones, K., & Higgins, S. (2008). *Relative difficulty of examinations in different subjects.* Retrieved from http://www.cem.org/attachments/SCORE2008report.pdf

Cook, W. (2013). How intake and other external factors affect school performance. *Rise Trust.* Retrieved from http://www.risetrust.org.uk/pdfs/Review_Performance.pdf

Creese, B., & Isaacs, T. (2016). International instructional systems: How England measures up. *The Curriculum Journal, 27*(1), 151–165. doi:10.1080/09585176.2015.1131171

DfE. (2010a). *Primary school performance tables 2010: User guide and resources.* Retrieved from http://webarchive.nationalarchives.gov.uk/20150812151035/http://www.education.gov.uk/schools/performance/archive/primary_10/p6.shtml

DfE. (2010b). *The importance of teaching: The schools white paper* (No.cm7980). London: Author. Retrieved from https://www.gov.uk/government/uploads/system/uploads/attachment_data/file/175429/CM-7980.pdf

DfE. (2011). *Youth cohort study and longitudinal study of young people in England: The activities and experiences of 19 year olds: England 2010.* London: Statistical Bulletin (No. B01/2011). Retrieved from http://www.education.gov.uk/rsgateway/DB/SBU/b001014/index.shtml

DfE. (2013a). *Changes to early entry at GCSE.* London: Author. Retrieved from https://www.gov.uk/government/news/changes-to-early-entry-at-gcse

DfE. (2013b). *Reforming the accountability system for secondary schools.* London: Author. Retrieved from https://www.gov.uk/government/speeches/reforming-the-accountability-system-for-secondary-schools

DfE. (2015a). *Consulting on implementing the English Baccalaureate.* London: Author. Retrieved from https://www.gov.uk/government/uploads/system/uploads/attachment_data/file/473455/Consultation_on_implementing_the_English_Baccalaureate.pdf

DfE. (2015b). *Nick Gibb: The social justice case for an academic curriculum.* London: Author. Retrieved from https://www.gov.uk/government/speeches/nick-gibb-the-social-justice-case-for-an-academic-curriculum

DfE. (2015c). *Nicky Morgan: Why knowledge matters.* London: Author. Retrieved from https://www.gov.uk/government/speeches/nicky-morgan-why-knowledge-matters

DfE. (2015d). *Nicky Morgan: Raising ambition for all.* London: Author. Retrieved from https://www.gov.uk/government/speeches/nicky-morgan-raising-ambition-for-all

DfE. (2015e). *Nicky Morgan: One nation education.* London: Author. Retrieved from https://www.gov.uk/government/speeches/nicky-morgan-one-nation-education

DfE. (2015f). *Progress 8 measure in 2016 and 2017. Guide for maintained secondary schools, academies and free schools.* London: Author. Retrieved from http://dera.ioe.ac.uk/22181/1/Progress_8_school_performance_measure.pdf

DfE. (2015g). *English Baccalaureate (EBacc) policy paper.* London: Author. Retrieved from https://www.gov.uk/government/news/new-reforms-to-raise-standards-and-improve-behaviour

DfE. (2015h). *SFR37/2015: Provisional GCSE and equivalent results in England, 2014 to 2015, 15 October 2015.* London: Author. Retrieved from https://www.gov.uk/government/uploads/system/uploads/attachment_data/file/467603/SFR37_2015.pdf

DfE. (2016a). *The importance of the curriculum.* London: Author. Retrieved from https://www.gov.uk/government/speeches/the-importance-of-the-curriculum

DfE. (2016b). *School performance tables: How to interpret the data.* Retrieved from https://www.gov.uk/government/publications/school-performance-tables-how-to-interpret-the-data/school-performance-tables-how-to-interpret-the-data

DfE. (2016c). *Nick Gibb: What is good education in the 21stcentury?.* London: Author. Retrieved from https://www.gov.uk/government/speeches/what-is-a-good-education-in-the-21st-century

DfE. (2016d). *SFR03/2017: Revised GCSE and equivalent results in England, 2015 to 2016, 19 January, 2017.* London: Author. Retrieved from https://www.gov.uk/government/uploads/system/uploads/attachment_data/file/584473/SFR03_2017.pdf

DfE. (2017a). *Progress 8 and attainment 8: Guide for maintained secondary schools, academies and free schools.* London: Author. Retrieved from https://www.gov.uk/government/uploads/system/uploads/attachment_data/file/583857/Progress_8_school_performance_measure_Jan_17.pdf

DfE. (2017b). *2017 secondary schools table.* Retrieved from https://www.compare-school-performance.service.gov.uk/schools-by-type?step=phase&geographic=all&region=0&phase=secondary&for=Performance&basedon=Overall%20performance&show=Low%20achievers%20at%20key%-20stage%202&&schoolTypeFilter=allSchools&dataSetFilter=prov

DfE. (2017c). *Implementing the English Baccalaureate: Government consultation response.* London: Author. Retrieved from https://www.gov.uk/government/uploads/system/uploads/attachment_data/file/630713/Implementing_the_English_Baccalaureate_-_Government_consultation_response.pdf

DfE. (n.d.). *English Baccalaureate (EBacc).* Retrieved from https://www.gov.uk/government/publications/english-baccalaureate-ebacc/english-baccalaureate-ebacc

Expressive Arts Subjects. (2016). Retrieved from https://hansard.parliament.uk/commons/2016-07-04/debates/EE71F434-AD11-4160-95A8-D616C6ED25F6/EbaccExpressiveArtsSubjects

Francis, B., Archer, L., Hodgen, J., Pepper, D., Taylor, B., & Travers, M. C. (2017). Exploring the relative lack of impact of research on 'ability grouping' in England: A discourse analytic account. *Cambridge Journal of Education, 47*(1), 1–17. doi:10.1080/0305764X.2015.1093095

Furnham, A., Monsen, J., & Ahmetoglu, G. (2009). Typical intellectual engagement, big five personality traits, approaches to learning and cognitive ability predictors of academic performance. *British Journal of Educational Psychology, 79*(4), 769–782. doi:10.1348/978185409X412147

Greevey, H., Knox, A., Nunney, F., & Pye, J. (2012). *The effects of the English Baccalaureate.* London: Ipsos MORI, Department for Education, Research report (No. DFE-RR249). Retrieved from https://www.education.gov.uk/publications/standard/publicationDetail/Page1/DFE-RR249

Hodgson, A., & Spours, K. (2011). Rethinking general education in the English upper secondary system. *London Review of Education, 9*(2), 205–216. doi:10.1080/14748460.2011.585882

House of Commons Education Select Committee. (2011). *The English Baccalaureate* (No. HC 851). London. Retrieved from http://www.educationengland.org.uk/documents/pdfs/2011-cesc-ebac.pdf

Hutchings, M. (2015). *Exam factories? The impact of accountability measures on children and young people.* London: National Union of Teachers. Retrieved from https://www.teachers.org.uk/sites/default/files2014/exam-factories.pdf

Iannelli, C. (2013). The role of the school curriculum in social mobility. *British Journal of Sociology of Education, 34*(5–6), 907–928. doi:10.1080/01425692.2013.816031

Isaacs, T. (2010). Educational assessment in England. *Assessment in Education: Principles, Policy & Practice, 17*(3), 315–334.

Jin, W., Muriel, A., & Sibieta, L. (2011). *Subject and course choices at ages 14 and 16 amongst young people in England: Insights from behavioural economics.* DFE (DFE-RR160). Retrieved from https://www.gov.uk/government/uploads/system/uploads/attachment_data/file/182677/DFE-RR160.pdf

Long, R., & Bolton, P. (2017). *English Baccalaureate briefing paper.* Retrieved from http://researchbriefings.files.parliament.uk/documents/SN06045/SN06045.pdf

McCrone, T., Morris, M., & Walker, M. (2005). *Pupil choices at key stage 3 – Literature review.* Slough: National foundation for educational research. Retrieved from https://www.nfer.ac.uk/publications/YPM01/YPM01.pdf

Muir, R. (2013). *The impact of league table reform on vocational education in schools.* London: Institute for Public Policy Research. Retrieved from https://www.ippr.org/files/images/media/files/publication/2013/01/league-tables-vocational_Jan2013_10247.pdf

National Association of Teachers of Religious Education. (2012). *An analysis of a Survey of teachers on the impact of the EBacc on student opportunity to study GCSE RS: A Fourth Study.* Retrieved from http://www.natre.org.uk/uploads/Free%20Resources/2012%20NATRE%20Survey%20on%20Impact%20of%20the%20EBacc%20on%20RE.pdf

Neumann, E., Towers, E., Gewirtz, S., & Maguire, M. (2016). *A curriculum for all? The effects of recent Key Stage 4 curriculum, assessment and accountability reforms on English secondary education.* London: NUT/King's College. Retrieved from https://www.teachers.org.uk/sites/default/files2014/curriculum-for-all-64 pp-10845.pdf

O'Neill, O. (2013). Intelligent accountability in education. *Oxford Review of Education, 39*(1), 4–16. doi:10.1080/03054985.2013.764761

Ofqual. (2014). *The assessment of a level modern foreign language.* Retrieved from https://www.gov.uk/government/uploads/system/uploads/attachment_data/file/387728/2014-09-26-the-assessment-of-a-level-modern-foreign-language-summary.pdf

Ofqual. (2015). *Inter-Subject comparability of exam standards in GCSE and a level: ISC working paper 3.* Retrieved from https://www.gov.uk/government/uploads/system/uploads/attachment_data/file/486936/3-inter-subject-comparability-of-exam-standards-in-gcse-and-a-level.pdf

Ofsted. (2015). *Key stage 3: The wasted years?* Retrieved from https://www.gov.uk/government/uploads/system/uploads/attachment_data/file/459830/Key_Stage_3_the_wasted_years.pdf

Ofqual. (2017). *A policy position on inter-subject comparability.* Retrieved from https://www.gov.uk/government/uploads/system/uploads/attachment_data/file/610111/Board_paper_-_Inter-subject_Comparability.pdf

Robertson, A. (2016, June 18). EBacc is leading to pupils being channelled into subject choices. *Schools Week.* Retrieved from http://schoolsweek.co.uk/ebacc-is-driving-subject-combinations/

Royal Society for the encouragement of Arts, Manufactures and Commerce. (2016). *Response to Department for Education's EBacc consultation.* Retrieved from http://www.rsaacademies.org.uk/response-department-educations-ebacc-consultation/

Russell Group. (2011). *Informed choices: A Russell Group guide to making decisions about post-16 education.* Russell Group. Retrieved October 26, 2012, from http://www.russellgroup.ac.uk/media/informed-choices/InformedChoices-latest.pdf

Schmidt, W. H., Burroughs, N. A., Zoido, P., & Houang, R. T. (2015). The role of schooling in perpetuating educational inequality: An international perspective. *Educational Researcher, 44*(7), 371–386. doi:10.3102/0012189X15603982

Schools Week. (2016). *The Progress 8 measure explained.* Retrieved from https://schoolsweek.co.uk/the-progress-8-measure-explained/

Sousa, S., & Armor, D. J. (2010). *Impact of family vs. school factors on cross-national disparities in academic achievement: Evidence from the 2006 PISA survey* (GMU School of Public Policy Research Paper No. 2010-25). Arlington, VA: George Mason University, School of Public Policy. doi:10.2139/ssrn.1688131

SSAT. (2015, June 17). *EBacc for all? The findings from SSAT's national survey of school leaders.* Retrieved from http://www.ssatuk.co.uk/ssats-national-survey-of-school-leaders/

Stables, A., & Wikeley, F. (1999). From bad to worse? Pupils' attitudes to modern foreign languages at ages 14 and 15. *The Language Learning Journal, 20*(1), 27–31. doi:10.1080/09571739985200231

Stokes, L., Rolf, H., Hudson-Sharp, N., & Stevens, S. (2015). Ethnic minorities and attainment: The effects of poverty. *National Institute of Economic and Social Research.* Report to the Department for Education. Retrieved from https://www.gov.uk/government/uploads/system/uploads/attachment_data/file/439861/RR439A-Ethnic_minorities_and_attainment_the_effects_of_poverty.pdf

Strand, S. (2015). *Ethnicity, deprivation and educational achievement at age 16 in England: Trends over time.* Report to the Department for Education. Retrieved from https://www.gov.uk/government/uploads/system/uploads/attachment_data/file/439867/RR439B-Ethnic_minorities_and_attainment_the_effects_of_poverty_annex.pdf.pdf

Taylor, R. C. (2016). The effects of accountability measures in English secondary schools: Early and multiple entry to GCSE Mathematics assessments. *Oxford Review of Education, 42*(6), 629–645. doi:10.1080/03054985.2016.1197829

Teaching Schools Council. (2016). *Modern foreign languages pedagogy review: A review of modern foreign languages teaching practice in key stage 3 and key stage 4.* Retrieved from http://tscouncil.org.uk/wp-content/uploads/2016/11/MFL-Pedagogy-Review-Report-2.pdf

TES. (2017, March 9). *Exclusive: DfE could water down 90 per cent EBacc target.* Retrieved from https://www.tes.com/news/school-news/breaking-news/exclusive-dfe-could-water-down-90-cent-ebacc-target

Thomson, D. (2017). *What might EBacc average point scores look like?* Retrieved from https://educationdatalab.org.uk/2017/08/what-might-ebacc-average-points-scores-look-like/

Vaughan, R. (2015, September 25). *Wilshaw and DfE on EBac collision course. TES.* Retrieved from https://www.tes.com/news/school-news/breaking-news/wilshaw-and-dfe-ebac-collision-course

Which. (2016). Retrieved from http://university.which.co.uk/advice/gcse-choices-university/how-important-are-my-gcse-grades

Wilkins, S., & Meeran, S. (2011). Student performance–university preference model: A framework for helping students choose the right A-level subjects. *Educational Studies, 37*(5), 541–555. doi:10.1080/03055698.2010.543550

Wolf, A. (2011). *Review of vocational education – The wolf report.* Retrieved from https://www.gov.uk/government/uploads/system/uploads/attachment_data/file/180504/DFE-00031-2011.pdf

Worth, J., & De Lazzari, G. (2017). *Teacher retention and turnover research. Research update 1: Teacher retention by subject.* Slough: NFER.

Young, M. (2011). The return to subjects: A sociological perspective on the UK Coalition government's approach to the 14–19 curriculum. *The Curriculum Journal, 22*(2), 265–278. doi:10.1080/09585176.2011.574994

National assessment policy reform 14–16 and its consequences for young people: student views and experiences of GCSE reform in Northern Ireland and Wales

Rhian Barrance and Jannette Elwood

ABSTRACT
This paper uses data from a mixed-methods research project which explored the views and experiences of students in Northern Ireland and Wales on the assessment and reform of GCSEs. The research found that while students were generally supportive of the substance of the reforms in each region, they raised concerns about the rapid pace of reform, and questioned whether changes were in their best interests. Participants expressed particular anxiety about the end of three-country regulation of GCSEs and the consequences of this development for students. As those most affected by changes to qualifications, they wanted a greater role in determining national assessment policies. Considering the impact of such reforms on young people, and recognising the important perspectives they can offer on how qualifications are enacted in practice, it is argued that the concept of student voice should be broadened to accommodate young people's involvement in national assessment and educational decisions.

Introduction

GCSEs are the main examinations taken by students at age 16 in England, Northern Ireland (NI) and Wales. Since their inception in 1988, GCSEs have been a 'common' examination (Gipps, 1986), jointly regulated by governments in these regions. However, this all came to an abrupt end in 2013, following a series of policy disagreements between England, Northern Ireland and Wales regarding plans for GCSE reform. The consequence is that while the label of 'GCSE' is used across the three regions, for the first time there are differences in the ways that students can achieve the qualification, which has major implications for the portability of GCSEs across England, Northern Ireland and Wales – meaning that qualifications obtained in one region many not be seen as equal currency in another. This paper considers a significant gap in the educational assessment and policy literature by focusing on the consequences of assessment policy reform from the perspectives of students, particularly in this case from students in Northern Ireland and Wales. While some existing research addresses students' views or experiences of particular assessment techniques, it is rare for their perspectives on assessment policy and/or its reform to be given consideration (Elwood, Hopfenbeck, & Baird, 2017). It is argued that not only do young people have a right for their views to be given due weight on public policy issues that affect them, but also that they have notable perspectives which can make an important contribution to our understanding of assessment policy implementation and success (Elwood, 2013).

The paper situates the debates around assessment policy reform within the context of devolved government arrangements for assessment and qualifications policy. The central UK Government has devolved particular public policy responsibilities to the separate jurisdictions of the UK (England, Northern Ireland, Wales and Scotland[1]). Such a context of devolved policy-making locates assessment policy reform within contexts of complex local processes driven by a range of different and competing factors and influences which force difficult decisions about the adequacy and appropriateness of existing assessment arrangements for local needs (Raffe & Spours, 2007). It also highlights how different priorities and ideological positions on the purposes of education are articulated through assessment reform programmes (Cadwallader & Tremain, 2013). So for example, while the significant changes taking place in England tend to emphasise the role of qualifications for school accountability measures (Gove, 2013), those taking place in Northern Ireland and Wales tend to focus more on the principles of inclusion and motivation (CCEA, 2013; Welsh Government, 2012), suggesting a greater emphasis on the needs of learners for the local contexts within which they are being educated. However, most of the rhetoric around these policy positions ignores the views of those most affected by them. This paper considers these assertions about the values inherent in qualification reform through a critical lens, by considering whether students in Northern Ireland and Wales perceive the current reforms as relevant and in their best interests.

Context: GCSE policy reform across England, Northern Ireland and Wales

In recent years, there has emerged an interesting situation where students in England, Northern Ireland and Wales are studying for the same qualification, labelled 'GCSE' but their experience of these qualifications is very different depending on where students live and on their teachers' choice of examination specifications and awarding organisations. This examination will no longer be common between the students who take it.

Until recently, GCSEs were regulated on a three-country basis: there was collaboration between Ofqual, the regulatory body for England, the Welsh Government and the Council for Curriculum, Examinations and Assessment (CCEA), the qualifications regulator for Northern Ireland. However, from 2010, political and educational disagreements regarding the fundamental purposes and quality of GCSEs emerged, and by 2013 they forced the collapse of three-country regulation. Since then, major (but not the same) reforms to GCSEs have been implemented in England, Northern Ireland and Wales. The consequence is that for the first time there are differences in the ways that students can achieve a GCSE across the three regions.

Reform of GCSEs: England

In May 2010, a coalition UK Government between the Conservative and Liberal Democratic parties was formed and the centrepiece of its education agenda was a concentration on reforming qualifications to make sure that 'existing qualifications are rigorous, challenging and properly prepare our young people for life, work and study' (Gibb, 2010). To meet the criteria of 'rigorous and challenging', the Department for Education in England specifically expressed concern about the structure of national examinations, notably course structures (modularity vs. linearity) and resits. They also raised concern about the use of early entry possibilities, where students are entered for some elements of the examinations in earlier sittings rather than all at the end of the two-year course. Both resits and early entry were practices seen as ways in which schools sought to raise examination outcomes and better their performance measures for accountability systems (Department for Education, 2010). Since 2012, the following major changes have been rolled out with regard to GCSEs in England: substantive reviews of syllabus content for core subjects to make GCSEs more rigorous; the re-introduction of linear qualifications (taken wholly at the end of a course) assessed solely by examinations; the removal of controlled assessment (internal to the school) in particular subjects; limitations to the number and extent of resits; and the introduction of a numerical grading scale at GCSE (9–1) for mathematics and English in 2017 and then rolled out to all subjects in subsequent years. Moreover, restrictions on tiering in GCSEs have also been introduced. This is a form of differentiation used to provide examination papers of appropriate levels of challenge for all students. For those subjects that use tiering at GCSE, there are normally two tiers with exam papers covering differing syllabus content and varied in cognitive demand – the higher tier with associated grades A*–D (9 to 4), and the foundation tier, with associated grades C–G (5–1). Following the latest reforms, tiering has been removed from most subjects.

Reform of GCSEs: Northern Ireland

Northern Ireland has diverged from England in its sated purposes of reform, by focusing on preparation for life and developing young people's skills, rather than the outcomes of assessments for accountability (CCEA, 2013, p. 2). The initial policy approach undertaken in Northern Ireland was based on the principle of flexibility and portability was considered a key concern (Perry, 2013); to have examinations equivalent in 'currency' in all aspects to their peers in England and Wales. This was because a large proportion of students from Northern Ireland enrol on university courses in England, with 22% of undergraduates doing so in 2011 (Higher Education Statistics Authority, 2013). Northern Ireland schools can choose syllabuses from English and Welsh awarding organisations as well as modular or linear qualifications, which means that they are not restricted to Northern Ireland qualifications only (O'Dowd, 2014). While modular GCSEs remain an option for those studying in Northern Ireland, only one resit opportunity is now allowed per unit (Department of Education Northern Ireland, 2014). Moreover, the use of controlled assessment and tiering has also been reduced (Department of Education Northern Ireland, 2014). Furthermore, Northern Ireland qualifications have retained the letter grading scale (A*–G) and introduced a C* grade to provide equivalency for the grade 5 to be used in England (Weir, 2016).

Reform of GCSEs: Wales

Decisions about reforms from the Welsh Government were based on 'the best interests of learners' (Welsh Government, 2012, p. 2) and were not 'allowed to simply emerge through a series of reactions to events or decisions in England' (Welsh Government, 2012, p. 18). This statement reflects suggestions generally that the business of governance in the UK's devolved administrations primarily consists of deciding whether or not to adopt policies developed in England (Fitz, 2000) and particularly that Wales's policy-making post-devolution has been criticised for focusing too much on distinguishing itself from England (Reynolds, 2008). However, even given these criticisms, Wales's approach to qualification reform has differed markedly to that in England, and reflects more those decisions taken in Northern Ireland. Thus, in Wales: both modular and linear course structures are now used; decisions about course structure, controlled assessment and tiering have been retained but it is emphasised that they should be used 'only where there is a clear case for doing so' (Welsh Government, 2012, p. 48); limited resits are now allowed per unit; generally early entries in to GCSEs are discouraged; and the current A*–C grade structure has been retained (Welsh Government, 2014).

Issues in assessment and qualifications policy reform

In recent years, a once relatively everyday area of education provision (national examinations), overseen by awarding organisations in direct communication with schools has become a significant policy frontline (Baird, 2011). Policy proliferation has become more problematic through multiple reforms being carried out in haste because of governments' general desire to have measurable impact on education within electoral terms (Baird & Lee-Kelley, 2009). In relation to changes in examination systems, while governments may want to see quick results that show considerable changes in standards and practices, tight timescales can pose significant threats to the validity of examinations (Cadwallader & Tremain, 2013), with insufficient time being allocated to certain stages of the work (e.g. curriculum development, identification of assessment criteria), instability creeping in to the system because of mass change all at once, and possible adverse consequences for students due to changes being introduced live without piloting (Elwood, 2012, 2013; Oates, 2007). Many of the problems experienced within assessment policy reform can be attributed to the increased politicised nature of reform programmes, and the expectation on examination results to fulfil multiple purposes (e.g. individual grades for students, performance measures for teachers and schools) (Cadwallader & Tremain, 2013). Such problems compound the underlying problems in the design of examination systems, impacting both the reliability and the validity of the final product as well as a lack of clarity over what is expected of key stakeholders (Baird & Coxell, 2009).

In practice, patterns emerge in assessment reform that show results on examinations dipping suddenly when new tests are introduced then improving slowly once teachers and students develop a better understanding of the assessment requirements. Over subsequent assessment sessions results tend to reach a plateau when teachers and students become very familiar with procedures and changes begin to show less variation (Koretz, 2005); performance tending to plateau after approximately three years (Ofqual, 2016). This pattern has been described as the 'sawtooth' effect (e.g. Koretz, 2005; Koretz & Barron, 1998; Linn, 1998,

2000). Research around this effect in the UK shows that performances on reformed qualifications are affected in similar ways (Cresswell, 2003; Ofqual, 2015). What is of interest within
this current paper are the repercussions for those students who take the new qualifications
in the first year of the reforms. If results dip following major changes to qualifications then
what are the consequences for students in terms of grades awarded and the impact of lower
than expected grades on future life chances[2]. Elwood (2013) emphasises that it is students
who disproportionately suffer the effects of successive changes which appear to be driven
by 'ideological and political agendas' (p. 109). Consequently, Elwood (2013) suggests that
young people should have a greater role in the development of qualification policy to ensure
that any reforms really are in their best interests as well as providing crucial information
about the ways in which reforms are enacted in practice.

Students as public policy actors

Conceptualisations of students as public policy actors call for young people to have their
views taken into account in policy decisions that affect them and to be afforded greater
opportunities to participate in political life at the public level (Arnott, 2008; Hinton, Tisdall,
Gallagher, & Elsley, 2008; Tisdall, 2008). A commonly cited reason for involving children
in public policy is their right to participation under article 12 of the UNCRC, which asserts
children's rights to participate in decisions which affect them (United Nations, 1989; see also
Lundy, 2007). While the UNCRC has been influential and has driven much research in the
area of children and participation, the drive for children to be recognised as public policy
actors is not only made on a legal basis. As users of public policy, children are affected by
reforms to public institutions and policies, and so, it is argued, they should be given the
opportunity to participate in decisions regarding change and development (Tisdall, 2008).
Underlying this is a shift in perceptions of young people as having the capacity to give valid
insights on institutions and services (Arnott, 2008).

In relation to assessment, there have been calls for test-takers' rights to be taken seriously,
in light of potential negative repercussions of testing, as well as significant power imbalances
between test-takers and highly influential global testing organisations (Shohamy, 2001).
Moreover, more democratic assessments which involve users in their production have been
proposed (Shohamy, 2001). Furthermore, Pavlou (2008) has suggested that adult test-takers' consumer rights should also be considered. However, these rights are limited as they
pertain to adults and to those designated as 'consumers' which is not often the case with
children. The UNCRC designates children as rights holders and as such demands that 'the
best interests of the child' guide decisions with regard to public policy actions that affect
children and young people directly (Elwood & Lundy, 2010: 335). With regard to assessment it has been argued that those devising national testing systems should abide by the
UNCRC's core principles and take positive action to ensure that young people's views are
taken into account in assessment decisions (Elwood & Lundy, 2010).

Student voice and assessment policy

While the inclusion of young people in policy decision-making is limited at the national
level, there are well-established arguments for their inclusion in decisions at a local level
within their own educational settings. This work is situated within that on 'student voice'

which refers to practices that have repositioned the worth of students' unique perspectives on teaching, learning and schooling more generally (Cook-Sather, 2006). Such work has included student participation in: school-level policy decisions (Thomson, 2011; Whitty & Wisby, 2007); teaching and learning decisions at the classroom level (Morgan, 2009); school-level committees alongside teachers and governors (Osberg, Pope, & Galloway, 2006); advisory groups for research projects with university researchers (Fielding, 2001); and in school and national councils focusing on key aspects of educational life (Davies & Yamashita, 2009).

However, there are shortcomings associated with the work around student voice reflecting the tendency to perceive some students' voices to be representative of all others (Bragg, 2007; Thomson, 2011) and assumptions that all student forums are effective and operating normally. Problems with ineffective student bodies can generate scepticism about voice initiatives amongst students themselves (Alderson, 2000) and indeed can be seen as mechanisms to reinforce student compliance (Fielding & McGregor, 2005). Furthermore, assumptions about a single 'student voice' denies diversity and difference in students' needs and opinions, hiding hierarchies of power and privilege within and across different student groupings (Cook-Sather, 2006). While keeping these limitations in mind, many calls have been made over the years for changes in mind-sets, structures and power relations to support respectful dialogue between students and adults in educational spheres. Such calls have emphasised the potential for student voice to enhance understanding of the impacts and effects of educational policies and practices as they are played out at both institutional and national levels (Cook-Sather, 2002; Cullingford, 1991; Fielding, 2001).

More recently, educational assessment research has also highlighted the importance of listening to students' experiences as an essential component of understanding the impact of national assessment systems (especially those at school-leaving age) on young people (e.g. Baird et al., 2010; Banks & Smyth, 2015; Chamberlain, 2012; Daly, Baird, Chamberlain, & Meadows, 2012; Elwood, 2012; Elwood et al., 2017). Hodgson and Spours (2003, p. 92) highlighted students feeling like 'guinea pigs' because of problems associated with reforms to national assessment programmes which play a highly significant role in young people's lives. Moreover, these studies have provided understandings of students' views on issues pertinent to assessment development such as variations in (un)reliable marking (Chamberlain, 2012), grade inflation and falling standards (Elwood, 2012) and implementing policy changes directly into 'live' examinations (Daly et al., 2012). Furthermore, this research has revealed a sense of disempowerment amongst young people in their lack of influence over 'higher level decisions' (Elwood, 2013, p. 108) and that 'ultimately they were the ones most affected if qualifications systems fail due to instabilities around syllabus and grading changes during examination cycles (Elwood, 2013, p. 108).

Emerging out of some of the studies considered above is a limited realisation by awarding organisations and regulators of the need to include students as participants in some of their own consultations into assessment reform (CCEA, 2013; Welsh Government, 2012; YouGov, 2017). Consultations like these present influential audiences for young people's views to be heard. However, as Elwood (2012) has emphasised, it is often difficult to determine the amount of influence young people have compared to other stakeholders in such consultations. While the involvement of young people is encouraging, it is clear that there is still a great deal to be done.

This paper aims to contribute to progress being made in this area by presenting the views and experiences of young people in the jurisdictions of Northern Ireland and Wales. The vast majority of the research around these issues derives from the English context, and yet the deviations between England, Northern Ireland and Wales in their approaches to GCSE reform set out an interesting case in relation to multiple changes across jurisdictions to ostensibly the same examination. Such changes, we believed, required further investigation.

Methodology

This paper draws on an original data-set of Northern Irish and Welsh students' views and experiences of GCSEs from a large mixed-methods research project (see Elwood et al., 2017). The methods employed within the study consisted of focus groups (20) conducted with GCSE students aged 15–16 across Northern Ireland and Wales (10 in each jurisdiction; 5–10 participants in each group) as well as a questionnaire survey completed by 1600 GCSE students (901 in Wales; 699 in Northern Ireland). The research aims were to seek out students' views about a range of different issues relating to GCSEs and their reform, such as the extent to which they were consulted about qualification reform and their opinions on the recent changes to qualifications in their regions. A particularly innovative aspect of the research instrument development was that it was designed in collaboration with groups of GCSE students who acted as advisors to the research. Working with students in this way reflected a direct children's rights approach to the research (Lundy & McEvoy, 2012) which aims to build young people's capacity within the topics under consideration so that they can act as advisors on issues relating directly to the research and to the lives of children and young people. In this case, capacity building sessions were delivered for advisory group members in NI and Wales on the purpose of assessment and reforms to GCSEs, as well as research processes such as survey design and data analysis and interpretation. It was important to take such an approach to ensure that the questions asked of the wider student participants were comprehensible, sensible and relevant to them as well as addressing issues that they themselves felt were important to ask of their peers. Moreover, the advisory groups' advice was key in formulating the capacity-building information, such as infographics on reforms, which were used in the questionnaires. This enabled students to give informed answers to questions, which was important, as very few participants in the focus groups were aware of the changes before the research visit.

Quantitative data from the survey was analysed using SPSS to identify relationships between key variables and patterns of responses of interest to the overall aims. Qualitative data was (i) coded by hand if it came from the open-ended questions on the survey and (ii) transcribed and coded using MAXQDA if it was from the focus groups. In analysing the data, the advisory group members were also involved in looking at anonymised extracts of qualitative data to help code and arrange into themes. Such a process offers new perspectives on ways in which the data can be considered, enhancing the quality of the analysis and the credibility of the findings with young people (Lundy, McEvoy, & Byrne, 2011). Students' analysis supported the researchers' interpretations, and helped inform the development of overall emerging themes from the data. While this paper will use both the quantitative and qualitative data to present key findings, it primarily focuses on the latter in order for the reader to 'hear' the voices of the young people and their views and experiences of GCSEs more generally. We present what were perceived to be the main issues for them in relation to qualification reform, their views on the changes to the GCSE within the devolved policy contexts as well as the impact of the removal of a common GCSE examination.

Presentation of the data

In the presentation of the data below, all extracts are labelled with information about the institution attended by students, the data source from which the extract is derived, e.g. focus group (FG) or open ended question on the survey. Additionally, the region, e.g. Northern Ireland (NI) or Wales will be identified. Where only one student is quoted, the gender will be indicated. The names of all institutions have been replaced with pseudonyms.

Students' perspectives on qualification reforms in Northern Ireland and Wales

Assessment structures and formats

As discussed earlier, wide ranging changes to GCSEs have come into play in England, Northern Ireland and Wales including the reduction on the use of controlled assessment, modularity and tiering. These changes have come about after only a few years after their introduction in 2009 (Department of Children, Schools & Families, 2008) and have been implemented in relative haste given government timeframes for change within parliamentary sessions.

In relation to what students thought about these changes, the survey data suggested that, on the whole, students in NI and Wales were relatively supportive of the decisions taken by the governments in their regions in relation to the reform of assessment structures and formats. With regards to the decision made in both NI and Wales to retain modularity, at least for some subjects, most students were in favour of keeping modular courses. In fact, as shown in Table 1, the majority of students wanted a choice to be available for all, or for only modular courses to be permitted. Very few students preferred the approach taken in England to mandate that all courses be linear.

Likewise, the majority of participants in both regions agreed with their governments' plans to retain controlled assessment (see Table 2). While it was clear that many students had reservations or were unsure about controlled assessment due to the high levels selecting 'neither agree nor disagree', only around a tenth of participants indicated that they disagreed with the policy.

Approval for the decision to retain tiering was also high, with over two thirds agreeing with their governments' plans in both regions (see Table 3).

While there was reasonably high support for the qualification policies taken by NI and Wales, the focus group data showed that students had concerns about a number of issues emerging from these changes relating as well as their exclusion from the policy process.

Table 1. Respondents' views on their government's plans to allow both modular and linear GCSE courses, by region.

Region	Only modular courses should be allowed %	Only linear courses should be allowed %	Both linear and modular courses should be allowed %
NI (n = 575)	39.1	7.7	53.2
Wales (n = 783)	28.0	9.7	62.3

Table 2. Respondents' level of agreement with their government's plans to keep controlled assessment, by region.

Region	Disagree %	Neither agree nor disagree %	Agree %
NI (*n* = 579)	10.4	15.7	74.0
Wales (*n* = 788)	12.4	28.2	59.4

Table 3. Respondents' level of agreement with their government's plans to retain tiering, by region.

Region	Disagree %	Neither agree nor disagree %	Agree %
NI (*n* = 578)	6.4	13.1	80.5
Wales (*n* = 788)	10.2	24.2	65.5

They were apprehensive about the impact of numerous reforms, and in particular, the consequences of the loss of a 'common' GCSE examination (from the end of three-country regulation) for their future educational and employment opportunities. These will be discussed further below.

Awareness of reforms and impact

From discussions with students in focus groups, there was not a great deal of awareness amongst students about the most recent decisions taken regarding GCSEs, but that many were knowledgeable about previous reforms or had a sense that there had been a number of changes to GCSEs over the last few years. For example, when given information about the current reforms, a student in Northern Ireland asked: 'Has it not been changed a good few times... has it not been chopping and changing?' (Male, Devlin High, FG 2, NI). In both regions, there was concern about the amount of change in the system and the impact it could have upon individuals, with one NI student noting that 'GCSEs are the way of having that achievement [to show] what you're good at, but this will not happen if it changes every time' (Female, Paulin High, Survey, NI). In Wales, this point was made even more emphatically, with students discussing their cohort as 'a test year' for new reforms (Female, Herbert High, FG 2), and another group discussing their experience as akin to being experimented upon:

S1   it's too much development like every year

S2   we're just an experiment for the next year basically

INTERVIEWER   an experiment for the next year?

S1   guinea pigs (Waters High, FG, Wales)

There was a sense of disempowerment amongst participants, with students expressing the view that they have no control over the reform process and that decisions are not made in their best interests. In describing themselves as being experimented upon, they echo research which has considered the problem of visiting unpiloted reforms on young people (Oates, 2007). They also resonate with the statements made by young people interviewed by Hodgson and Spours (2003) regarding the reform of A-levels in 2002, who also likened themselves to 'guinea pigs', suggesting that little has changed with regards to the ways that students experience qualification reform in the UK over the last decade and a half.

Some students went into more detail about the problems caused by reforms, noting that it was difficult to understand what was expected of them when new specifications were introduced:

'I do not agree with the exam boards changing the style of their examinations because this sometimes gives us no indication on what to expect in the GCSE exam.'(Male, Follett High, Survey, Wales)

Such statements resonate with research that shows lack of familiarity with new styles of assessment or the requirements of examinations can have a significant impact in the early years of the assessment (Ofqual, 2016). It shows that students can experience problems in understanding the requirements of new specifications and course types, emphasising again possible detrimental repercussions for young people of making changes to 'live' national systems.Students' responses indicated that they were not only concerned about the immediate consequences for the students in the cohorts who will sit these new qualifications but also the impact on all year groups, causing problems with inter-cohort comparability. This was a key issue for the participants in this study, with students revealing anxiety about the consequences of the changes on many cohorts of young people:

S1   they change too much

S2   like the differences between when our parents did it when our siblings did it and then now when we are doing it they just change all the time

S3   they're changing by the year and it's hard

S4   they all mean different things

S1   like the English exam last year was new so the English exam we are doing now our teachers know what to do but last year it just changed so everyone in last year failed or most of them (Waters High, FG, Wales)

Students were aware that they would not only be competing against pupils in their own year groups for educational and employment opportunities in the future, but with others from additional cohorts. They found this lack of consistency in assessment features across year groups concerning, especially if employers did not have sound knowledge of the different assessment arrangements in place for different cohorts, and therefore those who sat more challenging examinations could be disadvantaged.

I think if it was done then it would have to be like people who are like interviewing you would have to sort of know how you sort of sat the exam like how your exams are set and everything and you you they sort of knew more about it than just you got you got an A (Male, Herbert High, FG 2)

Thus, students considered wide-ranging implications for young people generally with respect to these new reforms. The range of significant consequences emerging from recent changes created for them a level of instability in the system that was difficult to understand. Students expressed anxieties about the impact and pace of change, seeing those being implemented at the time of the research as simply more change in a steady stream of changes, all of which contributed to problems in how their qualifications would be viewed by selectors for courses and jobs.

End of a 'common' GCSE: loss of three-country regulation and students' particular concerns

When GCSE was first introduced in 1988, it was described as a common examination for all students (Gipps, 1986). While over the years small differences in specifications might have been apparent, the GCSE maintained a common framework and approach across all three jurisdictions, who worked together to maintain comparability of standards, assessment criteria, awarding practices and stability of the examination. However, the new GCSEs coming on stream no longer look the same nor are structured in the same way. This present situation regarding regulation and the 'look' and 'feel' of the GCSE was one particular aspect of the recent reforms which concerned students to a significant extent. A particularly pertinent issue for students in Northern Ireland was the portability of the new qualifications, perhaps reflecting the fact that a relatively high proportion of students from this region apply for university in England (Higher Education Statistics Authority, 2013). In the focus groups, concern was expressed by those who were considering applying for university or for jobs in England:

> You'd almost worry that like if you ever wanted to try and get a job in England or anything that they would consider like a Northern Irish GCSE to be less relevant than an English one or somehow like insufficient (Female Heaney Grammar, FG 2, NI)

For participants, changes to the ways that the GCSE was now to be assessed resulted in differences in the skill-sets required to achieve good grades under very different assessment structures, raising questions about the fairness and validity of the qualifications across the three jurisdictions. For example, there was a perception that modular qualifications in Northern Ireland would not be perceived to be rigorous enough compared to linear qualifications in England, and that NI students would be disadvantaged as a result. The view in both NI and Wales was that standardisation of qualifications across all regions would be best for all students: 'I think all of Britain should just have the same course so if you're going for jobs it's equal' (Female, Sheers High).

Welsh students also raised concerns about the comparability of the GCSEs that they were studying compared with those in England which was perceived to have a more challenging assessment system:

> in England more people will be smarter because … they're doing it all at the end … where we're getting it easier cause we get controlled assessments to do over and over again (Male, Waters High, FG, Wales)

> it's a GCSE so if in three nations who are all taking the GCSE why isn't it the same as standard?' (Male, Herbert High, FG 3, Wales).

This is particularly pertinent for Welsh students with the land border between them and England, with some of their peers being educated across the border in England and taking very 'different' GCSEs. The data here suggests that while students are relatively supportive of modular courses, controlled assessment and tiering, they do not see decisions to remove or retain these features of GCSEs in isolation and balance these decisions with considerations about portability and comparability. Students were extremely concerned at what they saw as decisions which would, in the long term, affect the value of the qualifications they receive as well as their 'currency' in an ever competitive education and employment market. Overall, students seem to prefer adaptations to the current system; tweaks rather than extreme changes. In many cases, they suggest that problems within assessment systems could be solved by giving students a greater role in determining how they are enacted. It is often not the assessment feature itself that it is perceived to be problematic, but the way it is enacted and the fact that students are not routinely involved in decisions about them. We turn to this issue next.

Students' involvement in assessment policy-making

Some students attributed the problems in the examination system to politicians' failure to consult them before reforms were implemented. For example, at Sheers High in Wales, one student stated that 'I think politicians just say right we're going to do this because I think it's a really good idea just give me more votes ... but they don't get feedback when they make decisions ...' (Male, Sheers High, FG, Wales). There was a sense that reforms were sometimes made for political reasons, to win votes, and that the opinions of stakeholders such as young people were thus not considered relevant to the debates:

S1 but I think all of Britain should just have the same courses... cause I think Wales are overcomplicating it

S2 yeah they're trying to be independent with other countries

S3 yeah they're trying to be independent and it's not benefitting us I don't think

S2 it's benefitting the politicians because like they gain popularity but it doesn't really benefit us in any way because

(Sheers High, FG, Wales)

Here students' views reflect previous research on the politicised nature of assessment policy reform (Baird, 2011; Cadwallader & Tremain, 2013; Elwood, 2013) and a sense that the best interests of young people were not prioritised in the reforms. In a focus group discussion in Northern Ireland, it was argued that the government has 'made a system that's not suitable [and] they didn't know until they put it into practice. They need to know what we think so they know how to adjust it to suit the needs of the best from the youth' (Male, Friel High, FG, NI). For students, they expressed a sense of injustice that mistakes were made because of students' exclusion from the policy process. There were two reasons for this. First, because students' perspectives would help politicians understand how policies are being enacted in practice. The data on students' experiences of GCSE reform emerging from this project supports this view, showing that qualification features such as controlled assessment and modular courses are enacted in very different ways within different contexts (Barrance & Elwood, 2017). Thus students suggested that information on their experiences would be of benefit to politicians' understanding of the process of policy-making as a whole. Second, the data suggests that by consulting young people, governments can ensure that the qualification system developed reflects what students, as the main users of GCSEs, want from them. This could improve their utilitarian value and create a more fair system as choice and diversity of learning would be taken into account, rather than a 'one size fits all' approach.

There was a strong sense that students' views should be taken into account because they are the ones who are most affected by changes to qualifications:

because if it's affecting you – and like other students surely you should be the one to have a say in the decisions? (Female, Heaney Grammar, FG 1, NI).

Table 4. Percentages of students' according to the amount they report being asked about changes to GCSEs, by region.

Region	Not at all %	A little %	Quite a bit %	A lot %
NI ($n = 571$)	33.5	35.6	21.2	9.8
Wales ($n = 771$)	36.3	42.5	14.4	6.7

Student views on this issue accord with those expressed in the literature on student voice and children as policy participants (discussed earlier). These literatures argue that young people should be consulted because they have a legal right to participation in decisions that affect them (Lundy, 2007), and that without their views policy-makers will not have a complete picture of how their policies will work in practice (Cook-Sather, 2002; Tisdall, 2008).

These findings are also reflected in the quantitative data deriving from the survey. Students were asked 'how much are you asked your opinion about issues relating to GCSEs, such as those asked during this survey?' The results can be seen in Table 4:

As can be seen, the majority of participants in both regions indicated that they were not consulted, or were but only minimally. Moreover, most of the responses in the open-ended box which asked them to give details of who consulted them referred to parents or teachers and none referred to national governmental bodies, which indicates that their views had not been collected systematically by such organisations.

While the results of this question suggest that consultation with students on GCSE reforms is not routine, when asked whether they should be asked their opinions about GCSEs, the results were overwhelming positive. Over 90% of students in both regions agreed that students should be consulted on these kinds of issues before changes are introduced. On the whole, there was frustration over how decisions were being made currently by people who were not directly affected by the reforms and a belief that students themselves should have a greater involvement in policy-making. In focus groups from both NI and Wales, students offered ideas for facilitating students' participation in GCSE policy-making:

S1   I think maybe there should be a big vote on it

S2   … what's the point in a bunch of people who have went through education … all politicians, arguing, except young people […]

S3   well I think you'd have to ask the people who are about to go to do GCSEs–ones in like third year–give them all the options

S4   they may not know

S1   that's why you have to explain it to them, give them all the options …

S2   they wouldn't get the absolute 100 per cent final decision

S1   But they'd have an input (Longley High, FG 1, NI)

S1   … it's us we're doing it

S2   I think we should be taken into account

S1   I think that there should be more of these [focus groups]

S2   I feel like it's older people making our decisions when we are the ones being affected by it (Waters High, FG, Wales)

In both these cases, students have suggested that students' views should be taken into account, one through a democratic process which helps politicians understand students' views, and another through more consultations such as the focus groups they were participating in. Elwood (2012, 2013) and Elwood and Lundy (2010) have called for a shift in approaches from both governments and awarding organisations as to how they engage with young people on matters of assessment reform and development; the findings from this study support this call with students clearly articulating perspectives on how this could be operationalised. Notably, the views here are not that students should dictate policy, but that they should have 'an input' and that their views should be 'taken into account', as in keeping with Article 12 of the UNCRC (United Nations, 1989). Moreover, by arguing that young people have a valid contribution to make to the debate on reform, with active participation by adults in providing information and guidance, a considerable shift in the understanding of policy-makers, awarding organisations, teachers and school leaders as to the value that listening to young people on these matters can bring, especially to creating sustainable and fair assessment systems.

Discussion and concluding remarks

This research has shown that students are able to provide powerful insights on GCSE assessments both across structures and formats as well as how national systems of assessment are enacted within local schools and institutions. These insights have the potential to enhance our understanding of the ways in which national assessment systems are understood by those affected by them most; strengthening the case for the inclusion of students' views in policy-making in qualification reform. The idea that students should be involved in discussions regarding assessment is not new; it is a central principle of formative assessment, fostering students' engagement and active participation in their learning (Hayward, 2013). However, what is new from this research is the strength of concern from students about their lack of involvement in higher level decisions at a national level regarding changes to key summative assessments that determine their life chances and future opportunities. These findings challenge the view that students should not be consulted on assessment and qualification policies. They show young people with the capacity to make considered judgements and who do not automatically opt for what they perceive as the easiest option. It suggests that perhaps many of the arguments made against consulting young people are based on unfair assumptions about what young people will say; a perpetuation by adults of what Grace (1995, p. 202) termed the 'ideology of immaturity'. Cullingford (1991) articulated very clearly that young people are aware of the huge potential they offer adults in understanding educational issues but that their huge potential continues to go untapped. This is especially so in this research where young people do not see a valuing, by adults, of the potential of their contributions to informing high-risk policy domains such as educational assessment reform.

Students presented constructive ideas as to the ways in which they and their teachers could navigate the myriad of decisions about assessment at this level; they expressed clear wishes to be involved in both national and school-level determinations regarding GCSEs so that decisions made are in their best interests which they feel is not the case at present. Students were sceptical, not so much about what the actual changes were to GCSEs, but about their governments' *reasons* for introducing the latest reforms. They suggested that decisions were made for political reasons rather than educational ones, reflecting previous research on the politicised nature of policy-making in educational assessment (Cadwallader & Tremain, 2013). Thus, a sense of powerlessness emanated from students' responses through criticisms made about the lack of consultation with young people on these matters. Cullingford (1991) eloquently details how young people are conscious of, observe and discuss, the nature of power and influence in their own educational settings; they may not overtly describe what they observe and discuss as such, but they are aware of the politics of the social organisations within which they move. In the same vein, students were able to articulate an awareness that the changes introduced would affect them most, and as such 'power', in the guise of decision-making, should be shared with them, especially with regard to future systems. The majority of students were unaware of all of the changes to GCSEs, and yet they argued that, as the ones most affected by the reforms, they should be involved in making decisions regarding future assessment policies.

It is important to emphasise that students tended to agree with the *substance* of their governments' plans regarding changes to GCSEs; if not their *reasoning* for them. This is possibly because the reforms to GCSEs in NI and Wales were less radical than those introduced in England, and students tended to approve of the assessment system they were experiencing at the time of the research. The main problem, as students saw it, was that all these changes would remove the 'common GCSE' across the three jurisdictions with all the problems of comparability and portability which this raised. Students were concerned about how their different 'GCSEs' would now be viewed by HE institutions and future employers and the impact of variations in understanding for their future options. At the time of the research, there was less awareness about the changes also to the labelling of GCSE results (9–1 in England; and the retention of A*-G in NI and Wales) but concerns about this have emerged from other later studies (see YouGov, 2017). Students expressed concern about the nature of policy-making in devolved regions, which they suggested were designed to differentiate policies in their regions from those of England, resonating with suggestions in the policy literature that Wales's main concern is to distinguish itself from England (Reynolds, 2008). While participants tended to agree with the reforms themselves, it was their lack of any role in contributing to them that was problematic. In common with policy-making in other fields, it may be that a more collaborative model of policy-making (Raffe & Spours, 2007) with greater involvement of young people in decision-making may have engendered more support amongst young people for the reforms being implemented.

The results of this project are comparable with those detailed in the literature section above that show students as having the capacity to express valid opinions on complex assessment issues (Barrance, 2017; Chamberlain, 2012; Daly et al., 2012; Elwood (2012, 2013)). In this particular context, they showed a strong understanding of how GCSE assessment structures and practices are experienced by them within schools and colleges. Such findings contribute to education policy research that considers policy as being 'enacted' (Ball, Maguire, & Braun, 2012) rather than implemented, showing how students experience assessment reforms in a myriad of ways depending on their locations, schools, teachers and their own interpretation of events. Students may not have a formal role in assessment policy-making, but as this data has shown they are at the centre of the enacted policies and processes in their local contexts and their 'lived social participation across all the spheres of their [assessment] interactions (Horgan, Forde, Martin, & Parkes, 2017, p. 275). In this respect, they are as much 'policy actors' (Ball et al., 2012) as their teachers or school leaders with significant influence over the interpretation and implementation of assessment policy changes.

Findings from this research have the potential to contribute to the field of assessment research by showing that it is very easy to make assumptions about how assessment policy is enacted within institutions, without considering that the practice will be quite different from what we expect. There will be differences in how students experience assessment policy reform and it is these differences that should be made visible to inform both national and international policies as well as institutional practices. The data from this and other studies (Barrance, 2017; Elwood, 2012) highlight how young people feel positioned within assessment regimes and how considering their perspectives on these matters can only improve our knowledge of fundamental assessment practices.

The results of this study suggest that the notion of 'student voice' needs to be expanded to accommodate not only the multiple 'voices' of students within educational settings (Cook-Sather, 2002) but also the involvement of multiple student voices in national decision-making (Tisdall, 2008) regarding assessment policy. We argue that it is problematic that assessment decisions at both school and national levels tend to be discussed separately, with little recognition of the fluidity between national and local assessment policy. Broadening the concept of student voice to encompass students' participation in national decisions would also allow for a recognition of the diverse ways in which national governmental policies are enacted in different contexts (Ball et al., 2012), thus enabling a more fruitful, holistic discussion of policies and their impacts, based on students' accounts. By combining reflections from key concepts in the fields of student voice (Cook-Sather, 2002), children as public policy actors (Tisdall, 2008), and children's rights (Barrance, 2017; Elwood & Lundy, 2010), we can arrive at a far more nuanced conceptualisation of the experience of national assessment as it is perceived and experienced by young people.

Notes

1. Scotland is not considered in this paper as it has its own curriculum and assessment systems and also the project reported on focused on Northern Ireland and Wales with specific comparison to England as all three jurisdictions support GCSEs.
2. At the time of writing (May 2017) exam regulators in the UK, in attempting to deal with anticipated problems caused by the Sawtooth effect, have committed to using year-on-year 'comparable outcomes' to ameliorate any dips in results following the introduction of new qualifications (B. McDowell, Personal communication, 2017).

Disclosure statement

No potential conflict of interest was reported by the authors.

Funding

Rhian Barrance received a doctoral scholarship to complete the research for this project from the Department of Education Northern Ireland [grant number PhD scholarship].

References

Alderson, P. (2000). School students' views on school councils and daily life at school. *Children & Society, 14*, 121–134. doi:10.1111/j.1099-0860.2000.tb00160.x

Arnott, M. (2008). Public policy, governance and participation in the UK: A space for children? *The International Journal of Children's Rights, 16*, 355–367. doi:10.1163/157181808x311196

Baird, J. (2011). *Implementing examinations policy: How many hands make heavy work* (Inaugural Professorial Lecture). University of Bristol, UK.

Baird, J., & Coxell, A. (2009). Policy, latent error and systemic examination failures. *CADMO, 17*, 105–122. doi:10.3280/CAD2009-002011

Baird, J., Elwood, J., Duffy, G., Feiler, A., O'Boyle, A., Rose, J., … McWhirter, A. (2010). *14–19 centre research study: Educational reform in schools and colleges in England* (Annual report). Retrieved from OUCEA: http://oucea.education.ox.ac.uk/wordpress/wp-content/uploads/2013/04/CReSt-Annual-Report-Final-whole.pdf

Baird, J., & Lee-Kelley, L. (2009). The dearth of managerialism in implementation of national examinations policy. *Journal of Education Policy, 24*, 55–81. doi:10.1080/02680930802382938

Ball, S., Maguire, M., & Braun, A. (2012). *How schools do policy: Policy enactments in secondary schools*. London: Routledge.

Banks, J., & Smyth, E. (2015). 'Your whole life depends on it': Academic stress and high-stakes testing in Ireland. *Journal of Youth Studies, 18*, 598–616. doi:10.1080/13676261.2014.992317

Barrance, R. (2017). *The assessment and reform of GCSEs: The views and experiences of young people in Northern Ireland and Wales* (Unpublished doctoral dissertation). Belfast: Queen's University Belfast.

Barrance, R., & Elwood, J. (2017). *Inequalities and the curriculum: Young people's views on choice and fairness through their experiences of curriculum as examination specifications at GCSE* (CLS Working Paper). London: Institute of Education, UCL.

Bragg, S. (2007). 'Student voice' and governmentality: The production of enterprising subjects? *Discourse: Studies in the Cultural Politics of Education, 28*, 343–358. doi:10.1080/01596300701458905

Cadwallader, S., & Tremain, K. (2013). *How policy formation and implementation interacts with risks to high stakes qualifications*. Retrieved from CERP: https://cerp.aqa.org.uk/sites/default/files/pdf_upload/CERP_RP_SMC_25102013.pdf

Chamberlain, S. (2012). Public perceptions of reliability. In D. Opposs & Q. He (Eds.), *Ofqual's Reliability Compendium* (pp. 691–725). Coventry: Office of Qualifications and Examinations Regulation.

Cook-Sather, A. (2002). Authorizing students' perspectives: Toward trust, dialogue, and change in education. *Educational Researcher, 31*, 3–14. doi:10.3102/0013189X031004003

Cook-Sather, A. (2006). Sound, presence, and power: "Student voice" in educational research and reform. *Curriculum Inquiry, 36*, 359–390.

Council for the Curriculum, Examinations and Assessment. (2013). *Review of GCSE and A-level qualifications: Final report with appendices*. Retrieved from CCEA: http://ccea.org.uk/sites/default/files/docs/accreditation/projects/review/final_report.pdf

Cresswell, M. (2003). *Heaps, prototypes and ethics: The consequences of using judgements of student performance to set examination standards in a time of change*. London: University of London Institute of Education.

Cullingford, C. (1991). *The inner world of the school: Children's ideas about school*. London: Cassell.

Daly, A., Baird, J., Chamberlain, S., & Meadows, M. (2012). Assessment reform: Students' and teachers' responses to the introduction of stretch and challenge at A-level. *Curriculum Journal, 23*, 139–155. doi:10.1080/09585176.2012.678683

Davies, L., & Yamashita, H. (2009). Students as professionals: The London secondary school councils action research project. In B. Percy-Smith & N. Thomas (Eds.), *A handbook of children and young people's participation* (pp. 230–239). London: Routledge.

Department for Education. (2010). *The importance of teaching: Schools white paper*. Retrieved from Department for Education: https://www.gov.uk/government/publications/the-importance-of-teaching-the-schools-white-paper-2010

Department of Children, Schools and Families. (2008). *Delivering 14-19 reform: Next steps*. Retrieved from National Archives: http://webarchive.nationalarchives.gov.uk/20130401151715/http://www.education.gov.uk/publications/eOrderingDownload/7928-DCSF-Delivering%2014-19%20Reform%20Summary.pdf

Department of Education Northern Ireland. (2014). *Recommendations on the fundamental review of GCSEs and A-levels*. Retrieved from Department for Education Northern Ireland: https://www.education-ni.gov.uk/publications/recommendations-fundamental-review-gcses-and-levels

Elwood, J. (2012). Qualifications, examinations and assessment: Views and perspectives of students in the 14–19 phase on policy and practice. *Cambridge Journal of Education, 42*, 497–512. doi:10.1080/0305764X.2012.733347

Elwood, J. (2013). The role(s) of student voice in 14–19 education policy reform: Reflections on consultation and participation. *London Review of Education, 11*, 97–111. doi:10.1080/14748460.2013.799807

Elwood, J., Hopfenbeck, T., & Baird, J. (2017). Predictability in high-stakes examinations: Students' perspectives on a perennial assessment dilemma. *Research Papers in Education, 32*(1), 1–17. doi:10.1080/02671522.2015.1086015

Elwood, J., & Lundy, L. (2010). Revisioning assessment through a children's rights approach: Implications for policy, process and practice. *Research Papers in Education, 25*, 335–353. doi:10.1080/02671522.2010.498150

Fielding, M. (2001). Students as radical agents of change. *Journal of Educational Change, 2*, 123–141. doi:10.1023/A:1017949213447

Fielding, M., & McGregor, J. (2005). *Deconstructing student voice: New spaces for dialogue or new opportunities for surveillance*. Montreal: AERA.

Fitz, J. (2000). Governance and identity: The case of Wales. In R. Daugherty, R. Phillips, & G. Rees (Eds.), *Education policy-making in Wales: Explorations in devolved governance* (pp. 24–46). Cardiff: University of Wales Press.

Gibb, N. (2010). *Press release: Government announces changes to qualifications and the curriculum*. Retrieved from Gov.uk: https://www.gov.uk/government/news/government-announces-changes-to-qualifications-and-the-curriculum

Gipps, C. (1986). *The GCSE: An uncommon examination*. London: Institute of Education.

Gove, M. (2013). *Ofqual policy steer letter: Reforming Key Stage 4 qualifications*. Retrieved from Gov. uk: http://media.education.gov.uk/assets/files/pdf/l/ofqual%20letter.pdf

Grace, G. (1995). *School leadership: Beyond education management*. London: The Falmer Press.

Hayward, L. (2013). From why to why not? The conundrum of including learners' perspectives: A response to this special issue. *London Review of Education, 11*, 184–189. doi:10.1080/14748460.2013.799814

Higher Education Statistics Authority. (2013). *Higher education student enrolments and qualifications obtained at higher education institutions in the United Kingdom for the academic year 2011/12*. Retrieved from HESA: https://www.hesa.ac.uk/index.php?option=com_content&view=article&id=2667

Hinton, R., Tisdall, E. K., Gallagher, M., & Elsley, S. (2008). Children;s and young people's participation in public decision-making. *The International Journal of Children's Rights, 16*, 281–284. doi:10.1163/157181808X311132

Hodgson, A., & Spours, K. (2003). *Beyond A levels: Curriculum 2000 and the reform of 14–19 qualifications*. London: Kogan Page.

Horgan, D., Forde, C., Martin, S., & Parkes, A. (2017). Children's participation: Moving from the preformative to the social. *Children's Geographies, 15*, 274–288. doi:10.1080/14733285.2016.121 9022

Koretz, D. (2005). Alignment, high stakes, and the inflation of test scores. In J. Herman & E. Haertel (Eds.), *Uses and misuses of data in accountability testing. Yearbook of the National Society for the Study of Education* (pp. 99–118). Malden, MA: Blackwell Publishing. doi: 10.1111/j.1744-7984.2005.00027.x

Koretz, D., & Barron, S. (1998). *The validity of gains on the kentucky instructional results information system (KIRIS) (MR-1014-EDU).* Santa Monica: RAND. Retrieved from RAND: http://www.rand.org/pubs/monograph_reports/MR1014.html

Linn, R. (1998). *Assessments and accountability* (CSE Technical Report 490). Los Angeles, CA: National Center for Research on Evaluation. Retrieved from ERIC: https://eric.ed.gov/?q=Assessments+and+Accountability&ff1=autLinn,+Robert+L.&id=ED443865

Linn, R. (2000). Assessments and accountability. *Educational Researcher, 29*, 4–16. doi:10.3102/00 13189X029002004

Lundy, L. (2007). 'Voice' is not enough: Conceptualising Article 12 of the United Nations convention on the rights of the child. *British Educational Research Journal, 33*, 927–942. doi:10.1080/01411920701657033

Lundy, L., & McEvoy, L. (2012). Children's rights and research processes: Assisting children to (in) formed views. *Childhood, 19*, 129–144. doi:10.1177/0907568211409078

Lundy, L., McEvoy, L., & Byrne, B. (2011). Working with young children as co-researchers: An approach informed by the United Nations convention on the rights of the child. *Early Education & Development, 22*, 714–736. doi:10.1080/10409289.2011.596463

Morgan, B. (2009). 'I think it's about the teacher feeding off our minds, instead of us learning off them, sort of like switching the process around': Pupils' perspectives on being consulted about classroom teaching and learning. *The Curriculum Journal, 20*, 389–407. doi:10.1080/09585170903424922

O'Dowd, J. (2014). *Oral statement on evaluation and assessment.* Retrieved from CCEA: http://ccea.org.uk/sites/default/files/docs/news/2014/Mar/statement_-_evaluation_and_assessment_-_tuesday_11_march_2014.pdf

Oates, T. (2007). Protecting the innocent: The need for ethical frameworks within mass educational innovation. In L. Saunders (Ed.), *Educational research and policy-making: Exploring the border country between research and policy* (pp. 144–174). Oxford: Routledge.

Ofqual. (2015). *New GCSE grading structure.* Retrieved from Ofqual: https://www.gov.uk/government/uploads/system/uploads/attachment_data/file/460142/new_gcse_grading_structure.pdf

Ofqual. (2016). *An Investigation into the 'Sawtooth Effect' in GCSE and AS/A Level Assessments* (Ofqual/16/6098). Retrieved from Ofqual: https://www.gov.uk/government/uploads/system/uploads/attachment_data/file/549686/an-investigation-into-the-sawtooth-effect-in-gcse-as-and-a-level-assessments.pdf

Osberg, J., Pope, D., & Galloway, M. (2006). Students matter in school reform: Leaving fingerprints and becoming leaders. *International Journal of Leadership in Education, 9*, 329–343. doi:10.1080/13603120600895338

Pavlou, P. (2008). *Consumer's rights and language testing.* Retrieved from ealta.eu.org: http://www.ealta.eu.org/conference/2008/docs/saturday/Pavlou%20LT%20and%20CR.pdf

Perry, C. (2013). *GCSE and A-level reform: Research and information service research paper.* Retrieved from NI Assembly: http://www.niassembly.gov.uk/globalassets/documents/raise/publications/2013/education/11413.pdf

Raffe, D., & Spours, K. (2007). *Policy-making and policy learning in 14–19 education.* London: University of London, Institute of Education.

Reynolds, D. (2008). New Labour, education and Wales: The devolution decade. *Oxford Review of Education, 34*, 753–765. doi:10.1080/03054980802519019

Shohamy, E. (2001). *The power of tests: A critical perspective on the uses of language tests.* London: Pearson.

Thomson, P. (2011). Coming to terms with 'voice'. In G. Czerniawski & W. Kidd (Eds.), *The international handbook of student voice* (pp. 19–30). Emerald: Bingley.

Tisdall, E. (2008). Is the honeymoon over? children and young people's participation in public decision-making. *The International Journal of Children's Rights, 16*, 419–429. doi:10.1163/1571 81808X311240

United Nations. (1989). *United Nations Convention on the Rights of the Child (UNCRC)*. Retrieved from United Nations: http://www.ohchr.org/en/professionalinterest/pages/crc.aspx

Weir, P. (2016). *Oral statement on qualification market and grading*. Retrieved June 28, 2016, rom CCEA.org: http://ccea.org.uk/sites/default/files/docs/news/2016/Jun/minister_oral_statement_on_grading_june16.pdf

Welsh Government. (2012). *Review of qualifications for 14 to 19-year-olds in Wales: Final report and recommendations* (CAD/GM/0227). Retrieved from Welsh Government: http://gov.wales/docs/dcells/publications/121127reviewofqualificationsen.pdf

Welsh Government. (2014). *Qualified for life: How qualifications in Wales are changing*. Retrieved from Welsh Government: http://learning.gov.wales/docs/learningwales/publications/140616-qualified-for-life-how-qualifications-in-wales-are-changing-en.pdf

Whitty, G., & Wisby, E. (2007). Whose voice? An exploration of the current policy interest in pupil involvement in school decision-making. *International Studies in Sociology of Education, 17*, 303–319. doi:10.1080/09620210701543957

YouGov. (2017). *Perceptions of A levels, GCSEs and other qualifications in England – Wave 15. An Ofqual commissioned report* (Ofqual/17/6193). Retrieved from Gov.uk: https://www.gov.uk/government/uploads/system/uploads/attachment_data/file/606463/Ofqual_Perceptions_Survey_Wave_15_Report.pdf

Towards a national assessment policy in Switzerland: areas of conflict in the use of assessment instruments

Flavian Imlig 🆔 and Susanne Ender 🆔

ABSTRACT

This article reveals three emerging areas of conflict in the use of educational assessment instruments in compulsory education in Switzerland and outlines an analytical approach for detecting and analysing these areas of conflict. The approach combines a conceptual perspective, an evaluation perspective and a teaching perspective to show the different backgrounds and expectations of actors on the governmental and school levels. We apply our analysis to three assessment instruments, currently in use in Switzerland, retracing a rudimentary timeline of Swiss educational assessment, with a focus on the German-speaking region of the country. Combining the three perspectives and positioning the analytical approach within the context of political and historical developments enables us to discuss both the reasons for the conflicts and possible ways to respond to them.

Introduction

The educational assessment of students' performance has become a focal point of school governance and development and a possible way to support teaching and learning. As education policies have again become a 'hot topic on the political agenda', comparative assessment results are being intensely scrutinised in both the public and political spheres (Jakobi, Martens, & Wolf, 2010, p. 1). In its basic form, we understand educational assessment as any form of graded or evaluated work in schools, such as written or oral exams, essays and projects. Such assessment instruments are integral to the grading and evaluation processes that allow judgements on students' learning and achievement (Sun & Cheng, 2014). Several disciplines have explored the topic of educational assessment: Test developers are working to measure competences in more valid, reliable and objective ways (Lane, Raymond, & Haladyna, 2016); policy analysts are focusing on how international assessment studies shape governance mechanisms and power relations in the educational field (Martens, 2010); and educational scientists are analysing how instruments are or should be used in the teaching and learning process (Gordon & Rajagopalan, 2015).

In Switzerland, the assessment of students' performance has long been treated as a matter of instruction and teaching. Especially in compulsory education, assessment has been seen as a necessary tool for schools to fulfil their purpose of allocating and selecting students into different education paths. This purpose is, as Fend (2008) points out, one of the socially encoded functions of schools in society. In addition, assessment has been seen as a general core feature of schooling with high universal validity and stability over time (Tyack & Tobin, 1994). Beginning in the 1980s, Swiss teachers and politicians began to shift their judgement practices towards more scientific and standardised approaches, establishing a new culture of assessment within which assessment was discussed as a feature of educational and instructional quality (Vögeli-Mantovani, 1999). As a result, a wide range of development projects focusing on innovation and quality in compulsory schooling emerged all over Switzerland (e.g. Ambühl et al., 1986). In terms of assessment, relevant projects and tools were often developed locally and focused on actual educational practice in schools.

Since 2000, international discourse and, in particular, international large-scale assessments have again changed the perceptions and usage of information on students' performance. Throughout Switzerland, the use of such information in education-related policy-making has become the focus of intense discussion (Criblez, 2008a; Herzog, 2008). As a result, educational assessment has increasingly become seen as important beyond the levels of actual practice or single teachers or classes. Over time, new assessment instruments have become more and more connected to specific modes of monitoring, controlling and reporting. On a national level, Switzerland has introduced an educational governance system using standardised monitoring and reporting tools (Wolter, 2008). In 2016, the implementation of a nationwide performance assessment called 'Evaluation of basic competencies' (ÜGK) complemented this national assessment policy (Weber, 2016). As a whole, though educational assessment development in Switzerland started with locally implemented instruments for teaching and instruction, since 1990, assessment instruments have evolved towards systematic monitoring and increasing diffusion, culminating in a national performance assessment policy. However, more recent instruments did not replace existing ones. Teachers, schools and even cantons continued to develop and use various sorts of local assessment instruments.

In this article, we analyse the development of Switzerland's assessment policy from the bottom up. We begin by exploring the political and historical contexts of educational assessment in Switzerland. This first section presents a short overview of the principles of educational governance in Switzerland, a historical outline of the national reception of international discourses about indicators and large-scale assessments and a description of the subsequent shift towards evidence-based policy in Switzerland. In the second section, we present our analytical approach, which combines a conceptual perspective, an evaluation perspective and a teaching perspective. We then present in the third section three instruments with different aims and scopes, two of which are currently used in German-speaking Switzerland (Orientation test, Stellwerk test) and the 'Evaluation of Basic Competencies' test (ÜGK) which is now under implementation in the entire country (German-, French- and Italian-speaking regions). By applying our approach in the fourth section, we discuss three areas of conflict in the use of the three assessment instruments. Different opinions about the purposes of the instruments, the connection of aggregation levels to the sovereignty over test results, and the potential influence of assessment instruments on instruction bear conflicts that are revealed in our discussion. The conclusion explores the implications of the identified conflicts and summarises what needs to be taken into account in the processes of conceptualising, developing and implementing educational assessment instruments.

Political and historical contexts

The assessment of students' performance in Switzerland is situated in a threefold context both historically and politically. First, assessment policies are embedded in a particular landscape of education polity and governance within a federal, multilevel system of diverse actors and stakeholders. Moreover, assessment is thematically intertwined with Swiss policy traditions and international trends concerning both educational indicators and evidence-based policy-making. All three of these contexts shape the concepts, development processes and implementation of actual assessment instruments.

Educational governance in Switzerland

As a small state with a decentralised educational tradition and highly consensus-oriented policy institutions at all levels, federalist Switzerland is a special case when it comes to education policy-making. Over the last decade, the education systems of the federated states (cantons) have undergone a wide range of transformation processes, both structurally and in terms of governance (Bieber, 2010). Changes in school principles, systems of quality assurance and control, education monitoring and reporting and education standards can be observed at both the national and the canton level (Maag Merki & Büeler, 2002).

Like in other federal countries, compulsory education in Switzerland has been a primary policy field through which cantons have cultivated their autonomy throughout the twentieth century. At the same time, policies across the 26 Swiss cantons have moved towards a consensus, and cooperation has been maintained. The cantonal education departments coordinate at the intercantonal level via the Swiss Conference of Cantonal Ministers of Education (EDK). This harmonisation can be seen as a reaction to growing demands for education and mobility. In addition, cantonal education departments strive to coordinate their education policies in order to preserve their decentralised structure and authority in the education sector (Criblez, 2008c; Hega, 2000).

Despite this decentralised governance configuration, beginning in the 1980s, educational governance became a widely discussed national topic. Responding to international developments, such as the shift towards decentralised decision-making in the European Union (Green, 2002), most cantons began to move towards school autonomy. This development strengthened individual schools, fostered educational innovation from the bottom up and introduced new mechanisms of coordination and accountability between educational practice and educational policy (Maag Merki & Büeler, 2002; Nussbaum, Fischer, & Hildbrand, 2007). Concerning structural reforms on a national scale, the federal structure and high number of possible veto players created a backlog of unresolved policy issues that lasted well into the 1990s (Bieber, 2010).

From indicators to competence-based large-scale assessments

On an international level, educational assessment is closely intertwined with popular large-scale assessments like PISA (Programme for International Student Assessment), TIMMS

(Trends in International Mathematics and Science Study), PIRLS (Progress in International Reading Literacy Study), ALL (Adult Literacy and Life Skills Survey) and IALS (International Adult Literacy Survey). In Switzerland and many other countries, these large-scale assessments frame a majority of the policies surrounding assessment (Tillmann, Dedering, Kneuper, Kuhlmann, & Nessel, 2008; Windzio, Knodel, & Martens, 2014).

Since the first attempts of the IEA (International Association for the Evaluation of Educational Achievement) to survey a so-called 'attained curriculum' in the 1980s (Pelgrum, 1986, p. 6), the comparative assessment of students' achievement has been connected to the internationally shared aim of an indicator-based, comparative view of national education systems. At the same time, the OECD (Organisation for Economic Co-operation and Development) relaunched its programme of education indicators (Papadopoulos, 1994/1996; Tröhler, 2013). In the late 1980s, the OECD adopted the concept of monitoring output using students' performance and began the development of the later PISA. These PISA assessment data completed the OECD's neoliberally inspired concept of holistic and internationally comparable descriptions of education systems (Davies, Nutley, & Smith, 2012; Martens & Wolf, 2006; Sjøberg, 2007; Uljens, 2007).

The international large-scale assessments also (re)introduced paradigms of competence- or skill-based teaching and learning in compulsory schooling (Tyo, 2010). The concept of competence was originally introduced as an alternative to intelligence and was meant to describe a holistic capacity for reasonable and responsible action (McClelland, 1973). In international large-scale assessments, the notion shifted towards the measurability, assessment and evaluation of educational performance, often in relation to given standards (Oelkers & Reusser, 2008).

The Swiss Federal Statistical Office participated in the development of education indicators and published its first report according to OECD definitions in 1992 (BFS, 1992). In 2002, the first Swiss PISA results fell 'on fertile ground' and triggered fundamental discussions on the capacity and efficiency of schooling (Bieber, 2014, p. 186). The newness of this type of performance information and the backlog of structural reforms in federal Switzerland were two reasons for this fundamental impact. The PISA results were followed by a wide range of reforms, including, most recently, steps towards harmonising the cantons' education systems (Bieber, 2010; Criblez, 2008b; EDK, 2011). These harmonisation processes have also involved the introduction of national monitoring and reporting (Wolter, 2008).

The concept of competence has also played an important role in the implementation of educational standards on both national and regional levels (Criblez et al., 2009). It has been a critical concept in educational practice due to its influence on textbook development and teacher training. Competence-based assessment tools, as well as instruments for competence-based teaching and instruction, have been introduced (Bölsterli Bardy, 2015; Larcher & Smit, 2011).

Towards evidence-based policy

Ideas on evidence-based policy and practice have grown in popularity across all policy fields in many countries (Biesta, 2010, p. 492). This shift has been accompanied by changes to the guiding principles concerning polity, state organisation and public action (Jann & Wegrich, 2010), including the shift in regulatory responsibilities to international organisations and the shared provision of public goods (Hurrelmann, Leibfried, Martens, & Mayer, 2007). In education, the idea of evidence-based policy-making has led to widespread accountability reforms (Cibulka, 1990). A key component of these governance regimes, often referred to as 'new public management' (NPM), is the use of educational assessment (Green, 2011; Mitchell, Shipps, & Crowson, 2011).

In Switzerland, NPM concepts gained increasing popularity throughout the 1990s (Rieder, 2005). Most NPM-inspired reforms focused on management, supervision and accountability, leading to the introduction of head teachers and quality management procedures in most cantons (Hangartner & Svaton, 2013). The use of comparative data on educational outcomes has been intensely discussed in Switzerland. Unlike the UK or the Netherlands, Switzerland's political and scientific landscape has been characterised by critical positions on high-stakes testing, performance ranking and quasi-market models of education (Criblez, 2008a; Green, 2002; Herzog, 2008).

By positioning educational assessment within its complex and multifaceted historical and political contexts, we seek to set the stage for our analysis, which approaches actual assessment instruments via the three distinct analytical perspectives.

Analytical perspectives

Assessment in education is the subject of extensive research. Berry and Adamson's (2011) inventory of assessment reforms follows a political approach, which can also be found in the research on international assessments and how they shape national education policy (Davier, Gonzales, Kirsch, & Yamamoto, 2013; Martens, Knodel, & Windzio, 2014; Pereyra, Kotthoff, & Cowen, 2011). In critical policy analysis, traditional concepts of functionalism and rationalism have been rearranged to reveal policy contexts, traditions and overlooked actors and to introduce theorising methodologies and qualitative approaches to the field (Young & Diem, 2017). From a more technical perspective, there is a broad discourse on assessment quality, measurement accuracy and evaluation implementation (Goldstein, 2015; Lane et al., 2016). Purposes and quality criteria are key research subjects in the growing modern international assessment landscape (Broadfoot & Black, 2010). A relevant portion of this research also deals with the implications of assessment for educational practice (Gordon & Rajagopalan, 2015).

Our analytical approach seeks to integrate different aspects of this theoretical and empirical research on educational assessment. We seek to examine how educational assessment is embedded in education policy and education. To gain a coherent and plausible analysis of assessment instruments, we integrate three perspectives: a conceptual, an evaluation and a teaching perspective. This approach is not meant to fully cover all aspects of assessment tests, since there are, of course, topics that demand an extension of the analytical approach. The three perspectives allow us to discuss the broad questions surrounding the conceptual premises of assessment instruments, their evaluation policies and their practical impact on teaching, taking into account the complex interactions among educational governance, international influences and the adoption of evidence-based policy in Switzerland.

Conceptual perspective

From a conceptual perspective, student performance assessments need to fulfil either form ative or summative purposes. Formative assessments, sometimes referred to as assessments for learning, emphasise the connections between assessment and learning (Broadfoot & Black, 2010). From a formative perspective, assessment is an integral part of the learning process. It is a tool for communicating learning among actors at the level of educational practice (Ambühl et al., 1986). By contrast, summative assessments are used in communications related to classes, schools and education systems (Vögeli-Mantovani, 1999). They are meant to be public, and they relate to societal functions of allocation and selection and serve purposes of certification and accountability. Formative and summative assessments are just two of a bigger set of purposes for assessment instruments. Though they share common characteristics, the underlying assumptions and methods used by test developers differ (Harlen, 2012; Yates & Johnston, 2017). It is often argued that there are no good combinations of the two purposes and that summative assessments undermine the efficacy of formative assessments (e.g. Harlen & James, 1997). However, some evidence shows that multiple perspectives on purposes should be considered simultaneously and consciously during the conception of an assessment instrument (Newton, 2017). If summative assessments are combined with high stakes, then authorities will put stronger pressure on both teachers and students, since the results will be crucial for the course of education or the teacher's career. In using such tests, teachers face a conflict between accountability and their responsibility to the learning process. Therefore, the opposition between summative and formative assessment must be overcome, and teachers must be supported in adopting assessment for learning practice instead (Black, 2015).

From a conceptual perspective, we investigate the tensions between 'purpose purism' and 'purpose pluralism' (Newton, 2017) within the concepts and guidelines of assessment instruments in Switzerland. How are assessment instruments positioned in the interplay of different purposes and their respective assumptions? Which demarcations and boundaries in terms of functions or purposes can be drawn?

Evaluation perspective

Students' performance assessments are always directly connected to the level of educational practice. The results of single students are evaluated in either a prognostic or recapitulatory manner in order to look forward or backward in time. The evaluation perspective is strongly connected not only to educational practice, but also the political foundations of the school system. Educational governance points to a wide range of actors and their reciprocal influences of a multilevel system (Böttcher, 2007). The level of educational practice involves schools, teachers, students and parents. Above this level are multiple policy levels, ranging from school administrators to administrators of cantons, groups of cantons and the Swiss federation. The descriptions of educational governance in a multilevel system are based on sociological theories, such as neo-institutionalism and system and organisation theory (Berkemeyer, 2010; Koch & Schemmann, 2009). The trend towards evidence-based policy presented above establishes connections among actors on different levels. The evaluation of the results of educational assessment links the different levels by extending the results to levels above single students. Information can also be aggregated beyond the level of single students' performance, extending to the levels of classes, schools, regions, nations and other entities.

Evaluation theory differentiates among the various evaluation levels of educational assessment (Rhyn, 2009). For example, a teacher assesses the performance of his or her students, possibly compared to a broader standard. He or she then uses the resulting information to judge the students' performance and to reflect on his or her practice. At the next level, an educational organisation, typically a school, assesses the students' performance in order to gather information on quality and fulfil responsibilities for reporting and accountability. Finally, an education system (in Switzerland, typically a canton) assesses the students' performance to legitimate itself and inform processes of educational governance. When the results of educational assessment are projected to the system level on a regular basis, this is called education monitoring (Hovenga & Bos, 2009). At the level of the educational system, information on students' performance is often combined with other data indicators to support political conclusions (Wolter, 2008).

From an evaluation perspective, we investigate the levels of aggregation of performance data in relation to the political purposes of assessment instruments in Switzerland. Which actors use the assessment results? Which projections of students' performance can be observed?

Teaching perspective

The teaching perspective focuses on the instructional relevance of educational assessments, since forms and procedures of assessments express general understandings of teaching and learning (Vögeli-Mantovani, 1999). As presented above, educational assessments, especially popular large-scale assessments, imply competence-based teaching and learning. This concept follows a constructivist understanding that organises learning and teaching arrangements around individual students' learning processes. Therefore, teaching consists of different actions designed to initiate, support, coach, scaffold, review and consult students' learning. These actions are combined with an analytical, research-based teaching methodology designed to support the usability and applicability of learning outcomes (Wiater, 2013). A specific understanding of teaching and learning is also supported by the content of assessment instruments. The actual tasks represent certain underlying concepts of learning and play an important role in instructional processes (Drüke-Noe, 2014), since they structure teaching, learning and results (Knudson, 1993). Therefore, in recent educational assessments, task types have been important at the level of education practice. Especially in Switzerland, actors on the level of educational practice often raise concerns regarding 'teaching to the test'. It is assumed that teachers intuitively align their teaching towards various assessments, especially if the stakes are high (Yates & Johnston, 2017).

From a teaching perspective, we investigate the potential influences of assessment instruments and their included tasks on instruction. Which elements are explicitly and implicitly transported into the educational practice?

Instruments under scrutiny

To apply our analytical approach, we chose three assessment instruments that represent a rudimentary timeline of educational assessment in Switzerland, with a focus on the experience of the German-speaking cantons. Although teachers use many 'handmade' tests to evaluate the performance of their classes, only a few instruments exist that claim to either completely or partially fulfil the psychometrical criteria of valid, reliable and objective assessment.

One of the first such instruments, which is still used in the German-speaking part of Switzerland, is the 'Orientation test' (*Orientierungsarbeit*). The first iteration of this test was developed and published in 1994 by the canton of Lucerne and comprised a set of standardised mathematics questions for sixth graders. Since then, five other cantons have joined the project, and the tests now cover a wide range of subjects for grades 2–9 (BKZ, 2013). The teachers' use of the Orientation tests is regulated by cantonal guidelines (e.g. Frey, 2010). Orientation tests are paper-and-pencil tests that are published as brochures and resemble the types of tests teachers use in their classes. They are tailored to the current curriculum (Sutermeister-Christen et al., 2007). Though the evaluation of students' answers is neither standardised nor centralised, the Orientation tests contribute to a more objective grading practice and refer to external criteria (rather than individual teachers' instruction). Thus, they tackle the problem of teacher bias in class-oriented grading (Vögeli-Mantovani, 1999).

In 2006, a decade after the first release of the Orientation test and influenced by psychometrically shaped assessments like PISA, the 'Stellwerk test' was developed and implemented by the canton of St. Gallen. Since the Stellwerk test has been implemented by nearly all German-speaking cantons, its items are based on common educational goals of the cantons' different curricula (Wolter & Hof, 2014). The Stellwerk test is a computer-based test with items referring to Question and Test Interoperability (QTI) specifications, such as multiple-choice, short answer and drag-and-drop. Both the test development and the evaluation of the students' results are centralised and conducted by a professional organisation. The test seeks to build an individual profile of competencies of students in the eighth and ninth grades in order to prepare them for their transition from compulsory school to upper secondary school and/or vocational education and training (Staatskanzlei SG, 2006).

Most recently, in 2016, a decade after the first release of the Stellwerk test, the 'Evaluation of Basic Competencies' (ÜGK) assessment of the Swiss educational system was implemented. This assessment is rooted in the responsibilities shared by the federation and the cantons. It was developed by the EDK and is part of the national education monitoring strategy. It comprises a sample-based assessment of the competencies of second, sixth and ninth graders throughout Switzerland. In its final implementation, it will cover mathematics, science and both first and foreign languages. The ÜGK is a computer-based assessment that uses QTI item formats. It is designed to measure whether students have attained national education standards on both the national and cantonal levels (EDK, 2013).

Discussion: areas of conflict

The different aims and scopes of the described assessment instruments raise questions concerning their potential for governance, the availability of their data and the use of their results. Applying our analytical approach to the three assessment instruments described above reveals three areas of conflict in regard to these questions: from a conceptual perspective, there is a confusion of purposes; from an evaluation perspective, the different aggregation levels give rise to questions of sovereignty; and from a teaching perspective, the influence of assessment instruments on instruction is unclear. We seek to show how the specific political and historical contexts in Switzerland, as presented in the first section, produce conflicting ideas of educational assessment.

Confusion of purposes

We discuss the purposes of the three assessment instruments from a conceptual perspective. The instruments deal in a specific way with the distinction between formative and summative purposes and processes (Harlen, 2005). The ways in which these instruments are positioned between these purposes reveal conflicts.

The original aim of the Orientation tests was clearly and explicitly defined as summarising students' knowledge and skills in relation to the goals of the curriculum. In this respect, the tests were designed to make teachers' judgements more objective (Vögeli-Mantovani, 1999). Nevertheless, the first Orientation test in 1994 explicitly sought to formatively support teachers in planning individual support and teaching (Jost, 1994). This mix of functions was seen as a problem by governmental actors, especially because the assessment was positioned at the end of primary school, when students were assigned to a certain track of secondary school. On one hand, the 'results of the 'Orientation tests' should be used neither to give marks nor to justify assignment decisions', while, on the other hand, 'the results provide criteria for assignments to continuing schools' (Jost, 1994, p. 1). From the beginning, the guidelines and discussions surrounding the tests indicate a confusion of purposes. When the Orientation tests were expanded, the originally unintentional mix of formative and summative purposes persisted. Today, both the planning function and the performance function are highlighted in parallel (Frey, 2010). The educational administration is not clear in its communication of the purpose. In the canton of Lucerne, for example, the formative function of evaluating individual performance is clearly emphasised and set in contrast to the functions of other standardised and summative assessment tests (BKD LU, 2013). On the other hand, the instrument is also used during the process of assigning students to lower secondary school (Roos, Wandeler, & Mosimann, 2013).

Since the beginning of the Stellwerk concept, there has been an attempt to avoid confusion of purposes by clearly distinguishing summative and formative purposes. The first assessment, which is given to eighth graders, is meant to be formative, while the second one, which is given to ninth graders, is designed to be summative. The latter is meant to measure students' skills at the end of compulsory school, while the former is seen as a planning tool for the last year of compulsory school (Staatskanzlei SG, 2006). In actual practice, this two-step concept has seen little realisation. The eighth-grade test is used mainly as a certificate to apply for vocational education, and the formative function takes secondary importance (Goetze, Denzler, & Wissler, 2009). This change in the purpose of the assessment test has had a backwash effect, such that official guidelines issued by educational administrations that originally argued for a distinction of purposes now recommend that the eighth-grade test be used in a summative manner (e.g. BD SZ, 2015).

The ÜGK is based on a different concept than the Orientation test and the Stellwerk test. It has a clear summative function: It is meant to give information on the national and cantonal levels regarding whether students have achieved national education standards. Its results inform educational policy on the performance of the educational system with respect to education standards. The ÜGK does not aim to evaluate single students, schools or teachers (EDK, 2013). In fact, due to the assessment's sample-based approach and references to national education standards, a formative purpose is virtually impossible (Klausing & Husfeldt, 2015). However, though the concept of the evaluation seems to be distinctively summative, its connection to national education standards also suggests a formative aspect. The evaluation of the achievement of educational goals implies conclusions designed to support the development of educational system quality (EDK, 2015). Though the responsibility and processes for achieving such conclusions have not yet been defined, drawing development goals from performance data means going beyond using the evaluation for exclusively summative interpretations. In sum, the ÜGK reinterprets the traditional formative purpose of assessment instruments by relocating the responsibility of 'looking forward' to improve students' performance to policy-makers.

Aggregation levels and sovereignty

The needs of different actors (e.g. teachers, schools, cantons) and their expectations concerning the effects of various instruments are reflected by the instruments' levels of evaluation. As Goldstein (2004) pointed out with respect to PISA, there is a mismatch between the conceptual restrictions and the wide political use of the instrument. The ways in which the results of the three investigated assessment tests are evaluated reveal political conflicts.

The Orientation tests were developed from the bottom up in the context of instructional quality development. They were meant to support teachers' assessments of students' performance; therefore, they were orientated towards the processes of teaching and learning (Vögeli-Mantovani, 1996). The Orientation tests have also faced claims concerning aspects of their role as standardised assessments, such as the valid operationalisation of performance and the collection of context factors of instruction and learning techniques. Nevertheless, the tests remained bound to instruction. The tests' decentralised ways of evaluating students' performance also prevent the aggregation of results (BKD LU, 2013). Some cantons use a monitoring mechanism to supervise the Orientation tests, but not to aggregate their results (e.g. BD NW, 2015). The Orientation tests refer to the instructional level of education and are strongly connected to both individual teachers and their classes. They are not standardised in a way that allows comparisons across all kinds of classes, schools or even cantons. Misunderstandings of the possibilities of data aggregations can create political conflicts. Specifically, when Orientation tests tend to be used by communal or cantonal policy-makers in a comparative way, teachers become pressured by the accountability assigned to this originally instructional instrument. There is a conflict between educational practitioners and superordinate governing levels concerning sovereignty over the test and the right to use the produced information for their own purposes.

The Stellwerk test supports the aggregation of performance results across different levels, beginning with the individual student and going up to the level of the canton. In several Swiss cantons, the educational administration both prescribes and funds the test. There, student performance data are aggregated on four levels. Students receive profiles of their individual performance, teachers receive profiles of their classes in comparison to the cantonal standard, school boards receive profiles of their schools in comparison to the cantonal standard and cantons receive detailed reports showing anonymised differences among classes and schools (e.g. BD SZ, 2015). These evaluation practices illustrate the diminishing importance of the formative purpose of the eighth graders' test and imply accountability mechanisms that go beyond mere classroom instruction. The process of projecting assessment information to not only the levels of learning and instruction, but also the levels of schools and the cantonal education policy field opens up an area of political conflict regarding the sovereignty of the test and the use of its results. The results of the eighth graders' test are presented in a way that fosters their use at levels other than teaching and learning. Students use their test results for applications (a usage recommended by officials), and administrators are informed about the results of classes, schools and cantons.

The ÜGK explicitly excludes all evaluation levels below the cantons. No reporting will be made at lower levels, such as schools, classes, teachers or individual students (EDK, 2013). The results target the education system level and are made available to relevant research. The main evaluation level is that of the cantons. At the moment, there is no clear information concerning which data are provided and how they can be used. The cantons receive evaluation results concerning their own cantonal performance in relation to basic national competencies (Klausing & Husfeldt, 2015). Though all evaluation levels below the cantons' education systems are excluded, political conflicts arise from questions of responsibility and aggregation among cantons at the federal level. This conflict area specifically involves the Swiss governmental system. Though the cantons are in charge of their own education systems, they are requested by federal law to harmonise them. The EDK is a key actor concerning harmonisation at the intercantonal political level. Since the results of the ÜGK serve as an indicator of harmonisation, it is unclear which political level (i.e. the cantons, the EDK or the federal state) is responsible in the event that results do not match expectations. Finally, the inclusion of independent research in the evaluation process raises questions of autonomy and responsibility. The researchers engaging in evaluations of the ÜGK tend to come from Swiss teacher training colleges and universities. On one hand, they are committed to independent research; however, on the other, they are part of the educational system, not least because they are responsible for teacher training. Thus, they may contribute simultaneously to both problems and solutions, creating a challenging starting position for research. The ÜGK is a politically governed educational assessment that is meant to support evidence-based policy. Therefore, the extent to which policy-makers do or might hand over responsibility to supposedly independent researchers is currently unclear.

Influence on instruction

Current assessment instruments seek to inspire not only teachers' evaluations of students' performance, but also new methods of instruction. Through the nature of their tasks, assessment instruments transfer instructional elements into classes and interact with other teaching elements. The ways in which instruments are used in educational practice reveal instructional conflicts shaped by traditions and trends in teaching and learning. From a teaching perspective, it is unclear whether teaching and learning can contribute to educational steering policy or should be left unaffected by superordinate political aims (Maier, 2015). The discussions around teaching and testing during the implementation of the Orientation tests and the Stellwerk test in Switzerland represent areas of conflict that can be applied to other assessment instruments as well. Since these two were the first widely used instruments in German-speaking Switzerland, the conflicts can be seen as prototypical harbingers of the broad discussion today.

The Orientation tests are bound to their formative function and their close connection to teaching and instruction. Among other measures, these tests contributed to the 1990s reforms in teaching and instruction by introducing multidimensional, complex and challenging tasks (Vögeli-Mantovani, 1996). Several cantons' guidelines stress the model character of the tasks included in the Orientation tests (e.g. BKD LU, 2013), which are designed to be used as samples for teachers to convert and modulate (e.g. BKD OW, 2013). Educational conflicts emerge from the blurring of the frontiers between the tests and the instructional material. With the Orientation tests, the risk is that the tests could become the teaching, which would ultimately make the tests needless as assessment instruments. If instruction is too closely connected to the Orientation tests, then the tests will no longer be able to reflect students' performance from an external perspective. The strength of the Orientation test is that it challenges students to show their skills in new tasks. When incorporated into instruction, the Orientation tests can no longer maintain their objective position.

When the Stellwerk test was first introduced into schools, the main challenge was to acquaint teachers and school boards with the concept of a computerised assessment test. Preparing, organising and applying a computerised test clearly influenced the practice level. Teachers and students alike had to handle new educational material and get used to using computer systems. Even today, standardised tests like the Stellwerk test are surrounded by controversy concerning the differences between computerised feedback on students' performance and common teachers' evaluations. Students, teachers, school boards and instructors in vocational education must learn how to read such results and interpret them in formative and summative ways. Furthermore, in parallel to the Stellwerk tests, several training platforms were established. One of these platforms is directly connected to the tests themselves and serves as a possible preparation for the assessment. In relation to the new kind of standardised assessment in schools, the Stellwerk test was criticised as a kind of hidden curriculum that endangered instructional quality by encouraging teaching to the test and sanctioning teachers who did not design their teaching according to test contents (Schaller, 2011). The scope of tasks made possible by QTI has also been critically discussed. Item formats like multiple choice questions were not very common in Swiss paper-and-pencil tests (Husfeldt, 2007). Although teachers increasingly got used to these modes of testing, they examined the results with caution and suspicion. The educational conflicts surrounding the Stellwerk test are symptomatic of the clash between traditional educational practices and the new influence of educational assessment on teaching.

The ÜGK includes no training platforms or teaching materials. In this respect, the evaluation is uncoupled from the instructional level. Nevertheless, an implicit influence can be identified through the information published on students' performance, which is available to teachers and school boards. As yet, it is unclear which instructional conflicts can be expected in the upcoming implementation of the ÜGK. The assumption is that teaching will be more influenced by instruments and arrangements that are closer to the school level than the assessment of the educational system. However, at the same time, given previous experiences with PISA, it seems obvious that this type of system assessment will affect the level of education practice, too.

Implications and conclusion

The educational assessment of students' performance is embedded in a specific educational governmental system and influenced by international trends in educational assessment. By applying an analytical approach to three assessment instruments currently used in

Switzerland, we retrace the country's recent history of assessment, progressively complementing existing tests developed locally and from the bottom up with more recent instruments and moving towards a national assessment system of education monitoring.

From a conceptual perspective, we demonstrate that, although the function of newer standardised instruments is conceptualised in a more conscious and clear way than that of tests developed from the bottom up, the functions of actual instrument use tend to be blurred. For assessment policies, this illustrates the importance of defining use purposes and processes from the beginning and taking into account the possibility of serving several purposes simultaneously. But even with carefully developed and unambiguous concepts, assessment instruments inevitably are subject to recontextualisation processes in policy and practice. Test developers, policy-makers and practitioners might as well take these processes into account.

From an evaluation perspective, we demonstrate that the dictum of evidence-based policy leads to the integration of more and more levels of the educational system in the evaluation and information process. It is not always clear which stakeholders hold sovereignty over a given test or who is responsible for the several steps in the educational processes surrounding educational assessment. To address this issue, it is crucial for assessment policies to consider the significance and constraints of various instruments for acting at different levels of the education system and to create an assessment loop that connects the numerous stakeholders in a single dialogue. At the same time, stakeholders do not necessarily share common goals, a collective understanding of a reasonable use of the single instruments or a uniform set of information needs. To be aware of the different positions might already help establish common assessment policies.

From a teaching perspective, we demonstrate that assessment instruments influence instruction both intentionally and unintentionally. With respect to assessment policies, it is important to clarify whether assessment instruments are meant to improve instruction and how they relate to other instruction material and to teachers' professional backgrounds and routines. If assessment instruments are made a part of instruction and designed to contribute to the quality of education, they must be integrated into overarching systems. But still, the actual impact of assessment instruments on instruction and teaching depends on local perceptions of the instruments by school boards and teachers as well as parents and students. Stakeholders might not neglect this, but find a sensitive approach to handle it.

Following the rudimentary timeline our three instruments under scrutiny represent, the areas of conflict are both persistent and constantly adapting to current developments in education policy and educational assessment influences within Switzerland and beyond.

The confusion of purposes emerged in the early Orientation tests as a lack of coordination between political and instructional aims. Neither the attempts to create a functional divide in the Stellwerk tests nor the limitations of the ÜGK to a mere monitoring purpose fully eliminated this area of conflict. On the contrary, these confusions triggered a reshaping of the traditional differences between the summative and formative purposes of educational assessment both in Switzerland and on an international level. Currently, questions on the asymmetric relationship between the two purposes are combined with questions on appropriate evidence for assessment, assessment quality and the potential dangers and benefits of combinations of purpose (Harlen, 2012).

The influence of test development and the increasing ability to measure competences in more valid, reliable and objective ways opened the way for data aggregation at levels above that of the individual student. The Orientation tests and the ÜGK represent the two poles of this continuum of aggregation and evaluation possibilities. Increased aggregation involves a greater policy focus on schools, regions and nations. As Skedsmo (2011) pointed out for Norwegian evaluation policy, a high evaluative aggregation of assessment data enables the political usage of these data and introduces new inconsistencies between practice and policy.

Using assessment instruments to influence instruction can be seen as a key rationale for implementation in a majority of assessment instruments. The Orientation tests have served as both assessment instruments and instructional material. Furthermore, while the Stellwerk tests are supported by additional training platforms, the ÜGK offers no specific materials for teachers or students. Thus, the monitoring purpose of this assessment instrument inherently involves teaching and instruction. In other words, as Yates and Johnston (2017) state in their examination of teachers' conceptions of assessment in New Zealand, assessment regimes have a strong influence on educational practice and reignite the tension between summative and formative understandings.

Our investigation is meant to instigate a discussion that has not yet fully evolved in Switzerland. The assessment instruments currently in use have not been examined in a systematic or critical manner. Further research could focus on assessment beliefs, practices and policies in the multilevel Swiss education system. The wide variety of policy and practice levels, the multiple relevant stakeholder groups or the different linguistic regions in Switzerland offer possible starting points for such research. Although the political and historical contexts in which these educational assessments are embedded are nation-specific, the broad lines of federalism and such international developments as large-scale assessments and evidence-based policy can also be found in other countries. Thus, as long as both broad political and historical lines and particular backgrounds are taken into account, our analytical approach is transferable to other countries. Comparing assessment tests across different countries and periods from the presented analytical perspectives could support a discussion of the commonalities and differences of assessment policies.

Disclosure statement

No potential conflict of interest was reported by the authors.

ORCID

Flavian Imlig ⓘ http://orcid.org/0000-0002-6305-8088
Susanne Ender ⓘ http://orcid.org/0000-0002-7841-9114

References

Ambühl, E., Heller, W., Huldi, M., Oggenfuss, A., Rageth, E., Strittmatter, A., & Trier, U. P. (1986). *Primarschule Schweiz: 22 Thesen zur Entwicklung der Primarschule* [Primary school Switzerland: 22 propositions on the development of primary school]. Berne: EDK.

BD NW (Nidwalden Cantonal Education Department). (2015). *Orientierungsarbeiten: Rahmenbedingungen, Verbindlichkeiten ab Schuljahr 2015/16* [Orientation tests: Basic conditions, liabilities from school year 2015/16]. Stans.

BD SZ (Schwyz Cantonal Education Department). (2015). *Wegleitung für Stellwerk 8 und 9* [Manual for Stellwerk 8 and 9]. Schwyz.

Berkemeyer, N. (2010). *Die Steuerung des Schulsystems: Theoretische und praktische Explorationen* [Regulation of the school system: Theoretical and practical explorations]. Wiesbaden: Springer VS.

Berry, R. & Adamson, B. (Eds.). (2011). *Assessment reform in education.* Dordrecht: Springer.

BFS (Swiss Federal Statistical Office). (1992). *Bildungsmosaik Schweiz* [Education mosaic Switzerland]. Berne: BFS.

Bieber, T. (2010). Playing the multilevel game in education: The PISA study and the bologna process triggering Swiss harmonization. In K. Martens (Ed.), *Transformation of Education Policy* (pp. 105–131). Basingstoke: Palgrave Macmillan.

Bieber, T. (2014). Cooperation or conflict? Education politics in Switzerland after the PISA study and the Bologna process. In K. Martens, P. Knodel, & M. Windzio (Eds.), *Internationalization of education policy: A new constellation of statehood in education?* (pp. 179–201). New York, NY: Palgrave Macmillan.

Biesta, G. (2010). Why 'what works' still won't work: From evidence-based education to value-based education. *Studies in Philosophy and Education, 29*(5), 491–503. doi:10.1007/s11217-010-9191-x

BKD LU (Lucerne Cantonal Department of Education and Culture). (2013). *Orientierungsarbeiten: Merkblatt* [Orientation tests: Information sheet]. Lucerne.

BKD OW (Obwalden Cantonal Department of Education and Culture). (2013). *Orientierungsarbeiten: Verbindlichkeiten ab Schuljahr 2013/14* [Orientation tests: Liabilities from school year 2013/14]. Sarnen.

BKZ (Conference of Cantonal Ministers of Education of central Switzerland). (2013). *Orientierungsarbeiten im Kontext von Lehrplan und HarmoS* [Orientation tests in the context of Curriculum 21 and 'HarmoS']. Lucerne.

Black, P. (2015). Formative assessment – an optimistic but incomplete vision. *Assessment in Education: Principles, Policy & Practice, 22*(1), 161–177. doi:10.1080/0969594X.2014.999643

Bölsterli Bardy, K. (2015). *Kompetenzorientierung in Schulbüchern für die Naturwissenschaften* [Competence orientation in natural science schoolbooks]. Wiesbaden: Springer VS.

Böttcher, W. (2007). Zur Funktion staatlicher, Inputs' in der dezentralisierten und outputorientierten Steuerung [On the function of state 'inputs' for decentralized and output-oriented steering]. In H. Altrichter (Ed.), *Educational Governance: Handlungskoordination und Steuerung im Bildungssystem* (pp. 185–206). Wiesbaden: Springer VS.

Broadfoot, P., & Black, P. (2010). Redefining assessment? The first ten years of assessment in education. *Assessment in Education: Principles, Policy & Practice, 11*(1), 7–26. doi:10.1080/0969594042000208976

Cibulka, J. G. (1990). Educational accountability reforms: Performance information and political power. *Journal of Education Policy, 5*(5), 181–201. doi:10.1080/02680939008549071

Criblez, L. (2008a). Bildungsforschung und Bildungspolitik oder: Von überdauernden Problemen der Grenzziehung: Eine Replik auf Walter Herzog [Education research and education policy: On persistent problems in setting boundaries: A response to Walter Herzog]. *Schweizerische Zeitschrift für Bildungswissenschaften, 30*(1), 153–166.

Criblez, L. (2008b). Die neue Bildungsverfassung und die Harmonisierung des Bildungswesens [The new education constitution and the harmonisation of the education system]. In L. Criblez (Ed.), *Bildungsraum Schweiz: Historische Entwicklung und aktuelle Herausforderungen* (pp. 277–299). Berne: Haupt.

Criblez, L. (2008c). Zur Einleitung: Vom Bildungsföderalismus zum Bildungsraum Schweiz [Introduction: From educational federalism to the Swiss educational area]. In L. Criblez (Ed.), *Bildungsraum Schweiz: Historische Entwicklung und aktuelle Herausforderungen* (pp. 9–32). Berne: Haupt.

Criblez, L., Oelkers, J., Reusser, K., Berner, E., Halbheer, U., & Huber, C. (2009). *Bildungsstandards Education standards.* Zug: Klett und Balmer.

Davier, M. V., Gonzales, E., Kirsch, I., & Yamamoto, K. (Eds.). (2013). *The role of international large-scale assessments: Perspectives from technology, economy, and educational research.* Dordrecht: Springer.

Davies, H. T. O., Nutley, S. M., & Smith, P. C. (2012). Introducing evidence-based policy and practice in public services. In H. T. O. Davies, S. M. Nutley, & P. C. Smith (Eds.), *What works? Evidence-based policy and practice in public services* (pp. 1–11). Bristol: Policy Press.

Drüke-Noe, C. (2014). *Aufgabenkultur in Klassenarbeiten im Fach Mathematik: Empirische Untersuchungen in neunten und zehnten Klassen* [The culture of tasks in assessments in the subject of mathematics: Empirical studies in 9th and 10th grade]. Wiesbaden: Springer VS.

EDK (Swiss Conference of Cantonal Ministers of Education). (2011). *Die Interkantonale Vereinbarung über die Harmonisierung der obligatorischen Schule (HarmoS-Konkordat) vom 14. Juni 2007* [Intercantonal agreement on the harmonisation of compulsory school ('HarmoS-Konkordat') of 14 June 2007]. Berne: EDK.

EDK. (2013). *Überprüfung der Erreichung der Grundkompetenzen: Konzept* [Evaluation of the achievement of basic competencies: Concept]. Berne: EDK.

EDK. (2015). *Nationale Bildungsziele für die obligatorische Schule: In vier Fächern zu erreichende Grundkompetenzen* [National education standards for compulsory school: Basic competencies to be achieved in four subjects]. Berne: EDK.

Fend, H. (2008). *Neue Theorie der Schule: Einführung in das Verstehen von Bildungssystemen* [A new theory of school: Introduction to the understanding of education systems]. (2nd ed.). Wiesbaden: Springer VS.

Frey, P. (2010). Für die Praxis: Orientierungsarbeiten BKZ [For practical application: Orientation tests]. *Schulblatt Nidwalden, 3*, 6–8.

Goetze, W., Denzler, N., & Wissler, P. (2009). *Evaluation Stellwerk: Kurzbericht* [Evaluation Stellwerk: Short report]. Thalwil: BfB.

Goldstein, H. (2004). International comparisons of student attainment: Some issues arising from the PISA study. *Assessment in Education: Principles, Policy & Practice, 11*(3), 319–330. doi:10.1080/0969594042000304618

Goldstein, H. (2015). Validity, science and educational measurement. *Assessment in Education: Principles, Policy & Practice, 22*(2), 193–201. doi:10.1080/0969594X.2015.1015402

Gordon, E. W., & Rajagopalan, K. (Eds.). (2015). *The testing and learning revolution: The future of assessment in education.* New York, NY: Palgrave Macmillan.

Green, A. (2002). The many faces of lifelong learning: Recent education policy trends in Europe. *Journal of Education Policy, 17*(6), 611–626.

Green, J. (2011). *Education, professionalism and the quest for accountability: Hitting the target but missing the point.* New York, NY: Routledge.

Hangartner, J., & Svaton, C. J. (2013). From autonomy to quality management: NPM impacts on school governance in Switzerland. *Journal of Educational Administration and History, 45*(4), 354–369. doi:10.1080/00220620.2013.822352

Harlen, W. (2005). Teachers' summative practices and assessment for learning – tensions and synergies. *Curriculum Journal, 16*(2), 207–223. doi:10.1080/09585170500136093

Harlen, W. (2012). On the relationship between assessment for formative and summative purposes. In J. Gardner (Ed.), *Assessment and Learning* (2nd ed., pp. 87–102). Los Angeles, CA: Sage.

Harlen, W., & James, M. (1997). Assessment and learning: Differences and relationships between formative and summative assessment. *Assessment in Education: Principles, Policy & Practice, 4*(3), 365–379. doi:10.1080/0969594970040304

Hega, G. M. (2000). Federalism, subsidiarity and education policy in Switzerland. *Regional & Federal Studies, 10*(1), 1–35. doi:10.1080/13597560008421107

Herzog, W. (2008). Unterwegs zur 08/15-Schule? Wider die Instrumentalisierung der Erziehungswissenschaft durch die Bildungspolitik [On the way to the 'cookie-cutter' school? Against the instrumentalisation of educational science by education policy]. *Schweizerische Zeitschrift für Bildungswissenschaften, 30*(1), 13–31.

Hovenga, N., & Bos, W. (2009). *Bildungsmonitoring auf der Systemebene* [Education monitoring on the system level]. Düsseldorf: UDiKom.

Hurrelmann, A., Leibfried, S., Martens, K., & Mayer, P. (2007). The transformation of the golden-age nation state: Findings and perspectives. In A. Hurrelmann, S. Leibfried, K. Martens, & P. Mayer (Eds.), *Transforming the Golden-Age Nation State* (pp. 193–205). Basingstoke: Palgrave Macmillan.

Husfeldt, V. (2007). *Zum Stand der externen Schulevaluation in Verbindung mit Leistungsmessung: Leistungstests und Schulevaluation in der deutschsprachigen Schweiz und Blick in andere Länder* [The status of external school evaluation including performance measurement: Performance tests and school evaluation in German-speaking Switzerland and other countries]. Aarau: PH FHNW.

Jakobi, A. P., Martens, K., & Wolf, K. D. (2010). Introduction: A governance perspective on education policy. In A. P. Jakobi, K. Martens, & K. D. Wolf (Eds.), *Education in political science: Discovering a neglected field* (pp. 1–20). London: Routledge.

Jann, W., & Wegrich, K. (2010). Governance und Verwaltungspolitik: Leitbilder und Reformkonzepte [Governance and administrative policy: Guiding principles and reform concepts]. In A. Benz (Ed.), *Governance—Regieren in komplexen Regelsystemen. Eine Einführung* (2nd ed., pp. 175–200). Wiesbaden: Springer VS.

Jost, D. (1994). *Orientierungsarbeiten Mathematik 5./6. Klasse: Themenschwerpunkte Grundoperationen, Grössen, Brüche, Sachrechnen* [Orientation tests mathematics, 5th/6th grade: The topics of arithmetic, units, fractions, word problems]. Lucerne: BKD LU.

Klausing, A., & Husfeldt, V. (2015). Verknüpfung von Daten aus Bildungsstatistik und Leistungsmessungen auf Individualebene in der Schweiz [Linking data from education statistics and performance assessments at the individual level in Switzerland]. *Die Deutsche Schule, 107*(4), 352–364.

Knudson, R. E. (1993). Effects of different instructional tasks on students' narrative writing. *The Journal of Experimental Education, 61*(3), 205–214. doi:10.1080/00220973.1993.9943861

Koch, S., & Schemmann, M. (2009). Neo-Institutionalismus und Erziehungswissenschaft: Eine einleitende Verhältnisbestimmung [Neo-institutionalism and education science: Introduction to the determination of their relation]. In S. Koch & M. Schemmann (Eds.), *Neo-Institutionalismus in der Erziehungswissenschaft. Grundlegende Texte und empirische Studien* (pp. 7–18). Wiesbaden: Springer VS.

Lane, S., Raymond, M. R., & Haladyna, T. M. (Eds.). (2016). *Handbook of test development* (2nd ed.). New York, NY: Routledge.

Larcher, S., & Smit, R. (2011). Unterrichtskompetenz im Berufseinstieg: Mittels 'Mixed Methods' zum Kompetenzmodell [Teaching competency in early career: From 'mixed methods' to a competency model]. In M. Gläser-Zikuda, T. Seidel, C. Rohlfs, A. Gröschner, & S. Ziegelbauer (Eds.), *Mixed methods in der empirischen Bildungsforschung* (pp. 227–241). Münster: Waxmann.

Maag Merki, K., & Büeler, X. (2002). Schulautonomie in der Schweiz: Eine Bilanz auf empirischer [Basis autonomy of schools in Switzerland: A summary on an empirical basis]. In H.-G. Rolff (Ed.), *Jahrbuch der Schulentwicklung: Daten, Beispiele und Perspektiven* (pp. 131–161). Weinheim: Juventa.

Maier, U. (2015). *Leistungsdiagnostik in Schule und Unterricht: Schülerleistungen messen, bewerten und fördern* [Performance diagnostics in school and instruction: Measuring, evaluating and supporting student performance]. Bad Heilbrunn: Klinkhardt.

Martens, K. (Ed.). (2010). *Transformation of education policy*. Basingstoke: Palgrave Macmillan.

Martens, K., Knodel, P., & Windzio, M. (Eds.). (2014). *Internationalization of education policy: A new constellation of statehood in education?* New York, NY: Palgrave Macmillan.

Martens, K., & Wolf, K. D. (2006). Paradoxien der Neuen Staatsräson: Die Internationalisierung der Bildungspolitik in der EU und der OECD [Paradoxes of the new state: The internationalisation of education policy in the EU and the OECD]. *Zeitschrift für Internationale Beziehungen, 13*(2), 145–176.

McClelland, D. C. (1973). Testing for competence rather than for 'intelligence. *American Psychologist, 28*(1), 1–14.

Mitchell, D. E., Shipps, D., & Crowson, R. L. (2011). What have we learned about shaping education policy? In D. E. Mitchell, R. L. Crowson, & D. Shipps (Eds.), *Shaping education policy: Power and process* (pp. 286–296). New York, NY: Routledge.

Newton, P. E. (2017). There is more to educational measurement than measuring: The importance of embracing purpose pluralism. *Educational Measurement: Issues and Practice, 115*, doi:10.1111/emip.12146

Nussbaum, P., Fischer, S., & Hildbrand, J. (2007). Der Umgang mit Heterogenität in der Schule [Dealing with heterogeneity in school]. In H. Rhyn (Ed.), *Heterogenität, Gerechtigkeit und Exzellenz. Lebenslanges Lernen in der Wissensgesellschaft/OECD/CERI-Regionalseminar für die deutschsprachigen Länder in Nottwil (Schweiz) vom 26. bis 29. September 2005* (pp. 40–50). Innsbruck: StudienVerlag.

Oelkers, J., & Reusser, K. (2008). *Qualität entwickeln —Standards sichern—mit Differenzen umgehen* [Developing quality, securing standards, handling differences]. Berlin: BMBF.

Papadopoulos, G. S. (1994/1996). *Die Entwicklung des Bildungswesens von 1960 bis 1990: Der Beitrag der OECD* [The development of the education system from 1960 to 1990: The OECD's contribution]. Frankfurt am Main: Lang.

Pelgrum, W. J. (1986). *The implemented and attained mathematics curriculum: A comparison of eighteen countries. Second international mathematics study.* Washington, DC: Center for Education Statistics.

Pereyra, M. A., Kotthoff, H.-G., & Cowen, R. (Eds.). (2011). *PISA under examination: Changing knowledge, changing tests and changing schools.* Rotterdam: Sense.

Rhyn, H. (2009). Evaluation im Bildungsbereich in der Schweiz [Evaluation of education in Switzerland]. In T. Widmer, W. Beywl, & C. Fabian (Eds.), *Evaluation. Ein systematisches Handbuch* (1st ed., pp. 182–192). Wiesbaden: Springer VS.

Rieder, S. (2005). Leistungs-und Wirkungsmessung in NPM-Projekten: Erfahrungen, Konzepte, Ausblick [Performance and impact measurement in NPM projects: Experiences, concepts, outlook]. In A. Lienhard, A. Ritz, R. Steiner, & A. Ladner (Eds.), *10 Jahre new public management in der Schweiz. Bilanz, Irrtümer und Erfolgsfaktoren* (pp. 149–159). Berne: Haupt.

Roos, M., Wandeler, E., & Mosimann, M. (2013). *Das Übertrittsverfahren Primarschule—Sekundarstufe I des Kantons Luzern: Schlussbericht zur externen Evaluation* [The transition process from primary to secondary school in the canton of Lucerne: Final report of the external evaluation]. Baar: Spectrum3.

Schaller, R. (2011). Ein Stein im Mosaik der Gesamtbeurteilung': Stellwerk ['A piece of the puzzle of overall assessment': Stellwerk]. *ZLV Magazin, 6*, 6–12.

Sjøberg, S. (2007). PISA and 'real life challenges': Mission impossible? In S. T. Hopmann, G. Brinek, & M. Retzl (Eds.), *PISA zufolge PISA. Hält PISA, was es verspricht?* (pp. 203–224). Vienna: Lit.

Skedsmo, G. (2011). Formulation and realisation of evaluation policy: Inconcistencies and problematic issues. *Educational Assessment, Evaluation and Accountability, 23*(1), 5–20. doi:10.1007/s11092-010-9110-2

Staatskanzlei SG (St. Gallen Cantonal State Office). (2006). *Perspektiven der Volksschule: Bericht der Regierung* [Perspectives on compulsory school: Governmental report]. St. Gallen.

Sun, Y., & Cheng, L. (2014). Teachers' grading practices: Meaning and values assigned. *Assessment in Education: Principles, Policy & Practice, 21*(3), 326–343. doi:10.1080/0969594X.2013.768207

Sutermeister-Christen, R., Ackermann, U., Aeppli, J., Häcker, T., Luthiger, H., Reinhardt, V., & Zutavern, M. (2007). *Lernergebnisse beurteilen und Schülerinnen und Schüler beraten* [Evaluating learning outcomes and advising students]. Lucerne: PHZ.

Tillmann, K.-J., Dedering, K., Kneuper, D., Kuhlmann, C., & Nessel, I. (2008). PISA als bildungspolitisches Ereignis: Oder: Wie weit trägt das Konzept der, evaluationsbasierten Steuerung'? [PISA as an education policy event, or: How far does the concept of 'evaluation-based control' reach?]. In T. Brüsemeister & K.-D. Eubel (Eds.), *Evaluation, Wissen und Nichtwissen* (pp. 117–140). Wiesbaden: Springer VS.

Tröhler, D. (2013). The OECD and cold war culture: Thinking historically about PISA. In H.-D. Meyer & A. Benavot (Eds.), *PISA, power, and policy: The emergence of global educational governance* (pp. 141–161). Oxford: Symposium Books.

Tyack, D., & Tobin, W. (1994). The 'grammar' of schooling: Why has it been so hard to change? *American Educational Research Journal, 31*(3), 453–479.

Tyo, J. (2010). Competency-based education. *The Clearing House, 52*(9), 424–427. doi:10.1080/000 98655.1979.10113640

Uljens, M. (2007). The hidden curriculum of PISA: The promotion of neo-liberal policy by educational assessment. In S. T. Hopmann, G. Brinek, & M. Retzl (Eds.), *PISA zufolge PISA. Hält PISA, was es verspricht?* (pp. 295–303). Vienna: Lit.

Vögeli-Mantovani, U. (1996). *Orientierungsarbeiten: Überlegungen zur klassenübergreifenden Lernerfolgsmessung* [Orientation tests: Reflections on performance assessments across school classes]. Lucerne: ZBS.

Vögeli-Mantovani, U. (1999). *Mehr fördern, weniger auslesen: Zur Entwicklung der schulischen Beurteilung in der Schweiz* [More support, less selection: On the development of educational assessment in Switzerland]. Aarau: SKBF.

Weber, H. (2016). Jetzt kommt das Schweizer [PISA Swiss PISA is coming]. *Bildung Schweiz, 161*(2), 12–15.

Wiater, W. (2013). Kompetenzorientierung des Unterrichts: Alter Wein in neuen Schläuchen? [Competence-oriented teaching: Old wine in new bottles?]. *Bildung und Erziehung, 66*(2), 145–161.

Windzio, M., Knodel, P., & Martens, K. (2014). Reforming education policy after PISA and Bologna: Two logics of governance and reactions. In K. Martens, P. Knodel, & M. Windzio (Eds.), *Internationalization of education policy: A new constellation of statehood in education?* (pp. 247–260). New York, NY: Palgrave Macmillan.

Wolter, S. C. (2008). Purpose and limits of the education system through indicators. In N. C. Soguel & P. Jaccard (Eds.), *Governance and performance of education systems* (pp. 57–84). Dordrecht: Springer VS.

Wolter, S. C., & Hof, S. (2014). *Bildungsbericht Schweiz 2014* [Swiss Education Report 2014]. Aarau: SKBF.

Yates, A., & Johnston, M. (2017). The impact of school-based assessment for qualifications on teachers' conceptions of assessment. *Assessment in Education, Principles, Policy & Practice.* doi:10.1080/0 969594X.2017.1295020

Young, M. D., & Diem, S. (2017). Introduction: Critical approaches to education policy analysis. In M. D. Young & S. Diem (Eds.), *Critical approaches to education policy analysis: Moving beyond tradition* (pp. 1–13). Cham: Springer. doi:10.1007/978-3-319-39643-9_1

Teacher evaluation as a wicked policy problem

Sølvi Lillejord[ID], Eyvind Elstad[ID] and Håkon Kavli

ABSTRACT

While it is generally assumed that the aim of teacher evaluation is to *formatively* support teachers' professional development, research finds that teacher evaluation practices are predominantly *summative*. This paper describes a Norwegian governmental policy experiment aiming to overcome this fallacy through a bargaining process, where experience-based knowledge was combined with research evidence. When preparing to introduce teacher evaluation, the Ministry of Education and Research commissioned a group of researchers and a group representing practitioners to identify teacher evaluation practices that are conducive for educational quality. Drawing on experiences from the policy experiment, the article discusses three approaches to teacher evaluation: the political, the administrative and the professional. The analysis indicates that successful implementation of interventions needs a new educational infrastructure and professional school leadership. One conclusion is that teacher evaluation cannot be successfully implemented through traditional linear approaches. A more productive approach is to treat it as a wicked problem.

Introduction

Teacher evaluation has been defined as 'the process of arriving at judgements about an individual's past or present performance, against the background of his work environment, and about his future potential for an organisation' (Castetter, 1976, p. 232). Murphy, Hallinger, and Heck (2013) find that this definition, by foregrounding the personnel function, positions teacher evaluation in the hierarchical architecture of schooling, with principals as supervisors and teachers as subordinates. Over the last decades, more collaborative and participatory approaches to evaluation are developed, intended to support professional practice in general (Shulha, Whitmore, Cousins, Gilbert, & al Hudib, 2016) and in schools (Darling-Hammond, 2013). When describing less top-down teacher evaluation practices, some researchers use teacher *assessment* (e.g. McMahon & Jones, 2015), combine evaluation and assessment (Smagorinsky, 2014) or use teacher *appraisal* (e.g. Flores, 2012).

In one perspective, teacher evaluation may be perceived as an abstract policy idea that circulates globally (Popkewitz, 2000), entangled in a neoliberal discourse ignited by the report *A Nation at Risk* (National Commission on Excellence in Education, 1983), blaming schools for the recession in the US economy (Hursh, 2007), and holding teachers accountable for their students' learning outcome. In another, it is a practice yielding information leaders can use to enhance teaching quality (Goe, Biggers, & Croft, 2012). In theory, therefore, the purpose of teacher evaluation is twofold: to serve as a professional development process and as a quality assurance mechanism (Kraft & Gilmour, 2016). Difficulties in reconciling these two approaches (Firestone, 2014; Popham, 1988) may explain why teacher evaluation is a contested practice (Cohen & Goldhaber, 2016; Elstad, Lejonberg, & Christophersen, 2015b) and a hotly debated topic (Collins & Amrein-Beardsley, 2014).

Different countries have tried different approaches to evaluate teachers' work, and when Norwegian politicians during election year 2013 contemplated national initiatives for more systematic teacher evaluation, policy-makers in the Ministry of Education and Research initiated a process that will be described in detail later, of gathering knowledge from research and practice. The assumption was that ownership to a joint knowledge base might facilitate the process of implementing teacher evaluation nationwide.

While each country responds in its own way to international policy discourses (Hudson, 2011), researchers often find that across countries, systems for teacher evaluation are reduced to bureaucratic problem solving and fail to strengthen teachers' professional knowledge base (Darling-Hammond, 2013; Taut & Sun, 2014) or improve schools (Hallinger, Heck, & Murphy, 2014). This article presents a policy experiment that sheds light on why this happens.

The three authors had different roles in the policy experiment. The first author was the lead author of the systematic review, the second author headed the work in the group representing practitioners and the third author contributed to designing the policy experiment. We first explain the policy context and background for the experiment that drew on the Scandinavian bargaining model, then frame teacher evaluation as a wicked problem and discuss three approaches to teacher evaluation: the political; the administrative and the professional. The article analyses teacher evaluation as a *wicked problem* by asking: why is the formative purpose of teacher evaluation frequently reduced to administrative routines and technical practices? We finally indicate measures needed to strengthen the teaching profession.

Background and policy context

Educational policy in Norway (for instance, curriculum guidelines) is developed at the national level and adapted locally by autonomous local education authorities. The public-school system is pervasive; only about three per cent of primary and lower secondary school pupils and seven per cent of upper secondary pupils attend private schools. The Organisation for Economic Co-operation and Development (OECD) has commented on the high level of trust and lack of national quality control in Norwegian education (OECD, 1987). Schools are expected to conduct self-evaluations, and some of them do, but Norway has no nation-wide systematic evaluation of teachers' work and no national school inspectorate. The responsibility for quality in education rests on local municipalities (primary education) or counties (upper secondary) and the County Governor carries out inspections in accordance with the *Education Act* (1998) and *Kindergarten Act* (2005). Having reviewed Norwegian assessment and evaluation practices, the OECD more recently recommended that Norway connect teacher appraisal to professional learning and school development and integrate teacher evaluation in the unfinished National Quality Assessment System (Nusche, Earl, Maxwell, & Schrewbridge, 2011).

Norway is not the only country to get such advice from the OECD. Researchers (e.g. Anagnostopoulos, Lingard, & Sellar, 2016; Ozga, Dahler-Larsen, Segerholm, & Simola, 2011) argue that the OECD defines education quality and steers education systems through assessment. Teacher evaluation is an interesting case, as it has been identified as a means to increase student's learning outcome in an era of outcomes-based education policy (OECD, 2009). A recurring problem is, however, that while the intention is to implement evaluation practices that support teachers' professional development and promote quality in schools, many systems are reduced to instruments of accountability, burdening and demotivating schools and teachers instead of invigorating and empowering them (Santiago, Benavides, Danielson, Goe, & Nusche, 2013). This might happen if school leaders use bureaucratic levers of requirements and regulations when trying to solve problems that require professional skill and expertise (Mehta, 2013). The described policy experiment aimed to avoid these pitfalls by

(a) combining research evidence and knowledge from practice and
(b) anchoring the implementation process in broad, participative bargaining processes.

Before outlining the design of the policy experiment, we briefly present the policy context, research on implementation failure and the theory of wicked problems.

Outcomes-based policies and teacher evaluation

In 1990, a white paper introduced management by objectives (MbO) in the Norwegian education sector (White Paper no. 37, 1990–1991). The idea was simple. Politicians should formulate goals and steer from a distance; administrators should interpret the goals, divide them into smaller, manageable goals, explain these to the schools, and oversee how teachers followed up on the politicians' intentions. An essential but initially under-communicated part of MbO was the reporting of results and the measurement and comparison of each employee's performance with set standards. In the wake of MbO, developed by Drucker (1954) for private business companies, new public management (NPM) emerged, modelled on multidivisional private sector corporations, with corporate headquarters overseeing business units, controlled through monitoring performance outcomes. Central to managerialism has been a rational-technical approach to decision-making, with an aim to simplify and favouring general managerial skills over professional or technical content knowledge (Head & Alford, 2015). Both MbO and NPM assume the existence of an infrastructure that is lacking in complex education systems. Therefore, neither of them is appropriate for wicked environments, characterised by uncertainty, complexity and disagreement.

When the Programme for International Student Assessment (PISA) shock hit Norway and other countries in 2001 (Lundgren, 2011), a focus on measurable results rapidly overshadowed other political visions for education. Drawing on research arguing that the teacher is the most important factor explaining improved student learning outcomes (Hanushek, 1971, 1999), politicians wanted to know how they could increase the 'value added' of teachers. Teacher evaluation emerged as one solution (Berliner, 2013) with three interest groups: politicians; administrative staff and teachers. Typical political arguments were that teacher evaluation secures pupils' democratic participation (Elstad et al., 2015b) and that schools more readily will strive for improvement in a competitive market system (Hanushek & Raymond, 2005). Administrative arguments were that accountable and efficient school leaders should evaluate teachers' work and inform them about how to improve their teaching, while teachers expect teacher evaluation to support their broader mandate and professional learning (Smylie, 2014; Smylie, Murphy, & Louis, 2016). As these interests are not easily reconciled, teacher evaluation turns into a policy implementation problem.

Implementation challenges

There is a growing realisation that major social issues of modern life are grounded in value perspectives. Gathering more information for scientific analysis or initiating further research is insufficient when the goal is to understand and resolve social problems (Head & Alford, 2015). Both public and private institutions now realise that a strong knowledge base is necessary, but does not in itself guarantee successful implementation.

Having reviewed the research on implementation failure, Decker et al. (2012) find that failure rates for organisational change have been hovering around 73 per cent since the 1960s and range somewhere between 28 per cent and 93 per cent. One reason, they suggest, is that traditional linear problem-solving models, such as MbO, assume that the leaders' job is finished when the goals are formulated. This assumption no longer holds, they argue, because organisations are handling increasingly complex problems in increasingly complex contexts. Leaders can no longer formulate goals and expect others to finish the job; they must keep their attention on the entire implementation chain. Because the politics of implementation differs from the politics of enactment, McDonnell and Weatherford (2016) suggest that implementation should be understood as a *continuous* political process.

This insight yields the question: is teacher evaluation reduced to technical procedures and bureaucratic documentation, not fulfilling the formative intentions, because it is treated as a benign problem while it – more appropriately – should be treated as a 'wicked' problem? Characteristically, wicked problems are difficult to solve because contradictory intentions, for instance, formative *and* summative ambitions, are embedded in the problem. Wicked problems are ambivalent, resist resolution and cannot be 'solved' in the sense that they disappear. Merton (1976) has shown that ambivalence is central to modern societies, and warns of unintended consequences when solving problems in ambiguous contexts. Evaluation and assessment are practices with high probability for unintended consequences (Lavigne, 2014), causing potential problems for actors involved.

Teacher evaluation as a wicked problem

The term wicked problem (Rittel & Webber, 1973) is used to describe social problems in modern, pluralistic societies. According to Buchanan (1992), Horst Rittel borrowed the phrase from Karl Popper during the 1960s and modified it for his own use. Wicked problems are characterised by ambiguity and uncertainty (Head, 2008), generating conceptual difficulties and practical challenges. Efforts to solve one aspect of a wicked problem often breed new problems. The greater the disagreement between stakeholders, the more wicked the problem (Camillus, 2008). Table 1 highlights general characteristics of wicked problems.

In modern organisations, stakeholders with different values and priorities are struggling with problems that are difficult to come to grips with (Camillus, 2008), with no 'right' answers. Head and Alford (2015, p. 717) distinguish between Type 1 situations, where both the definition of the problem and the likely solution are clear, Type 2 situations where the definition of the problem is clear but not the solution, and Type 3 situations where both problem definition and solution are unclear. Teacher evaluation appears to be a Type 3 situation, as goals are ambiguous or contradictory, the expected outcome is broad and vaguely defined (evaluation should contribute to professional development, quality in school, improved learning outcomes for students, etc.) and various actors have their personal interpretations of how this outcome may be achieved. This kind of 'inescapable wickedity' is, according to Jordan, Kleingasser, and Roe (2014, p. 415), frequent in education.

Head and Alford (2015) argue that efforts to deal with wicked problems are impeded by the public sector's characteristic ways of decision-making, organising routines, financing and staffing. Hierarchical organisation and control, focused on input monitoring and process compliance, limit the opportunities to think expansively about complex policy issues. Instead, they suggest the following strategies: (a) going beyond technical/rational thinking; (b) collaborative working; (c) new models of leadership; and (d) reforming the managerial infrastructure of government. For the Norwegian Ministry of Education and Research, a way forward when designing a scheme for teacher evaluation that could be implemented nationally, was to draw on the Scandinavian bargaining model, based on influence, joint decision-making and mutual respect. The term Scandinavian bargaining model refers to inter-party collaboration between employer and employee organisations (and, in some instances, the state). The policy experiment follows Head and Alford (2015) points a, b and c, as it goes beyond technical/rational thinking, by collecting knowledge both from research and experience, is innovative in terms of collaborative policy leadership, and therefore, meets three of the four above suggested requirements for successful implementation strategy. Having presented the policy experiment, we will return to the question of infrastructure (point d).

Policy design for teacher evaluation

The policy experiment is anchored in the current Norwegian government's political platform (2013–2017) which opens for students in upper secondary to evaluate their teachers' instructional practice, and aims at implementing teacher evaluation more systematically nationwide. In Norwegian schools, teacher evaluation is rarely used as an instrument for quality assurance (Anderson, Terras, & Dagfinrud, 2013) and schemes vary considerably nationwide. In some secondary schools, deputy heads perform appraisal interviews with groups of teachers (Abrahamsen, 2017), and in one county, student ratings are found to

Table 1. General characteristics of wicked problems (Rittel & Webber, 1973, pp. 161–167).

Unique – no definition	Don't know when the problem is solved
May be the symptom of another problem	No way to test out solutions
Disagreements have multiple explanations	Every solution is unique
Solutions are not right/wrong, but good/bad	No available set of possible solutions

provide teachers in upper secondary with constructive feedback they can use to improve the quality of their teaching (Elstad, Lejonberg, & Christophersen, 2017). When planning the policy experiment, the Ministry of Education and Research drew upon EU and OECD recommendations defining teacher evaluation as a method of developing and improving the quality of teaching, strengthening teachers' status and recognition as professionals, raising the attractiveness of teaching, and supporting professional development for individual teachers throughout their careers. Guided by a Centre for Educational Research and Innovation, CERI/OECD project, *Governing Complex Education Systems*, the introduction of teacher evaluation was perceived as a *systemic* organisational change effort (Senge, 1990), and treated as a bargained solution amongst stakeholders.

To facilitate the process, the Ministry designed a project with several phases, starting with involving relevant stakeholders and establishing a knowledge base. The aim was that a parallel and participatory process would result in agreement on characteristics of high quality teaching, guidelines for teacher evaluation and requirements for teacher professionalism that could later be used in national recommendations. The Ministry simultaneously commissioned a systematic review on teacher evaluation from a group of researchers (Lillejord et al., 2014) and established a stakeholder group with teachers' and headmasters' unions, an employer association, a teacher educator and student association, etc., to summarise assessment experiences from schools and municipalities (Elstad et al., 2015a). This policy design, where stakeholders are engaged in bottom-up processes, provides ownership and empowerment, but may also produce confounding compromises, complicating the implementation processes.

The Scandinavian bargaining tradition and the GNIST partnership

The hallmark of successful policy making is to reconcile disagreements. While contradictory interests give something to bargain *about*, common interests give something to bargain *for* (Schelling, 1980). Scandinavian countries have a long tradition of significant employee influence, collective agreements and centralised bargaining (Byrkjeflot, 2001). For long periods, the open economies in Scandinavia have had high productivity and work effort, small wage differentials, and a generous welfare state (Barth, Moene, & Willumsen, 2014). The system is based on mutual respect, influence, and joint decision-making (Brandal, Bratberg, & Thorsen, 2013), aiming to reduce the negative effects of inherent inter-party conflicts of interest, which in some instances can disrupt processes (Moene & Wallerstein, 2002). This model for reconciling conflicts has been regarded with both astonishment and interest by non-Scandinavians (Barth et al., 2014; Lindbeck, 1997).

The tradition of negotiating compromises through giving and taking is fruitful for many purposes. However, when teacher evaluation is on the bargaining table, a relevant question is: Which are the common and potentially contradictory interests?

In line with the bargaining tradition, the Norwegian Ministry of Education and Research in 2009 initiated the establishment of GNIST ('SPARK'), a partnership for teacher professional development and arena for cross-collaboration between stakeholders (leaders of teacher and teacher educator unions, student teachers, headmaster and student associations, an employer association, etc.). The partnership's mandate was to 'strengthen the schools' academic platform and the prestige of the teaching profession' (GNIST, 2009, p. 3). One key initiative identified by the partners was teacher evaluation. The GNIST partnership was subsequently mobilised in this policy experiment with three phases, described below.

Phase 1: The two groups: knowledge from experience and research

In autumn 2013, the GNIST partnership appointed a working group (Elstad et al., 2014) with a mandate to '... identify and assess important prerequisites for teacher evaluation contributing to the development of schools as learning organisations, to teachers' professional development, and with a positive effect on pupils' learning and development' (p. 5). The report concluded with these preconditions for successful teacher evaluation:

- mutual trust between the parties;
- appraisal schemes should be systematic, predictable and practically feasible;
- specific, immediate feedback is deemed better than general and delayed feedback;
- teacher appraisal should focus on development and not serve to monitor the teachers' work;
- teacher appraisal schemes should be based on research evidence.

In parallel to appointing the working group, the Ministry commissioned a systematic review from the Norwegian Knowledge Centre for Education (Lillejord et al., 2014). The review question was: Which teacher evaluation schemes may promote quality in school? Initial searches did not identify previous systematic reviews on the topic. The search process was complicated as the Ministry asked the group of researchers to include quantitative *and* qualitative studies, studies about formative *and* summative assessment, and information about process *and* outcome quality. Systematic searches (search period 2009–2013) yielded around 12.000 entries. Five expert researchers supported the review team in the process of assessing studies, following predefined criteria for inclusion and exclusion. Finally, 79 studies were included in the review that concluded with four preconditions for successful teacher evaluation:

- Active participation, responsibility and trust;
- Involved parties need scientific methods and data use literacy;
- Clear and direct communication (not too many goals);
- Responsible and competent leaders with attention to dialogue and follow-up.

The systematic review revealed that the amount of time and resources needed for successful teacher evaluation is frequently underestimated. Main findings were that evaluation is unsuccessful when the scope is too broad, the object unclear or no plans are in place for how to deal with unintended consequences that emerge during the evaluation. Also, key actors in successful implementation of teacher evaluation are active school leaders and local school authorities and results are better when teachers' professional learning is prioritised over bureaucratic evaluation procedures aiming at control. The two groups did not collaborate, but met twice during 2013 and 2014 to exchange information about work processes. For some of the practitioners it was unclear what they could expect from research. During the meetings, misunderstandings were clarified. Because of the meetings and overlapping findings from the two reports, the GNIST partners developed a sense of ownership to the overall process.

In the GNIST group, disagreements occurred, for instance, on the name of the activity (teacher evaluation or *teaching* evaluation) and on the anonymity of students' feedback to teachers. Further, in February 2014, one teacher association (Norwegian Union of School Employees) resigned from the partnership as it had lost its confidence in the employer body (KS, the Norwegian Association of Local and Regional Authorities), due to a breakdown in negotiations over regulations of working hours. In April 2014, the Minister of Education and Research invited all participants to discuss the knowledge base (from research and practice) and plan for the next phase. All remaining GNIST partners adhered to the knowledge gathered during Phase 1, underlined the importance of avoiding the pitfalls and unintended consequences revealed in the systematic review, and agreed to move on to Phase 2.

Phase 2: Designing teacher evaluation

Next, the working group outlined guidelines for teacher evaluation to be piloted and tested in Norway, based on these recommendations from the partnership organisations, (Elstad et al., 2015a):

1. Students' evaluations of teaching via anonymous surveys;
2. Observation of teachers' work by school leaders or external experts, with subsequent feedback;
3. Students' learning progress: information about their learning, self-formation ('Bildung'), and development;
4. Feedback on teachers' educational practice.

Based on these recommendations a trial scheme for teacher appraisal was developed, inspired by teacher evaluation practices in upper secondary schools in two Norwegian counties (Vestfold and Akershus), endorsed by the local teachers' unions and perceived as an interesting model for a pilot. It included anonymous student surveys and follow-up through individual performance reviews and group sessions for each discipline.

According to Camillus (2008), traits of wicked problems include confusion, discord, and lack of progress. In hindsight, such sentiments may have characterised Phase 2. Even though all three authors attended meetings and were involved in parts of the process, we find it difficult to identify one single event that caused the process to slow down. It could be a growing realisation in the GNIST group that the work ahead was overly complex, partly related to research findings in the systematic review, about potential pitfalls and unintended consequences of teacher evaluation. Some of the partners may have wanted not to be interpreted as distrusting teachers; some teacher representatives may have felt that evaluation indirectly signalled a lack of trust in teachers' work and therefore did not embrace the process whole-heartedly. Or, the process may have revealed that there were more conflicting than common interests to bargain for.

The policy experiment rests on the assumption that successful implementation of political decisions presupposes ownership and commitment to bargained solutions. Munneke, Andriessen, Kanselaar, and Kirschner (2007) have reviewed research indicating that serious argumentation only emerges when serious problems are encountered. Normally, when people reason in groups, they take the correctness of their supportive theories for granted and most evidence brought to the table is not evidence, but anecdotal pseudo-evidence. Because thinking about alternative theories, counterarguments and rebuttals are very difficult, more time is spent on supporting theories and less attention given to the opponents' views. The main goal is to persuade the other, not explore together. Much policy debate takes the form of bargaining to achieve temporary compromises (small-scale symbolic wins), while the wicked, underlying differences persist. This might also have happened in the policy experiment described in this article.

During this phase, the divergent interests between the stakeholders were not *on* the bargaining table, but rather *under* the table and difficult to grasp. Political goals are broad and ambitious; supposed to 'trickle down' to administrators who are responsible for the successful implementation of political visions. Administrators realise that their job is to transform the idea into a feasible project, reduce the ambitions and narrow the scope while remaining faithful to the overarching ideals. Teachers know, from experience, that they are left with the challenge of realising ambitions that are often at odds with what may possibly be achieved in their everyday 'reality'. Consensus on the surface may have concealed the uncertainty underneath, causing uncertainty and hesitance. Before presenting the pilot scheme (Phase 3), we will outline two categories of problems that, according to our interpretation, seem to have influenced the deliberations in the GNIST working group during Phase 2.

First category of problems: tensions between summative and formative purposes of teacher evaluation

The most consistent finding in the systematic review (Lillejord et al., 2014), reported from countries as diverse as Belgium (Delvaux et al., 2013), Chile (Taut & Sun, 2014), China (Zhang & Ng, 2011), and Portugal (Flores, 2012), was that teacher evaluation procedures seem to fail when they violate insights from evaluation research such as (a) sufficient resources (expertise, money, time) must be made available and efforts balanced against expectations (Cousins & Earl, 1992); (b) evaluation must be planned and conducted in ways that are experienced by the person(s) being evaluated as valid and reliable (Smagorinsky, 2014), and performed by *knowledgeable* evaluators (Darling-Hammond, 2014); (c) evaluation should concentrate on specific parts of the work while not neglecting that each part is integral to a bigger whole (Darling-Hammond, 2013, 2014); (d) evaluation should not only measure outcomes but contribute to strengthening the learning environment (Cousins, Whitmore, & Shulha, 2013); and (e) because evaluation has a huge impact on practice, it should be planned and conducted in ways that minimise unintended consequences (Lavigne, 2014) (Table 2).

Researchers found that while negotiations over teacher evaluation schemes were consensual at the national or central level, implementation problems occurred locally. Divergence between political visions, administrative procedures and expected teacher professional development reduced teacher evaluation to technical procedures, paper work and little attention to teachers' professional learning. The sudden lack of progress in the group may be ascribed to a suspicion that this might also happen in Norway.

Second category of problems: stakeholder groups with divergent interests

The GNIST partners (representing teachers, school leaders, district and National level authorities) had different expectations to the bargaining process. In a system based on MbO, politicians are formulating vision goals. When implementing their interpretation of the political visions for teacher evaluation (accountability, improved learning outcomes, transparent democratic processes and better schools), administrators at district- and school-level use available tools and familiar quality assurance procedures (Pupala, Kascak, & Tesar, 2016). Teachers expect formative feedback from school leaders, but frequently find themselves victims to bureaucratic procedures, narrowing the scope of their job and constraining their professional discretion (Kraft & Gilmour, 2016). Figure 1 illustrates this:

The political-bureaucratic discourse is holistic and normative, favouring general tools and procedures. Teachers, however, continuously relate to concrete problems in need of specific solutions and immediate attention. While politicians and bureaucrats give direction from a distant *system* perspective, teachers sort out complex *life-world* issues (Habermas, 1984). Such tensions, inherent to MbO as a steering system, driven by increased control, were not initially identified by the bargaining partners as contradictory interests, but appear to have surfaced when more concrete practices and procedures were specified in Phase 2. Discussions about whether future teacher evaluation activities should be labelled *teacher* or *teaching* evaluation may seem trivial, but might have had significant symbolic bearings as indicators of trust or distrust for some stakeholders. The theory of wicked problems addresses these subtle mechanisms of inter-party tensions by showing that disagreements

Table 2. Challenges encountered in teacher evaluation when requirements and principles from evaluation and assessment research are violated (from Lillejord et al., 2014).

Challenges encountered across countries (Chile, China, Belgium, Portugal)	Principles violated
• Additional work for the teachers	• *Resources must be available:* Not sufficient time for the evaluation and the follow-up
• Trust in assessors and confidence in their assessment competency	• *Results should be valid and reliable:* Teachers often question the assessors' legitimacy, competence and thrustworthiness
• Unclear object of assessment, combined with a multitude of assessment methods: too complex, difficult to handle	• *Assessment must have a clear scope:* The object of evaluation is not clearly defined
• Problems when following up evaluation results formatively • Teacher evaluation turns summative and bureaucratic	• *The evaluation should contribute positively to learning in school:* Problems realising the formative purpose of the assessment

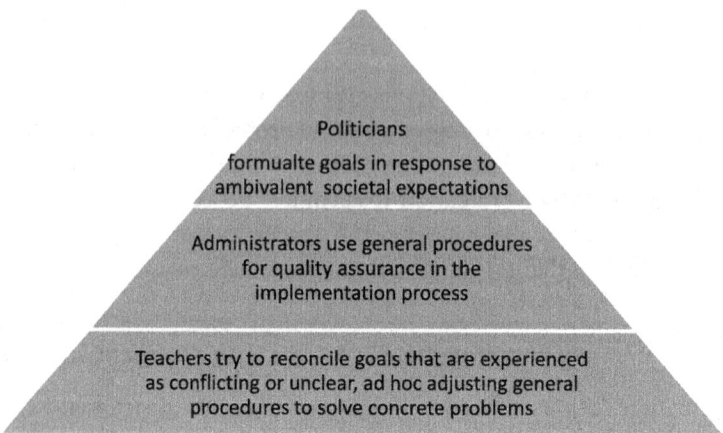

Figure 1. Illustration of the hierarchical structure of MbO as a steering system.

may have multiple explanations, be symptoms of other problems than the one discussed and that solutions are experienced as good or bad, not right or wrong.

To gain further insight, Phase 3 of the experiment was therefore designed as a pilot.

Phase 3: Trial scheme

The trial scheme proposed by the GNIST working group was designed as a follow-up study at eight schools with supervision from a consultancy firm (IMTEC), actively guiding teachers and school leaders in improvement processes. IMTEC is expected to collect, organise, and analyse schools' experiences related to the testing of a system labelled 'evaluation of professional development' in schools. The questions guiding Phase 3 are developed by the Directorate for IMTEC to answer in a report after the trial scheme:

1. What impact did anchoring at school and school owner level have for participation in evaluation for professional development?
2. How was the trust between participants, based on agreement to use the information for development and not control, safeguarded during the period schools participated in the evaluation of professional development?
3. Are there signs that the four elements mentioned in Phase 2 were used formatively and systematically? Did they contribute to teacher professional learning and, more broadly, school development? Did they strengthen the general feedback culture in schools? Did they develop schools as learning organisations?

The report from IMTEC (Stranden, 2017) does not provide sound empirical answers to the questions, and serves to confirm a slowdown in the process that was successfully brought through Phase 1 by the Scandinavian bargaining model, where the participants agreed on a joint knowledge base from research and practice, to Phase 2, when unclear responsibilities and conflicting interests between the stakeholders, in line with the theory of wicked problems, may have contributed to a sense of confusion and lack of progress. As previously mentioned, no single event appears to have caused the process to slow down, more a growing suspicion that the task at hand was more complicated than anticipated, and the realisation that teacher evaluation may have unintended consequences. Apparently, at this stage, a complex implementation process with several stakeholders with divergent interests needs a different approach.

Discussion and way forward

The purpose of this study was to shed light on the question why teacher evaluation often is reduced to bureaucratic routines and technical practices and fails to support teachers' professional learning. One reason, we have indicated, may be that teacher evaluation is perceived as a benign and technical problem, while it should be treated as a wicked problem. The policy experiment has shown that the bargaining approach is well suited to establish agreement at the initial stages, as consensus was established in the group during Phase 1. However, the fact that problems occurring at later stages require alternative approaches should have been anticipated and planned for. Partners with diverse interests may endorse the knowledge base and agree on the general intention to establish a system for teacher evaluation. At the same time, however, they envision different outcomes and end results of the process. Tensions emerge when the more specific questions are raised about *what* should be done, *how* it should be done and by *whom*.

We have identified a slowdown in the implementation process during Phase 2 of the policy experiment, and have tried to indicate why this may have happened. Here, we will elaborate on what was learned from the policy experiment and what must be taken into consideration if future politicians want to implement teacher evaluation more systematically at the national level in Norway.

When analysing educational organisations, Weick (1976) noticed that in schools, two *loosely coupled* systems appear to work separately from each other. In this analytical perspective, one system consists of teachers, parents, students and curriculum, another of the principal, vice-principal and superintendent. The two systems are somehow attached, but each part preserves its own identity. While teachers have the responsibility for the schools' 'technical core', the principal holds the authority of office. Loosely coupled organisations are stable, allow for self-determination and provide a sense of autonomy and efficacy. However, Meyer and Rowan (1977) observe that decoupled organisations tend to employ a logic of confidence and good faith – in place of coordination, inspection and evaluation. Quite often, teachers' autonomy and reluctance to change is cited as the prime reason for reform implementation failure in schools. Instead, Mehta (2013, 463) argues that a root problem in the educational sector is that it is organised as a bureaucracy rather than as a profession, and suffers under the absence of an 'educational infrastructure' to support practice. While he relates this to the US late 1800 and early 1900, Ramirez and Boli (1987) show that in most Western countries education was bureaucratised when mass schooling was institutionalised. According to Weber (1947), the hallmark of a successful bureaucracy is impartiality. The bureaucrat is an expert on general and domain-specific rules and regulations, and as bureaucrats are socialised into an ethos of rule-following, one bureaucrat may – in principle – be replaced by another bureaucrat who would reach the same conclusion.

If school leaders historically have belonged to a different 'system' than teachers, they may identify more with bureaucrats than with the profession and even perceive themselves as detached, top-down general managers. Many problems in education can therefore be ascribed to the current educational infrastructure where politicians, administrators and teachers, work in a 'layered' and loosely coupled system largely based on linear top-down communication and principal-agent relationships. The three groups have different knowledge bases, divergent interests and problem-solving procedures that will be discussed below.

Tyack (1974) and Tyack and Hansot (1982) show how Taylorism, between 1890 and 1920, inspired the development of the modern school system. Following business models, (mostly male) superintendents were empowered as CEOs to lead schools, while low status (mostly female) teachers worked in relative isolation from each other, following rules and programmes prescribed by the superintendents. One by-product of this institutional form has been relatively weak professionalisation among teachers (Elmore, 2000) and the idea that the complex practice in need of attention in education was not teaching, but administration. The training of administrators provided an opportunity for education departments to produce a new class of mostly male professionals who brought findings from research to the teachers. Mehta (2013, p. 471) comments that already John Dewey did not believe in the model where administrative 'experts' dictated educational methods to passive teachers and warned against partitioning researchers and teachers, as the two groups have a shared interest in understanding and improving practice.

Tschannen-Moran (2009) argues that school leaders adopt a bureaucratic orientation at the expense of cultivating professionalism in schools. The OECD observes that, in Chile, school leaders have traditionally played more of an administrative and managerial role than a pedagogical leadership role, and asks if school leaders have the necessary competencies to lead the effective implementation of teacher evaluation (Santiago et al., 2013). Kraft and Gilmour (2016) find that not only do19 of 24 interviewed principals express concern about their ability to provide meaningful feedback to teachers, they also regard this as outside of their area of expertise. If school leaders see themselves as administrators in a top-down system and lack the necessary competence to give formative feedback to the teachers, we are narrowing in on the question why teacher evaluation is predominantly summative and why the policy process lost its energy during Phase 2, when the more concrete questions about who should do what were raised.

Rittel and Webber (1973) claim that because governance, since the 1960s, is built on goal-setting and measuring outcomes, modern professions, initially expected to solve definable problems, have become victims of their own success. Formulating actionable goals is a complicated task, and it has turned out to be 'terribly difficult, if not impossible', to make various systems operational (Rittel & Webber, 1973; p. 157). One solution is to move beyond dichotomies (Blömeke, Gustafsson, & Shavelson, 2015) and perceive teacher professionalism as a developing continuum. This aligns with insights from the theory of wicked problems and the argument that leaders cannot communicate goals and step aside, because successful implementation requires leaders' continuous attention.

Education is a highly politicised field with a growing, but still weak, knowledge base and no strong tradition for collaborative professional work. Having reviewed the literature on assessment of professionalism, Goldie (2013) finds that peer assessment is the most commonly used instrument among medical doctors. In the systematic review that represents one part of the knowledge base for the policy experiment (Lillejord et al., 2014) peer assessment was frequently mentioned as an underutilised resource in teacher evaluation. Studies also identified assessment literacy as a prerequisite for teacher evaluation to be successful. Sahlberg (2010) describes the ambivalence in ongoing reforms where teachers are trapped in a dilemma between schooling for social capital and moral purpose with student-centred pedagogy and learning on the one side, and, on the other, efficiency-driven education with teacher-centred instruction and achievement. He calls for intelligent accountability (O'Neill, 2002), which combines internal accountability, self-evaluations, critical reflection and school-community interaction with external accountability. When discussing how teachers develop assessment capacities, Livingston and Hutchinson (2016) suggest ongoing enquiry-based training and mentoring focused on pupils' *and* teachers' learning. This may distribute the responsibility to the professional collective of teachers and school leaders and move the attention away from the teacher being individually accountable for the students' learning outcome. One implication is that steering from a distance must be supplemented with organising schools for continuous development – two approaches that require different structures and leadership skills.

Ideally, teacher evaluation should support teacher professionalism. However, argue Cohen and Mehta (2017), teaching is not a full-fledged profession because professions have features that regulate and organise the quality of work; standards for training and licencing, prohibiting those without such credentials from joining the profession; agreement on definitions of problems the profession can solve; appropriate approaches to tackling those problems; and mechanisms to ensure that standards are applied in practice. Professional work therefore requires adherence to a joint and continuously renewed knowledge base, ethical standards, collaboration and a self-critical approach to practice (Gardner & Valentine, 2015; Simons & Ruijters, 2014). In professions, leaders and employees typically share knowledge base, standards, principles and guidelines.

Conclusion

Based on experiences from a Norwegian policy experiment, we have argued that teacher evaluation has traits of a wicked problem and should not be treated as a benign problem. Ashforth, Rogers, Pratt, and Pradies (2014) have identified organisational responses to ambivalence as avoidance, domination, compromise, and holism. In the described policy experiment, several of these responses were observed, related to the fact that teacher evaluation is expected to reach two goals not easily reconciled: professional development *and* quality assurance – in Popham's (1988) words – a *dysfunctional* marriage of formative and summative approaches. The expected outcome of the process is vaguely defined (professional development for teachers, quality schools, improved learning outcome for students, etc.), and various interest groups and stakeholders have their personal interpretation of goals and outcome.

According to Ingvarson (2005), policy-makers can have quite naïve expectations about how easy it is to bring about educational change. This may result in a technical approach to professional development, based on the assumption that the goal is reached if skilled administrators guide teachers step by step in pre-prescribed processes towards the realisation of the political vision for education. While administration today is modernised, certain bureaucratic ground rules persist. March (1984) ascribes the success and longevity of the bureaucracy to adaptivity and lose coupling between what is said and done.

One ambition of the study was to shed light on the question: Why is teacher evaluation often reduced to bureaucratic routines and technical procedures? The analysis indicates that when the policy issue at hand is wicked and ambivalent, traditional bargaining approaches only help part of the way as compromises fail to give direction and impetus. It appears that the political problem-solving approach (holistic compromises) and the administrative problem-solving approach (reducing complexity) produce more problems for the teaching profession than they solve. The policy experiment has also revealed that a core problem in the case of teacher evaluation is the historic loose-coupling between school leaders and teachers. The top-down linear MbO-approach, combined with NPM, appears to have broadened the distance between the two 'systems'.

Governments everywhere face the challenge of translating national policy into implementation strategies that work on the ground and fit the varying conditions in different parts of a country (Kettl, 2015). When political decisions are holistic compromises, and there are no policy feedback loops in place, several local interpretations of centrally initiated intentions may be expected. We have argued that MbO and NPM both assume the existence of an infrastructure that is lacking in educational institutions, where loose-coupling appears to be a major impediment to implementation efforts. Because wicked problems always are only temporarily 'solved'; there is a need for an organisational infrastructure with feed-back loops where professionals continuously relate to the problems, knowing that they are not expected to solve them once and for all. Realising that all solutions are temporary lies at the heart of continuously learning, self-renewing systems and requires that school leaders exercise their authority with a professional orientation; perceive teachers as competent and knowledgeable contributors (Spillane & Diamond, 2007) and extend adaptive discretion to teachers in the conduct of their work (Tschannen-Moran, 2009).

Transformational leadership, where the leader formulates a vision, sets the direction, and inspires others to follow, does not work when circumstances are wicked (Head & Alford, 2015). Top-down bureaucratic structures tend to adopt an implicit distrust towards subordinates; an orientation that is counterproductive when the goal is productive learning and development (Lillejord & Dysthe, 2008). A lesson learned from the GNIST partnership is that relational trust among the parties involved in this kind of managerial structure lubricates the endeavour of common interests. Another lesson learned is that narrowing the loose-coupling by adopting practices that engage school leaders more directly in teacher's work is fundamental to the further development of the teaching profession.

Following this argument, a possible next step when moving teacher evaluation forward, is to perceive teaching an intellectual activity (Stroupe, 2016) and engage teachers more directly in the evaluation process. Professionals' knowledge consists of research (theory) and acknowledged good practice, and Darling-Hammond (2015) suggests that educators should design systems for teacher evaluation based on their knowledge of how students are learning in relation to how teachers are teaching. This has support in implementation research arguing that leaders must keep their attention on the entire implementation chain (Decker et al., 2012). One approach is to establish an educational infrastructure where knowledge from research and experience supports professional work and give the responsibility of evaluating, improving and professionalising teaching jointly to teachers and school leaders.

There is, currently, increased interest in how the teaching profession may become a more mature profession (Sachs, 2016). This article has shown that in parallel to this debate, the question where school leaders are positioned in relation to the profession should be raised. Formative teacher evaluation presupposes knowledgeable evaluators who understand the complex and contextual nature of teaching and can engage in informed dialogue about it. Professionalisation of teachers presupposes a collective effort within the profession to establish a joint research- and experience-based knowledge base that will serve as a centrepiece of a modernised educational infrastructure. This work needs leadership.

Disclosure statement

No potential conflict of interest was reported by the authors.

ORCID

Sølvi Lillejord ⓘ http://orcid.org/0000-0002-4246-0393
Eyvind Elstad ⓘ http://orcid.org/0000-0003-4369-0040

References

Abrahamsen, H. (2017, February 20). Redesigning the role of deputy heads in Norwegian schools – tensions between control and autonomy? *International Journal of Leadership in Education*, 1–17. doi:10.1080/13603124.2017.1294265

Anagnostopoulos, D., Lingard, B., & Sellar, S. (2016). Argumentation in educational policy disputes: Competing visions of quality and equity. *Theory Into Practice, 55*(4), 342–351.

Anderson, S. K., Terras, K. L., & Dagfinrud, M. (2013). Appraising teacher quality in Norwegian schools. *International Journal of Business, Humanities and Technology, 3*(8), 16–42.

Ashforth, B. E., Rogers, K. M., Pratt, M. G., & Pradies, C. (2014). Ambivalence in organizations: A multilevel approach. *Organization Science, 25*(5), 1453–1478.

Barth, E., Moene, K. O., & Willumsen, F. (2014). The Scandinavian model – an interpretation. *Journal of Public Economics, 117*, 60–72.

Berliner, D. C. (2013). Problems with value-added evaluations of teachers? Let me count the ways! *The Teacher Educator, 48*(4), 235–243.

Blömeke, S., Gustafsson, J. E., & Shavelson, R. J. (2015). Beyond dichotomies. *Zeitschrift für Psychologie, 223*(1), 3–13. doi:10.1027/2151-2604/a000194

Brandal, N., Bratberg, Ø., & Thorsen, D. E. (2013). *The Nordic model of social democracy*. London: Palgrave Macmillan.

Buchanan, R. (1992). Wicked problems in design thinking. *Design Thinking, 8*(2), 5–21.

Byrkjeflot, H. (2001). *The Nordic model of democracy and management*. Bergen: Fagbokforlaget.

Camillus, J. C. (2008). Strategy as a wicked problem. *Harvard Business Review, 86*(5), 98–108.

Castetter, W. B. (1976). *The personnel function in educational administration*. New York, NY: Macmillan.

Cohen, J., & Goldhaber, D. (2016). Building a more complete understanding of teacher evaluation using classroom observations. *Educational Researcher, 45*(6), 378–387.

Cohen, D. K., & Mehta, J. D. (2017). Why reform sometimes succeeds: Understanding the conditions that produce reforms that last. *American Educational Research Journal, 54*(4), 644–690.

Collins, C., & Amrein-Beardsley, A. (2014). Putting growth and value-added models on the map: A national overview. *Teachers College Record, 116*(1), 1–32.

Cousins, J. B., & Earl, L. M. (1992). The case for participatory evaluation. *Educational Evaluation and Policy Analysis, 14*(4), 397–418.

Cousins, J. B., Whitmore, E., & Shulha, L. (2013). Arguments for a common set of principles for collaborative inquiry in evaluation. *American Journal of Evaluation, 34*(1), 7–22.

Darling-Hammond, L. (2013). *Getting teacher evaluation right: What really matters for effectiveness and improvement*. New York, NY: Teachers College Press.

Darling-Hammond, L. (2014). One piece of the whole: Teacher evaluation as part of a comprehensive system for teaching and learning. *American Educator, 38*(1), 4.

Darling-Hammond, L. (2015). Can value added add value to teacher evaluation? *Educational Researcher, 44*(2), 132–137.

Decker, P., Durand, R., Mayfield, C. O., McCormack, C., Skinner, D., & Perdue, G. (2012). Predicting implementation failure in organization change. *Journal of Organizational Culture, Communication and Conflict, 16*(2), 29–49.

Delvaux, E., Vanhoof, J., Tuytens, M., Vekeman, E., Devos, G., & Van Petegem, P. (2013). How may teacher evaluation have an impact on professional development? A multilevel analysis. *Teaching and Teacher Education, 36*, 1–11.

Drucker, P. (1954). *The practice of management*. New York, NY: Harper.

Education Act. (1998). Retrieved from https://lovdata.no/dokument/NL/lov/1998-07-17-61

Elmore, R. F. (2000). *Building a new structure for school leadership*. Washington, DC: Albert Shanker Institute.

Elstad, E., Lejonberg, E., & Christophersen, K. A. (2015b). Teaching evaluation as a contested practice: Teacher resistance to teaching evaluation schemes in Norway. *Education Inquiry, 6*(4), 375–399.

Elstad, E., Lejonberg, E., & Christophersen, K. A. (2017). Student evaluation of high-school teaching: Which factors are associated with teachers' perception of the usefulness of being evaluated? *Journal of Educational Research, 9*(1), 99–117. Retrieved from http://www.j-e-r-o.com/index.php/jero/article/view/735

Elstad, E., Lysa, I., Baklien, R., Standal, E. O., Johansen, A., Filmberg, G., … Rimeslåtten, A. (2014). *Rapport til drøfting i GNIST-partnerskapet [Report to the GNIST partnership]*. Oslo: GNIST. ISBN 978-82-999655-0-7. Retrieved from http://udirbeta.udir.no/wp-content/uploads/2015/11/rapport-fra-arbeidsgruppa.pdf

Elstad, E., Lysa, I., Standal, E. O., Buan, A., Hvidsten Dahl, S., Trudeng, M., & Furulund, M. (2015a). *Forslag til hvordan et system for lærervurdering kan utformes og prøves ut i Norge* [How can a system for teacher evaluation be designed and tried out in Norway?]. Oslo: GNIST. ISBN 978-82-999655-0-7.

Firestone, W. A. (2014). Teacher evaluation policy and conflicting theories of motivation. *Educational Researcher, 43*(2), 100–107.

Flores, M. A. (2012). The implementation of a new policy on teacher appraisal in Portugal: How do teachers experience it at school? *Educational Assessment, Evaluation and Accountability, 24*(4), 351–368.

Gardner, H. K., & Valentine, M. (2015). Collaboration among highly autonomous professionals: Costs, benefits and future research directions. In Shane R. Thye & Edward J. Lawler (Eds.), *Advances in group processes* (Vol. 32, pp. 209–242). Emerald Group Publishing Limited.

GNIST. (2009). *GNIST - partnership for a coherent and comprehensive effort for teachers*. Oslo: Norwegian Ministry of Education and Research.

Goe, L., Biggers, K., & Croft, A. (2012). *Linking teacher evaluation to professional development: Focusing on improving teaching and learning. Research & policy brief*. Washington, DC: National Comprehensive Center for Teacher Quality.

Goldie, J. (2013). Assessment of professionalism: A consolidation of current thinking. *Medical Teacher, 35*(2), 952956. doi:10.3109/0142159X.2012.714888

Habermas, J. (1984). *The theory of communicative action* (Vol. 2). Cambridge MA: MIT Press.

Hallinger, P., Heck, R. H., & Murphy, J. (2014). Teacher evaluation and school improvement: An analysis of the evidence. *Educational Assessment, Evaluation and Accountability, 26*(1), 5–28.

Hanushek, E. (1971). Teacher characteristics and gains in student achievement; estimation using micro data. *American Economic Review, 61*, 280–288.

Hanushek, E. (1999). The evidence on class size. In S. E. Mayer & P. E. Peterson (Eds.), *Earning and learning: How schools matter* (pp. 131–168). Washington, DC: Brookings Institution.

Hanushek, E. A., & Raymond, M. E. (2005). Does school accountability lead to improved student performance? *Journal of Policy Analysis and Management, 24*, 297–327.

Head, B. W. (2008). Wicked problems in public policy. *Public Policy, 3*(2), 101–118.

Head, B. W., & Alford, J. (2015). Wicked problems: Implications for public policy and management. *Administration & Society, 47*(6), 711–739.

Hudson, C. (2011). Evaluation – the (not so) softly-softly approach to governance and its consequences for compulsory education in the Nordic countries. *Education Inquiry, 2*(4), 671–687.

Hursh, D. (2007). Assessing no child left behind and the rise of neoliberal education policies. *American Educational Research Journal, 44*(3), 493–518.

Ingvarson, L. (2005). *Getting professional development right*. Australian Council for Educational Research. Retrieved from http://research.acer.edu.au/professional_dev/4

Jordan, M. E., Kleinsasser, R. C., & Roe, M. F. (2014). Wicked problems: Inescapable wickedity. *Journal of Education for Teaching, 40*(4), 415–430.

Kettl, D. F. (2015). Syncing the instruments and missions of government: Re-thinking the roots of decay. *Asia Pacific Journal of Public Administration, 37*(4), 247–252.

Kindergarten Act. (2005). Retrieved from https://lovdata.no/dokument/NL/lov/2005-06-17-64

Kraft, M. A., & Gilmour, A. F. (2016). Can principals promote teacher development as evaluators? A case study of principals' views and experiences. *Educational Administration Quarterly, 52*(5), 711–753.

Lavigne, A. L. (2014). Exploring the intended and unintended consequences of high-stakes teacher evaluation on schools, teachers, and students. *Teachers College Record, 116*(1), 1–29.

Lillejord, S., Børte, K., Ruud, E., Hauge, T. E., Hopfenbeck, T. N., Tolo, A., ... Smeby, J.-C. (2014). *Former for lærervurdering som kan ha positiv innvirkning på skolens kvalitet: En systematisk kunnskapsoversikt.* Oslo: Kunnskapssenter for utdanning. Retrieved from www.kunnskapssenter. no.

Lillejord, S., & Dysthe, O. (2008). Productive learning practice–a theoretical discussion based on two cases. *Journal of Education and Work, 21*(1), 75–89.

Lindbeck, A. (1997). The Swedish experiment. *Journal of Economic Literature, 3*, 1273–1319.

Livingston, K., & Hutchinson, C. (2016). Developing teachers' capacities in assessment through career-long professional learning. *Assessment in Education: Principles, Policy & Practice, 24*(2), 290–307.

Lundgren, U. P. (2011). PISA as a political instrument. In M. A. Pereyra, H. G. Kotthoff, & R. Cowen (Eds.), *Pisa under examination. Changing knowledge, changing tests, and changing schools* (pp. 17–30). Dordrecht: Sense Publishers.

March, J. G. (1984). How we talk and how we act: Administrative theory and administrative life. In T. J. Sergiovanni & J. E. Corbally (Eds.), *Leadership and organizational cultures* (pp. 18–35). Urbana, IL: University of Illinois Press.

McDonnell, L. M., & Weatherford, M. S. (2016). Recognizing the political in implementation research. *Educational Researcher, 45*(4), 233–242.

McMahon, S., & Jones, I. (2015). A comparative judgement approach to teacher assessment. *Assessment in Education: Principles, Policy & Practice, 22*(3), 368–389.

Mehta, J. (2013). From bureaucracy to profession: Remaking the educational sector for the twenty-first century. *Harvard Educational Review, 83*(3), 463–488.

Merton, R. K. (1976). *Sociological ambivalence and other essays.* New York, NY: The Free Press. Macmillan Publishing.

Meyer, J. W., & Rowan, B. (1977). Institutionalized organizations: Formal structure as myth and ceremony. *American Journal of Sociology, 83*(2), 340–363.

Moene, K. O., & Wallerstein, M. (2002). *Social democracy as a development strategy.* Princeton, NJ: Princeton University Press.

Munneke, L., Andriessen, J., Kanselaar, G., & Kirschner, P. (2007). Supporting interactive argumentation: Influence of representational tools on discussing a wicked problem. *Computers in Human Behavior, 23*(3), 1072–1088.

Murphy, J., Hallinger, P., & Heck, R. H. (2013). Leading via teacher evaluation: The case of the missing clothes? *Educational Researcher, 42*(6), 349–354.

National Commission on Excellence in Education. (1983). *A nation at risk: A report to the nation and the Secretary of Education.* Washington, DC: U.S. Department of Education.

O'Neill, O. (2002). *A question of trust: The BBC Reith Lectures 2002.* Cambridge: Cambridge University Press.

OECD. (1987). *Reviews of national policies for education.* Norway: Draft of February 1988. Copy from the National Library of Norway, Depot.

OECD. (2009). *Teacher evaluation. A conceptual framework and examples of country practices.* OECD Review on Evaluation and Assessment Frameworks for Improving School Outcomes. Retrieved from http://www.oecd.org/edu/school/44568106.pdf

Ozga, J., Dahler-Larsen, P., Segerholm, C., & Simola, H. (2011). *Fabricating quality in education: Data and governance in Europe.* London: Routledge.

Popham, W. (1988). The dysfunctional marriage of formative and summative teacher evaluation. *Journal of Personnel Evaluation in Education, 1*(3), 269–273.

Popkewitz, T. S. (2000). Globalization/regionalization, knowledge, and the educational practices: Some notes on comparative strategies for educational research. In T. S. Popkewitz (Ed.), *Educational knowledge: Changing relationships between the state, civil society, and the educational community* (pp. 3–27). Albany, NY: State University of New York Press.

Pupala, B., Kascak, O., & Tesar, M. (2016). Learning how to do up buttons: Professionalism, teacher identity and bureaucratic subjectivities in early years settings. *Policy Futures in Education, 14*(6), 655–665.

Ramirez, F. O., & Boli, J. (1987). The political construction of mass schooling: European origins and worldwide institutionalization. *Sociology of Education, 60*(1), 2–17.

Rittel, H. W., & Webber, M. M. (1973). Dilemmas in a general theory of planning. *Policy Sciences, 4*(2), 155–169.

Sachs, J. (2016). Teacher professionalism: Why are we still talking about it? *Teachers and Teaching, 22*(4), 413–425.

Sahlberg, P. (2010). Rethinking accountability in a knowledge society. *Journal of Educational Change, 11*(1), 45–61.

Santiago, P., Benavides, F., Danielson, C., Goe, L., & Nusche, D. (2013). *Teacher evaluation in Chile. Main conclusions*. Paris: OECD Reviews of Evaluation and Assessment in Education.

Schelling, T. C. (1980). *The strategy of conflict*. Boston, MA: Harvard University Press.

Senge, P. (1990). *The fifth discipline: The art and science of the learning organization*. New York, NY: Currency Doubleday.

Nusche, D., Earl, L., Maxwell, W., & Schrewbridge, C. (2011). *OECD reviews of evaluation and assessment in education. Norway*. Paris: OECD. Retrieved from https://www.oecd.org/norway/48632032.pdf

Shulha, L. M., Whitmore, E., Cousins, J. B., Gilbert, N., & al Hudib, H. (2016). Introducing evidence-based principles to guide collaborative approaches to evaluation: Results of an empirical process. *American Journal of Evaluation, 37*(2), 193–215.

Simons, P. R. J., & Ruijters, M. C. (2014). The real professional is a learning professional. In S. Billet, C. Harteis, & H. Gruber (Eds.), *International handbook of research in professional and practice-based learning* (pp. 955–985). Dordrecht: Springer.

Smagorinsky, P. (2014). Authentic teacher evaluation: A two-tiered proposal for formative and summative assessment. *English Education, 46*(2), 165–185.

Smylie, M. A. (2014). Teacher evaluation and the problem of professional development. *Mid-Western Educational Researcher, 26*(2), 97–111.

Smylie, M. A., Murphy, J., & Louis, K. S. (2016). Caring school leadership: A multi disciplinary, cross-occupational model. *American Journal of Education, 123*(1), 1–35.

Spillane, J. P. & Diamond, J. B. (Eds). (2007). *Distributed leadership in practice*. New York, NY: Teacher College Press.

Stranden, K. (2017). *Profesjonsutvikling i skolen. Rapport fra et utviklingsprosjekt initiert av Utdanningsdirektoratet* [Professional development in school. Report from a developmental project initiated by the Directorate for Education and Training]. Retrieved from https://www.udir.no/tall-og-forskning/finn-forskning/rapporter/profesjonsutvikling-i-skolen/

Stroupe, D. (2016). Beginning teachers' use of resources to enact and learn from ambitious instruction. *Cognition and Instruction, 34*(1), 51–77.

Taut, S., & Sun, Y. (2014). The development and implementation of a national, standards-based, multi-method teacher performance assessment system in Chile. *Education Policy Analysis Archives, 22*(71), 1–33.

Tschannen-Moran, M. (2009). Fostering teacher professionalism in schools: The role of leadership orientation and trust. *Educational Administration Quarterly, 45*(2), 217–247.

Tyack, D. B. (1974). *The one best system*. Cambridge, MA: Harvard University Press.

Tyack, D., & Hansot, E. (1982). *Managers of virtue: Public school leadership in America 1820–1980*. New York, NY: Basic Books.

Weber, M. (1947). *The theory of social and economic organization*. (A. M. Henderson & Talcott Parsons, Trans.). New York, NY: Macmillan Publishing.

Weick, K. E. (1976). Educational organizations as loosely coupled systems. *Administrative Science Quarterly, 21*(1), 1–19.

White Paper (Stortingsmelding) No. 37. (1990–1991). *Om organisering og styring i utdanningssektoren* [Organization and steering in the education sector]. Oslo: Ministry of Education and Research.

Zhang, X. F., & Ng, H. M. (2011). A case study of teacher appraisal in Shanghai, China: In relation to teacher professional development. *Asia Pacific Education Review, 12*(4), 569–580.

The development of assessment policy in Ireland: a story of junior cycle reform

Ann MacPhail ⓘ, John Halbert and Hal O'Neill

ABSTRACT

The more recent discussion in Ireland around post-primary teachers being responsible for assessing their own students' work continues. The new junior cycle reform (covering the first three years of post-primary education) is concerned with making fundamental changes in approaches to learning, teaching, curriculum and assessment, with school-based assessment as an important element of the reform. This paper sets out to map assessment policy in a changing and contested assessment environment in the Republic of Ireland. The paper tells the story of assessment in junior cycle from the first progress report in 1999 on a review of the curriculum that had been introduced for students in the junior cycle of post-primary schools in 1989 to the 2015 *Framework for Junior Cycle*. We document the intention to move away from assessment as solely a means of making summative judgements towards assessment as a support of learning and teaching.

Introduction

Berry and Adamson's edited text (2011) explores assessment reform initiatives in a number of countries. They suggest that 'the nature of assessment that is prevalent in a particular system at a particular time reflects particular priorities, with some functions strongly emphasised and others neglected' (Berry & Adamson, 2011, p. 7). The associated text explores assessment reform initiatives in a number of countries and present differing scenarios. Such reforms are strongly influenced by the traditional view of examinations (Berry, 2011), embraced by those with a strong tradition of teacher empowerment through practices such as externally moderated classroom-based assessment (Klenowski, 2011). Such reforms can also encounter unexpected problems such as a tendency to displace learning with assessment (Tan, 2011). Berry (2011) suggests that outcomes of international assessment reforms favouring more of a reliance on formative assessment appear to have been undermined by (i) the dominance of high stakes summative discourse, (ii) issues of accountability and, (iii) the readiness of the teachers for the change necessitated by the assessment reforms. This paper sets out to share the extent to which Berry's (2011) observation on the dominance of summative discourse aligns with the experience of Irish assessment reform at lower secondary, i.e. age 12–15 years. Such is the continuing dominance of high stakes summative discourse in Ireland that the space for discussion of assessment and its reform by teachers has been slow to emerge. In particular, assessment is seen much more as a means of making summative judgements and less as a support of learning and its role in supporting learning and teaching is not always explicitly recognised.

In a paper published in this journal in 2006, Anne Looney, then Chief Executive of the National Council for Curriculum and Assessment (NCCA) in Ireland, noted that assessment reform in Ireland's post-primary schools was marked by a silence. She suggested that the silence was 'filled with the deafening noise of two formal public examinations, which, despite the efforts of the NCCA in its Assessment for Learning (AfL) Initiative, drowns out the whispers of other assessment discourse' (Looney, 2006, p. 352). Since then, the locus of assessment discourse has become a somewhat noisier place but the progress of reform in curriculum and assessment has been marked more by questions than answers. Nowhere, perhaps, is this more so than in the story of assessment policy and practice in junior cycle. In this paper, we trace the development of that policy from the conclusion of *The Junior Cycle Review* (National Council for Curriculum & Assessment, 1999) to its current articulation in the *Framework for Junior Cycle 2015* (Department of Education & Skills, 2015). The paper charts this policy journey by describing curriculum and assessment documentation and system-wide initiatives that sought to move practice away from the influence of externally conducted assessments. In turn, the move was towards a greater emphasis on school-based, teacher-led assessment in support of learning and teaching. This paper provides an essential platform for future exploration of factors (such as system readiness and teacher trade unions' perspectives) associated with, and impacting on, policy directions.

International assessment reform

Recent major assessment reform initiatives across the globe have resulted in problematising teacher assessment literacies (Leirhaug, Annerstedt, & MacPhail, 2016; Willis, Adie, & Klenowski, 2013), high-stakes examinations (Carless & Harfitt, 2013), and formative classroom assessment (Clark, 2015; De Lisle, 2015; Heitink, Van der Kleij, Veldkamp, Schildkamp, & Kippers, 2016). National education systems' engagement with reforming curriculum, pedagogies and assessment have also been explored (Hayward, 2015; Mills & McGregor, 2016; So & Kang, 2014; Tveit, 2014; Yan, 2015). Aligning more closely with the primary focus of this paper, authors highlight what a shift in assessment practices in specific jurisdictions means for how particular school subjects are taught and learned. These include the introduction of high-stakes assessment (East, 2015) and classroom-based assessment issues for language teacher education (Leung, 2014), formative assessment in the teaching of English (Chen, Kettle, Klenowski, & May, 2013), and a mathematics teacher's evolving beliefs and practices of changing assessment practices in the US (Pourdavood, Wachira, & Pitre, 2015). Science is represented through teachers' experiences of science curriculum reform in England and assessment in science education, respectively (Erduran & Msimanga, 2014; Ryder, Banner, & Homer, 2014), and mapping curriculum innovation in science, technology, engineering and mathematics (STEM) schools to assessment requirements (Tan & Leong, 2014). Within an Irish context, authors have explored the new direction for curriculum and assessment developments in science (Erduran & Dagher, 2014; Kennedy,

2014), mathematics (Kirwan, 2015; Prendergast & Treacy, 2017) and history (Waldron & McCully, 2016).

A contextual note

In Ireland, junior cycle (lower-secondary) covers the first three years of post-primary education, typically from the ages of 12 to 15 years. While the minimum school-leaving age is 16 years, the school retention rate to the end of senior cycle, typically up to age 18 years, was 90.2% for those students who began their post-primary education in 2009 and completed in 2015 (DES, 2016). Prior to their progression to senior cycle, students sit the Junior Certificate examination, which is set, marked and certificated by the State Examinations Commission (SEC). Students sit the examination in June and the SEC sends the results to the schools in mid-September, when the students have already progressed to senior cycle. At the end of senior cycle students sit the Leaving Certificate for which the results are converted to a 'points' rating, governing to a large extent entry to tertiary education. Although for most students the Junior Certificate fulfils no such 'gateway' function, the perception of its value as a 'dry run' for the Leaving Certificate persists (Looney, 2006).

Established as a statutory body in 2001, the NCCA advises the Minister for Education and Skills on matters relating to the curriculum for early childhood education, primary and post-primary schools and the assessment procedures employed in schools and examinations on subjects which are part of the curriculum. The NCCA is a representative structure, comprising nominees of the partners in education, industry and trade union interests, parents' organisations and one nominee each of the Minister for Education and Skills and the Minister for Children and Youth Affairs. While the NCCA carries out its developmental work through its representative structures and through its engagement with the education and research communities, it is ultimately the Minister for Education and Skills who determines policy in the areas of curriculum and assessment.

In mapping the development of curriculum and assessment policy in Ireland, we have chosen to begin with the 1999 review of junior cycle, the first progress report on a review of the curriculum that had been introduced for students in the junior cycle of post-primary schools in 1989. Following that review, there appeared to be three parallel strands of development, each of which the paper discusses. Firstly, the AfL initiative that emerged from a subsequent 2004 review. Secondly, an attempt to address a perceived content overload in the subject syllabuses and need for modernisation. And thirdly, a longitudinal study focused on capturing students' experience of the junior cycle. We then briefly allude to a political intervention, made while these three strands were proceeding, which had a significant impact on that work and future junior cycle development activity. That development activity ultimately led to the publication in 2012 of *A Framework for Junior Cycle* (DES 2012) and subsequently to a later 2015 *Framework for Junior Cycle* edition (DES, 2015). It is with these latter developments that we conclude our mapping of the curriculum and assessment developments in Ireland.

Moving from external summative assessment to school-based assessment

While a profile of assessment in the Republic of Ireland presented in 2006 (Looney, 2006) reported suggestions that neither assessment policy nor assessment practice featured as strengths in the Irish education system, this was not to deny that teachers had been engaging in assessment practices in their classrooms. Rather, the concern was that teachers had not been informed or supported by national policy on assessment in schools. Looney and Klenowski (2008) argued that the focus in Ireland had been on curriculum- rather than assessment-led reform as a driver of change in education.

This paper describes what we believe to be the origin and impact of an assessment-led reform in the Irish post-primary education system. The paper tracks the challenge presented by system-wide change in Irish post-primary schools, moving from a reliance on external summative assessment towards a greater role for school-based assessment in the recognition of student learning. In this context the term 'school-based assessment' implies assessment that is developed, administered and reported on by the individual school. The system-wide change eventually proposed the blending of school based and external summative assessment rather than a sole reliance on one or the other (not dissimilar to the focus in Egypt – Gebril & Brown, 2014). The paper does not allow room to explore the national implementation of a system of school-based assessment. Consequently, future work in this area might allow for the expansion of that particular literature base (see *Assessment in Education: Principles, Policy & Practice*, 22(1) 2015).

External summative assessment tends to be aligned with the term 'high-stakes' testing, with the intention of feeding into national assessment programmes (e.g. Australia – Klenowski & Wyatt-Smith, 2012) and/or being used to select students for access to further educational opportunities (Gebril & Brown, 2014). High-stakes tests in Ireland have been discussed in the Irish context with respect to student experiences of transitioning from high-stakes tests (i.e. Leaving Certificate at upper secondary education) to leaving school (Smyth, Banks, & Calvert, 2011) and more recently the predictability of such examination requirements (Baird, Caro, & Hopfenbeck, 2016; Elwood, Hopfenbeck, & Baird, 2017).

The Irish external summative assessment discussed in this paper has a different connotation again to the above references to 'high-stakes'. Given that the external summative assessment that is the focus of this paper takes place at the end of the third year of Irish post-primary education, with the outcomes having minimal bearing on the students' remaining years at school, the assessment could be considered as having low-stakes for the students completing it (Stobart & Eggen, 2012). However, in spite of the absence of many of the relevant characteristics, the public perception remains that the assessment and its associated certification are high stakes elements of young people's education. Attempts to shift the focus to the high stakes learning that is part of junior cycle (and away from a pre-occupation with preparation for and participation in the perceived high stakes assessments at the end of junior cycle) have not always been successful.

Few Irish studies have explored the changing assessment landscape arising from the introduction of the Framework for Junior Cycle (Erduran & Dagher, 2014; Lenihan, Hinchion, & Laurenson, 2016).

We contend that learning and assessment within the Irish post-primary school system have been treated as separate and not always related processes, with the former concerned with the students' accumulation of knowledge and skills and the latter taking stock of what had or had not been learned (Baird, Andrich, Hopfenbeck, & Stobart, 2017). The integration of assessment through learning (a central feature to what Cohen (1987) terms 'instructional alignment') continues to be strongly advocated for as the most effective way to encourage meaningful student learning and achievement (DeLuca, LaPointe-McEwan, & Luhanga,

2016). Readers are directed to two texts for further insight into Irish policy examples of the enactment of assessment in Irish schools (Murchan & Shiel, 2017) and a research-informed analysis of the Irish education system at the present time that identifies the main strengths, the main shortcomings, and the main opportunities for development in the Irish school system (Coolahan, Drudy, Hogan, Hyland, & McGuinness, 2017).

Many countries have adopted assessment policies that prioritise learning, commonly informed by developments in the AfL discourse (e.g. Scotland and Wales – Leung & Scott, 2009). A consensus throughout the literature notes that formative assessment by the teacher is more effective in motivating students and facilitating meaningful, relevant and worthwhile student learning than high-stakes testing assessment. There is continuing support for the enactment of AfL in the Irish context (Birenbaum et al., 2015; Lysaght, 2015; Lysaght & O'Leary, 2013).

A global movement towards accountability in education is related to student assessments occurring at numerous levels, resulting in an expectation that school-based assessment, through the capacity of teachers to understand assessment and assess appropriately, is now considered a fundamental competency for all educators (Xu & Brown, 2016). However, increasing concern about the over-reliance on teacher judgement in the allocation of summative grades has also been noted (Murchan, Shiel, & Mickovska, 2012).

In mapping the development of curriculum and assessment policy in Ireland, we begin with *The Junior Cycle Review: Progress Report: Issues and Options for Development* (NCCA, 1999). This was the first progress report on a review of the curriculum that had been introduced for students in the junior cycle of post-primary schools in 1989.

The junior cycle review

Introduced to schools in 1989, the Junior Certificate programme aimed to ensure that students received a broad, balanced education that introduced them to all the areas of experience relevant to the needs of learners at their age and stage of development. It offered students an educational experience marked by continuity with the primary curriculum through which they had come and with the curriculum at senior cycle to which the clear majority would in time progress. Regarding assessment, the intention of the Junior Certificate was to move school subject areas away from a sole reliance on a terminal written examination paper to a combination of external and internal assessment, using oral, aural, and practical components, project work, and assignments.

Four year after the first students were awarded the new Junior Certificate, the curriculum was under review. In 1996 the Minister for Education, Niamh Bhreathnach, asked the NCCA to conduct a review, mainly exploring subject status and availability and school flexibility. A year later, when the 'new' Junior Certificate programme was not yet a decade into its existance, the NCCA was asked to give particular attention in its curriculum review to a number of additional perspectives including 'whether the principles which underpin the curriculum are being fully realised' and 'whether the current assessment arrangements are appropriate to the curriculum and syllabus aims and objectives' (NCCA, 1999). It would appear that even after a relatively short period, the effectiveness of the Junior Certificate was being reflected upon and, in particular, methods of assessment were being fundamentally called into question.

In March 1999, the NCCA issued The *Junior Cycle Review: Progress Report: Issues and Options for Development* (NCCA, 1999), a progress report on its review of the curriculum that had been introduced for students in the junior cycle of post-primary schools in 1989. The report focused on two issues of relevance to this paper: (i) the extent to which the curriculum had met the needs of all students; and (ii) whether the current assessment arrangements were appropriate to the curriculum aims and objectives. Arising from the first concern it was suggested that schools have greater levels of flexibility in determining the curriculum to meet their students' needs. The second concern raised an awareness of the need for a changed approach to assessment of student achievement.

The report noted that, for most students, the terminal written examination papers remained the sole means of assessing their achievement in subjects and the only reporting of achievement that had significant status were the grades earned in those terminal examinations. It was also noted that Ireland remained unique in its commitment to wholly externally assessed examinations at the interim stage of post-primary education. The report acknowledged that while several assessment options were available, no associated training or support had been provided for teachers. The report noted a number of adverse consequences arising from an over-reliance on a terminal written examination paper and these included (i) a mismatch between curriculum aims and objectives and assessment through the vehicle of the examination paper, (ii) a bias in teaching and learning methodologies that focus heavily on the preparation for the exam paper, (iii) favouring what is relevant to the examination at the expense of a broad, well-balanced general education relevant to the student, (iv) no direct relationship between formative assessment and formal assessment for certification purposes, (v) the likelihood that potential early school-leavers were not motivated by a terminal exam at the end of three years, and (vi) the operational difficulties associated with recruiting sufficient examiners to assess student work for summative purposes.

The report drew attention to the expectation that, due to assessment proposals and practices in the revised primary curriculum, future students transferring from primary school to first year in post-primary would arrive with an experience of assessment as an integral part of the learning process. The report noted that assessment at junior cycle had the intention of serving both a professional purpose (supporting teaching and learning as an integral part of the education process) and public dimension (accountability). The report suggested that the examination at the end of the junior cycle favoured serving the accountability function over supporting learning and teaching. The report also questioned the necessity for such a high stakes examination in what is a low stakes context, i.e. at a time in post-primary schooling where, for most students, the Junior Certificate is not their final examination.

The role of the teacher in assessment was also a focus of the *Progress Report*, which noted that minimal (if any) responsibility for assessment was devolved to the teacher and to school-based assessment.

Concluding the section on assessment, the *Progress Report* outlined proposals for a developmental project 'focused on the exploration of possible future directions for assessment in junior cycle' (NCCA, 1999, 47). The three strands of the initiative – (i) the development of formative assessment, (ii) the implementation of a wider range of modes and techniques of assessment for certification and, (iii) a move towards assessment for certification through school-based assessment – aimed to address shortcomings in assessment practice in junior cycle identified in the report. In essence, the report argued that the quality of assessment in junior cycle suffered because of a fundamentally misplaced 'high stakes perception' of the role of the Junior Certificate examination:

> The Junior Certificate examination does not have a 'gatekeeper' function. It is an important certificate for students and for schools, but it is, in common with similar certification in other lower secondary systems, a 'low stakes' examination (NCCA, 1999, p. 46).

To reiterate, the Junior Certificate examination contrasted markedly with the English General Certificate of Secondary Education (GCSE), which is high stakes, both for students (because it has a bearing on what they can do post-16) and for schools (because GCSE outcomes are the main accountability mechanism) (West, 2010).

We now focus our attention, in turn, on three parallel strands of development that followed the 1999 Progress Report (NCCA, 1999) discussed above. We begin with the AfL initiative that emerged from a subsequent 2004 review.

Supporting teacher judgement for better reporting on student achievement

The focus of NCCA work on school-based assessment from 2003–2005 centred on support for teachers and schools in using school-based assessment and in reporting to parents. The update on the junior cycle review provides the following summary of developmental work in assessment:

> The work of the NCCA in relation to summative assessment at junior cycle has focused on implementing a wider range of modes and techniques of assessment in the Junior Certificate examination, such as in the new Religious Education syllabus and the revised Science syllabus, and in adopting a common syllabus template which, as mentioned above, expresses syllabus content in terms of learning outcomes. The NCCA has been conducting a developmental initiative in AfL. The aim of the initiative is to give assistance to teachers in the use of assessment in the classroom to support students' learning, and to assist schools and teachers in reporting to parents on students' progress (NCCA, 2004, p. 7).

The initiative in AfL comprised three strands: web-based support, liaison with teacher support services, and work with a small number of school networks (NCCA, 2005a). A significant output from the initiative was the web-based support it provided for teachers and schools who wished to expand their 'assessment toolkit' by exploring the potential of school-based assessment to improve students' motivation and learning (NCCA, 2005a). The continuing review of junior cycle recognised that assessment had been a neglected area in the professional and in-career development of teachers. Through a focus on AfL, it sought to expand the assessment literacy of teachers, in support of a move away from the identification of assessment with examinations and the perception that in the assessment role the teacher was primarily coaching for externally administered tests. To this end, the NCCA collaborated with in-career support services in the dissemination of supports for AfL (NCCA, 2005a). This initiative emphasised reporting on student achievement in the form of highly focused teacher feedback, and an important dimension of the initiative in AfL was the support it could offer teacher judgement for this purpose. This support was offered through a range of annotated examples of student work linked to criteria for assessment. The examples were generated by teachers in the school networks. These examples were quality assured for the process of selection and annotation. The examples, designed to support teachers in making effective judgements and in giving high-quality feedback to learners, were published on the NCCA website.

The initiative in AfL issued two reports in 2005 (NCCA, 2005a, 2005b) which indicated that teachers found that participation in the initiative made a positive contribution to learner motivation and enhanced the teacher/learner relationship. These outcomes of participation were seen as preparing the way for high quality reporting on student progress and achievement. This, in turn, was likely to contribute significantly to the quality of school reporting to students and their parents. The participant responses recounted in the reports related to a small sample of self-reporting teachers and the reports can make no claims as to the authority or generalisability of their findings. We reference them here not as a proof of the efficacy of the initiative. There is no shortage of research evidence of the beneficial impact of school-based assessment on teaching and learning (Assessment Reform Group, 1999; Hanover Research, 2014; Tindal & Marston, 1990; Wiggins, 1998).

The reports captured for the first time in an Irish context a changed perspective on the role of focused feedback in promoting effective learning. The impact of this changed role of feedback became evident in later work on the development of the 2012 *Framework for Junior Cycle* which will be described later in this paper.

The second parallel strand of development that followed the 1999 Progress Report (NCCA, 1999) was the attempt to address a perceived content overload in the subject syllabuses and need for modernisation.

Rebalancing the curriculum

The rebalancing process arose from concerns about curriculum overload and overlap articulated during the junior cycle review. The NCCA began a phased review of all junior cycle subject syllabuses when course committees for five subjects (Business Studies, English, History, Home Economics and Music) were convened in 2003. To ensure that the relative 'size' of the subjects could be determined more easily, a template was developed into which each syllabus would be re-articulated. The main purpose of rebalancing was:

> to reduce overload and overlap in the junior cycle curriculum to provide more time and space for students to have the quality of engagement with learning that teachers would like – the type of learning that was envisaged when the Junior Certificate was first introduced (NCCA, 2008, p. 7).

A critique of the assessment in a given subject was not part of the remit, except that each 'rebalanced' syllabus was required to have a 'Statement of Assessment'. This was, in effect, a description of how the subject was to be examined. The course committees for those first subjects set out primarily to delve into matters of content, i.e. reducing the amount, defining the reach, and modernising as they went. However, the interim and final reports to the NCCA (2004b, 2008) reaffirmed that assessment design had significant implications for the learning and teaching experiences. For a process that was not intended to delve deeply into assessment, the work of the first set of course committees resulted in two significant amendments to the syllabus template's assessment section. Firstly, that it be moved 'towards the back' of the document 'to reduce any perceived over-emphasis on assessment for examination'. Secondly, that as well as the examination information the section should 'include a statement on the purposes and principles of assessment'. These amendments were notable because they represented to some extent a recognition of the importance of developing teachers' assessment literacy and challenged the prominence of the terminal examination in the curriculum discourse.

The third parallel strand of development that followed the 1999 Progress Report (NCCA, 1999) was a longitudinal study focused on capturing students' experience of the junior cycle.

Students' experiences and perspectives on junior cycle

In 2002, the NCCA commissioned the Economic and Social Research Institute (ESRI) to undertake a longitudinal study of students' experiences of the junior cycle curriculum. The study followed the educational experiences of 900 students in twelve schools from first year to third year. The three research phases corresponded with the three years of junior cycle and two phases are more aligned to the focus of this paper. The phase titled *Pathways Through the Junior Cycle: The Experiences of Second Year Students* (Economic & Social Research Institute, 2006), set out to capture second year students' experiences of teaching, learning and the curriculum, and to trace the changes in student attitudes to school and schoolwork over the course of second year. This phase reported that the Junior Certificate examination students would complete at the end of their third year was already becoming more prominent in their lives. The impending examination exerted a considerable influence on the curriculum offered and the nature of teaching and learning and also placed increasing demands on students (and by association was linked to student disengagement) (NCCA, 2007). The phase titled *Gearing up for the Exams* (Economic & Social Research Institute, 2007), captured students' expectations and views regarding the impending Junior Certificate exam as well as the performance of the students in the examination.

In a related publication, Smyth (2016) explored the potential impact on student experiences of an orientation to exam-based assessment. The prevalence across the study schools of an 'over-reliance on a terminal exam and the 'all or nothing' nature of assessment' (Smyth, 2016, p. 52) did not result in an interrogation of alternative assessment practices that were being supported and enacted in schools. Rather, the study focused on the implication of the assessment system, i.e. the terminal examination at third and sixth year, for young people's construction of themselves as learners. Smyth (2016) reported a greater mismatch in third year (the Junior Certificate exam year) between the active learning favoured by students and teachers focusing on ensuring they covered the content for the exam. In turn, students became more instrumentalist in their views as they approached their final exams, 'The dominance of exam-based assessment in the Irish context has, in many ways, distorted the nature of teaching and learning away from more authentic experiences towards a more instrumentalist approach' (Smyth, 2016, p. 213). While the study did not focus on assessment practices, Smyth (2016) suggested that the use of different forms of assessment might have the potential to change the focus of teaching and learning to one which better facilitates student engagement.

When students were asked directly about their assessment preferences, they noted hands-on, practical approaches to assessment in favour of written examinations, believing that the former assessment approaches involved less pressure, allowed more time for completion and reflected a broader range of skills. A preference for continuous assessment rather than a terminal examination was noted by a number of students. In responding to such findings, the NCCA (2007) proposed that the continuing review of the junior cycle would support and engage with a wider range of possibilities in summative assessment as part of the process of syllabus rebalancing. As that work continued a newly appointed

Minister for Education was about to have a significant meeting with a newly convened Council of the NCCA.

We briefly allude to this political intervention, made while the above three strands were proceeding, which had a significant impact on that work and future junior cycle development activity.

Ministerial intervention

The parallel strands of junior cycle deliberation noted above were abruptly drawn together in 2009. Indeed, the Minister for Education and Skills Batt O' Keeffe's address (O'Keeffe, 2009) to the newly assembled Council in June of 2009 came at a critical juncture in the junior cycle project begun some ten years earlier. As has been described, initiatives in assessment had conspired to bring together a number of threads in the assessment discourse. These included a range of new components, a stronger focus on formative assessment, a clearer link between school-based assessment and reporting, and a growing acceptance that Ireland's externally administered examination at the end of junior cycle was out of step with international practice. Outlining his policy directions, Minister O'Keeffe used ten of the speech's twenty-two paragraphs to speak directly to what he saw as the shortcomings of the existing junior cycle programme and the priorities for review and reform. In this, he focused on the nature of junior cycle, the time available for deeper learning and the issue of assessment reform:

> There is no easy solution to these issues. It is important that the Council should review international practice in this area, examine what should be prioritised within the totality of the junior cycle experience, the nature and form of assessment which would be most appropriate in the context of what is no longer a high-stakes environment. In doing so, the issue of overload and time for active learning should be taken particular account of, to see how best these challenges can be dealt with (O'Keeffe, 2009, p. 4).

The NCCA was being requested to re-state the meaning of assessment in junior cycle while reducing what the Minister perceived as the damaging influence of the examination system. Within three months Council considered the discussion paper, *Junior Cycle Curriculum and Assessment: a question of identity?* (NCCA, 2009a). By December of that year, the Council discussed the first of a series of seminal papers on the future of lower secondary education. *Innovation and Identity: Towards a New Junior Cycle* (NCCA, 2009b) linked two demands emerging from the work during the preceding decade in its title: a focus on innovation in learning and teaching and a need to be explicit about what the system values in the educational experience of 12- to 15-year-olds. The culmination of this work formed the basis of the first comprehensive framework for the development of junior cycle curriculum and assessment. Its publication, in 2012, led to a somewhat startling intervention by another Minister for Education. It is to the publication in 2012 of a *Framework for Junior Cycle* and subsequently to a later 2015 edition that we now turn to conclude our mapping of the curriculum and assessment developments in junior cycle.

The evolution of the various frameworks explored below had as a central feature the shifting balance between approaches to assessment. On one side of this balance the external involvement in the assessment process was limited, with the school playing the significant part in administering assessments and reporting achievement. This would effectively see the end of national certification of student examination performance (DES, 2012a). The opposite balancing effect was to retain the external involvement in setting and administering assessments while providing for a limited school influence. In this model the certification of learning achievement would attempt to reflect performance in external as well as school-based assessments (DES, 2015).

A framework for junior cycle 2012

The Junior Cycle reform initiated by Minister O'Keeffe in 2009 was progressed within the NCCA's representative structures for three years. In the autumn of 2012, the then Minister for Education and Skills, Ruairí Quinn T.D., announced a reform plan (DES, 2012b), contained in a *Framework for Junior Cycle* (DES, 2012a), that would see students, rather than examinations, at the centre of the new approach to assessment. If the curriculum was seen as being constrained by the assessment for certification, he proposed to bring about what he saw as essential curriculum change by effectively abolishing the Junior Certificate, an examination which he described as no longer being 'high stakes'. In advocating for the very radical proposals being presented in the *Framework* (DES, 2012a), Quinn (DES, 2012b) was anxious to highlight the benefit of reforms as he saw them in terms of the people who would be most directly affected:

> This is not about our schools, students and teachers doing more work at junior cycle. It is about them doing things differently. Teachers are already doing a great job, but they are often hamstrung by pressure to teach to the test. The new reformed junior cycle will liberate teachers and their students. Parents too will benefit by knowing much more about their children's achievements over the three years of junior cycle than they could ever find out from a State Exam certificate at the end of Junior Cert.

The Minister's announcement on the abolition of the Junior Certificate examination was met with vehement disapproval on the part of both teacher trade unions, the Teachers Union of Ireland (TUI) and the Association of Secondary Teachers of Ireland (ASTI). Their opposition took the form of non-cooperation with the introduction of the new junior cycle based on the 2012 *Framework* (TUI & ASTI, 2014). However, the 2012 *Framework* provided the basis for ongoing development work while negotiations between the Department of Education and Skills and the teacher unions continued. These negotiations ultimately led to the re-iteration of the *Framework* in 2015 which we visit in due course.

The most significant change to junior cycle education proposed by the *Framework for Junior Cycle* (DES, 2012a) was in the area of assessment. Eight principles informed the planning, development and implementation of junior cycle programmes. Twenty-four statements of learning (underpinned by the eight principles) conveyed a broad set of outcomes to be achieved by the junior cycle student. Literacy and numeracy and six additional key skills were identified as being necessary for successful learning across the curriculum and beyond school. The 2012 *Framework* promised fundamental improvement in the learning experiences of students through changes to curriculum and assessment, where the traditional Junior Certificate examination was to be replaced by a new school-based model of assessment.

'AfL' and 'assessment of learning' directed the new focus on school-based assessment. This was to include formative and summative assessment and involve schools and teachers in ongoing assessment and reporting of students' progress and achievement. Other assessment-related elements to be addressed included the introduction of standardised testing in second year, the provision of an assessment and moderation toolkit and an improvement in how students' learning was to be reported to parents effectively.

All junior cycle subject specifications were to include features that would lead to a greater focus on assessment at both classroom and school levels, with a reduced emphasis on the final assessment at the end of junior cycle. It was expected that a percentage of the marks (likely to vary dependent on the subject and suggested to be worth 40% of the overall marks) would be allocated to the school work component completed during second and third year of junior cycle. The remaining marks (suggested to be 60% of the overall marks) would be allocated to the final assessment set by the State Examinations Commission and taken, administered and marked in the school at the end of the third year. In the event where schools choose to opt to provide alternative options to the subjects, i.e. Short Course and/or Priority Learning Unit, all of the marks awarded for each were to be from school work. Short courses were to require 100 hours of student engagement over the three years of junior cycle and be assessed through school-based assessment. Priority Learning Units were to focus on the social, personal and pre-vocational skills that prepare students for further study, work and life and were designed to meet the needs of students with specified general learning difficulties.

A School Certificate was to be presented to students and parents after completion of year three and would list achievement in all the subjects, Short Courses and Priority Learning Units undertaken by the student. The report would also provide an opportunity for the school, parent, and student to comment on other learning experiences not captured as part of the certification process. The proposal to recognise the learning of students with significant special education needs on the same basis (through a School Certificate) as all other students marked a substantial departure for the system.

While the 2012 *Framework* did provide a substantive basis for curriculum and assessment development, its existence as the definitive guide for this work was ultimately short lived. As a result of intensive negotiations between the DES and teacher unions in post-2012, a revised document was published in 2015. As might be expected, union concerns went beyond purely those related to curriculum and assessment with industrial relations issues such as provision of additional time to allow for increased teacher workload featuring in the negotiations (TUI & ASTI, 2015). However, in curriculum and assessment terms, while many of the original innovations contained in the 2012 *Framework* remained, fundamental changes to a number of aspects emerged in the 2015 *Framework* and most of these related to the provisions relating to assessment and certification.

Framework for junior cycle 2015

The headline shift between the 2012 and 2015 *Framework* documents emerged in the area of certification of achievement. Where the 2012 *Framework* effectively ended state involvement in examining students in lower secondary, by 2015 the state was once again engaged in providing examinations. This change arose predominantly in response to policy positions held by teacher trade unions supporting the retention of externally set and administered examinations. The 2015 *Framework* shied away from re-instating the Junior Certificate, or any certificate for that matter, referring instead to the existence of national examinations for subjects and the incorporation of the results of these examinations in a Profile of Achievement to be issued by the school at the end of the student's time in junior cycle. The

Profile of Achievement was to be the new award for all junior cycle students to replace the Junior Certificate, and would document the full range of the student's learning achievements. The 2012 and 2015 editions of the *Framework* articulated two significantly different approaches to assessment in junior cycle. The vision for assessment in the 2012 *Framework* promised, 'The current Junior Certificate examination will be phased out and replaced by a classroom-based approach to assessment. Junior cycle assessment, both formative and summative, will be school-based and focus on supporting learning' (DES, 2012a, p. 26). The 2015 *Framework* viewed the matter differently, 'All assessment in junior cycle, formative or summative, moment-in-time or ongoing, SEC, NCCA or teacher-designed, should have as its primary purpose, the support of student learning' (DES, 2015, p. 35). For this reason, the 2015 *Framework* looked for what it termed 'an appropriate balance':

> A dual approach to assessment, involving classroom-based assessment across the three years and a final externally-assessed, national examination can enable the appropriate balance between preparing students for examinations and also facilitating creative thinking, engaged learning and better outcomes for students. This approach will recognise and value the different types of learning that take place in schools and will allow for a more rounded assessment of the educational achievements of each young person (DES, 2015, p. 35).

The shifts evident in the 2015 *Framework* represented compromise rooted, at least in part, in the desire to restore a semblance of industrial relations peace to post-primary schools. When the impetus towards innovative curriculum reform came up against this reality, the outcome was bound to lead to disappointment. While a level of stability might well have returned to the school environment, the cost in reform terms was very significant.

Conclusion

The paper has described how, in assessment terms, the 2012 *Framework for Junior Cycle* represented a significant evolution in the post-primary landscape and was in some way the logical outcome of development and research initiatives. The launch of the 2012 *Framework* contained within it the seeds of a dispute which has continued to confound the junior cycle reform agenda to the present day, a topic we alluded to briefly and that warrants further discussion. The enduring point of contention has been assessment change. Given that assessment was such a significant lever for change in the preceding years, it is not surprising that reform in the area attracted and continues to attract such attention.

The pressures on, and changes to, the junior cycle assessment landscape described in this paper led in 2012 to a very significant, though not radical by international standards, move away from what had been very familiar surroundings in Ireland. What followed in the period 2012–2015 represented retrenchment and renewal, i.e. a substantial willingness to embrace change balanced by profound resistance to any engagement with the reform agenda. The historical and ongoing resistance to engagement with the junior cycle reform agenda is extensive and requires space not possible in this paper.

It is clear, however, that the students who completed their English junior cycle studies in 2017 (English was the first school subject to follow the new junior cycle framework) received not a Junior Certificate but for the first time a Junior Cycle Profile of Achievement (explained earlier). This recorded new assessment elements which are part of the revised English specification, assessments in Short Courses if studied, other learning (at the school's discretion) as well as results of national examinations.

This paper has mapped the extent to which the junior cycle reform scenario was strongly influenced by the traditional view of examinations (Berry, 2011), with the intention for assessment reforms to favour more of a reliance on formative assessment appearing to have been undermined by the dominance of high stakes summative discourse. This was somewhat compounded by the strong common perspective by many education stakeholders that the Junior Certificate is considered as a 'high-stakes' examination, even though the outcome of such examinations appear not to have a significant bearing on the students' remaining years at school.

While this paper documented the intention though policy documents to move away from assessment as solely a means of making summative judgements towards assessment as a support of learning and teaching, there are aligned developments in the Irish context that require further exploration. These include factors (such as system readiness and teacher trade unions' perspectives) associated with and impacting on policy directions and the national implementation of school-based assessment through training and support. Such explorations will allow commentary on the extent to which there may be an increasing concern about the over-reliance on teacher judgement in the allocation of summative grades (Murchan et al., 2012). There would also be the intention of serving both a professional purpose and public dimension. The professional purpose would be supporting teaching and learning as an integral part of the education process. The public dimension would be to ensure there is a level of accountability for the assessment judgements that are made.

Disclosure statement

No potential conflict of interest was reported by the authors.

ORCID

Ann MacPhail (iD) http://orcid.org/0000-0003-1875-0582

References

Assessment Reform Group. (1999). *Assessment for learning: Beyond the black box*. Cambridge: University of Cambridge School of Education.

Baird, J. A., Andrich, D., Hopfenbeck, T. N., & Stobart, G. (2017). Assessment and learning: Fields apart. *Assessment in Education: Principles, Policy & Practice, 24*(3), 317–350.

Baird, J. A., Caro, D. H., & Hopfenbeck, T. N. (2016). Student perceptions of predictability of examination requirements and relationship with outcomes in high-stakes tests Ireland. *Irish Educational Studies, 17*(1), 1–19.

Berry, R. (2011). Assessment reforms around the world. In R. Berry & B. Adamson (Eds.), *Assessment reform in education. Policy and practice* (pp. 89–102). London: Springer.

Berry, R., & Adamson, B. (Eds.). (2011). *Assessment reform in education. Policy practice*. London: Springer.

Birenbaum, M., DeLuca, C., Earl, L., Heritage, M., Klenowski, V., Looney, A., … Wyatt-Smith, C. (2015). International trends in the implementation of assessment for learning: Implications for policy. *Policy Futures Education, 13*(1), 117–140.

Carless, D., & Harfitt, G. (2013). Innovation in secondary education: A case of curriculum reform in Hong Kong. In D. Carless & G. Harfitt (Eds.), *Innovation and English language education* (pp. 172–185). London: Routledge.

Chen, Q., Kettle, M., Klenowski, V., & May, L. (2013). Interpretations of formative assessment in the teaching of English at two Chinese universities: A sociocultural perspective. *Assessment & Evaluation in Higher Education, 38*(7), 831–846.

Clark, I. (2015). Formative assessment: Translating high-level curriculum principles into classroom practice. *Curriculum Journal, 26*(1), 91–114.

Cohen, S. A. (1987). Instructional alignment: Searching for a magic bullet. *Educational Researcher, 16*(8), 16–20.

Coolahan, J., Drudy, S., Hogan, P., Hyland, A., & McGuinness, S. (2017). *Towards a better future: A review of the Irish school system*. Kildare: NAPD & IPPN.

De Lisle, J. (2015). The promise and reality of formative assessment practice in a continuous assessment scheme: The case of Trinidad and Tobago. *Assessment in Education: Principles, Policy & Practice, 22*(1), 79–103.

DeLuca, C., LaPointe-McEwan, D., & Luhanga, U. (2016). Teacher assessment literacy: What is it and how do we measure it? *Educational Assessment, Evaluation, and Accountability, 28*, 251–272.

Department of Education and Skills. (2012a). Retrieved from http://www.education.ie/en/Press-Events/Press-Releases/2012-Press-Releases/PR12-10-04.html

Department of Education and Skills. (2012b). *A framework for junior cycle*. Dublin: Author.

Department of Education and Skills. (2015). *Framework for junior cycle 2015*. Dublin: Author.

Department of Education and Skills. (2016). *Retention rates of pupils in second-level schools. 2009 entry cohort*. Dublin: Author.

East, M. (2015). Coming to terms with innovative high-stakes assessment practice: Teachers' viewpoints on assessment reform. *Language Testing, 32*(1), 101–120.

Economic and Social Research Institute. (2006). *Pathways through the junior cycle: The experiences of second year students*. Dublin: Author.

Economic and Social Research Institute. (2007). *Gearing up for the exams*. Dublin: Author.

Elwood, J., Hopfenbeck, T., & Baird, J. A. (2017). Predictability in high-stakes examinations: Students' perspectives on a perennial assessment dilemma. *Research Papers in Education, 32*(1), 1–17.

Erduran, S., & Dagher, Z. R. (2014). Regaining focus in Irish junior cycle science: Potential new directions for curriculum and assessment on nature of science. *Irish Educational Studies, 33*(4), 335–350.

Erduran, S., & Msimanga, A. (2014). Science curriculum reform in South Africa: Lessons for professional development from research on argumentation in science education. *Education as Change, 18*(sup 1), S33–S46.

Gebril, A., & Brown, G. T. L. (2014). The effect of high-stakes examination systems on teacher beliefs: Egyptian teachers' conceptions of assessment. *Assessment in Education: Principles, Policy & Practice, 21*(1), 16–33.

Hanover Research. (2014). *The impact of formative assessment and learning intentions on student achievement*. Washington, DC: Hanover Research.

Hayward, L. (2015). Assessment is learning: The preposition vanishes. *Assessment in Education: Principles, Policy & Practice, 22*(1), 27–43.

Heitink, M. C., Van der Kleij, F. M., Veldkamp, B. P., Schildkamp, K., & Kippers, W. B. (2016). A systematic review of prerequisites for implementing assessment for learning in classroom practice. *Educational Research Review, 17*, 50–62.

Kennedy, D. (2014). The role of investigations in promoting inquiry-based science education in Ireland. *Science Education International, 24*(3), 282–305.

Kirwan, L. (2015). Mathematics curriculum in Ireland: The influence of PISA on the development of project maths. *International Electronic Journal of Elementary Education, 8*(2), 317–332.

Klenowski, V. (2011). Assessment reform and educational change in Australia. In R. Berry & B. Adamson (Eds.), *Assessment reform in education. Policy and practice* (pp. 63–74). London: Springer.

Klenowski, V., & Wyatt-Smith, C. (2012). The impact of high stakes testing: The Australian story. *Assessment in Education: Principles, Policy & Practice, 19*(1), 65–79.

Leirhaug, P., Annerstedt, C., & MacPhail, A. (2016). 'The grade alone provides no learning': Investigating assessment literacy among Norwegian physical education teachers. *Asia-Pacific Journal of Health, Sport and Physical Education, 7*(1), 21–36.

Lenihan, R., Hinchion, C., & Laurenson, P. (2016). A changing assessment landscape in Ireland: The place of oral language. *English in Education, 50*(3), 280–296.

Leung, C. (2014). *Classroom based assessment issues for language teacher education. The companion to language assessment.* Wiley Online Library.

Leung, C., & Scott, C. (2009). Formative assessment in language education policies: Emerging lessons from Wales and Scotland. *Annual Review of Applied Linguistics, 29*, 64–79.

Looney, A. (2006). Assessment in the Republic of Ireland. *Assessment in Education: Principles, Policy & Practice, 13*(3), 345–353.

Looney, A., & Klenowski, V. (2008). Curriculum and assessment for the knowledge society: Interrogating experiences in the Republic of Ireland and Queensland, Australia. *Curriculum Journal, 19*(3), 177–192.

Lysaght, Z. (2015). Assessment for learning and for self-regulation. *International Journal of Emotional Education, 7*(1), 20–34.

Lysaght, Z., & O'Leary, M. (2013). An instrument to audit teachers' use of assessment for learning. *Irish Educational Studies, 32*(2), 217–232.

Mills, M., & McGregor, G. (2016). Learning not borrowing from the Queensland education system: Lessons on curricular, pedagogical and assessment reform. *The Curriculum Journal, 27*(1), 113–133.

Murchan, D., & Shiel, G. (2017). *Understanding and applying assessment in education.* London: Sage.

Murchan, D., Shiel, G., & Mickovska, G. (2012). An education system in transition: Assessment and examinations in the Republic of Macedonia. *Assessment in Education: Principles, Policy & Practice, 19*(4), 487–502.

National Council for Curriculum and Assessment. (1999). *The junior cycle review: Progress report: Issues and options for development.* Dublin: Author.

National Council for Curriculum and Assessment. (2004). *Update on junior cycle review.* Dublin: Author.

National Council for Curriculum and Assessment. (2005a). *Interim report on the developmental initiative in assessment for learning in junior cycle.* Dublin: Author.

National Council for Curriculum and Assessment. (2005b). *Assessment for Learning. Report on Phase 2 of the developmental initiative.* Dublin: Author.

National Council for Curriculum and Assessment. (2007). *ESRI research into the experiences of students in the third year of junior cycle and in transition to senior cycle. Summary and commentary.* Dublin: Author.

National Council for Curriculum and Assessment. (2008). *Rebalancing of junior certificate syllabuses. Report on the consultation.* Dublin: Author.

National Council for Curriculum and Assessment. (2009a). *Junior cycle curriculum and assessment: A question of identity?* Document presented to the NCCA Council. September 2009.

National Council for Curriculum and Assessment. (2009b). *Innovation and identity: Towards a new junior cycle.* Dublin: Author.

O'Keeffe, B. (2009). Retrieved from www.ncca.ie/en/About_Us/Council/Minister_meets_Council_ Members/Ministers_speech.pdf

Pourdavood, R. G., Wachira, P., & Pitre, S. (2015). A case study of a secondary mathematics teacher's beliefs and practices relative to NCTM principles: Implication for teacher education, curriculum change, and school reform. *Global Journal of Mathematics, 6*(2), 592–600.

Prendergast, M., & Treacy, P. (2017). Curriculum reform in Irish secondary schools – A focus on algebra. *Journal of Curriculum Studies*, 1–18.

Ryder, J., Banner, I., & Homer, M. S. (2014). Teachers' experiences of science curriculum reform. *School Science Review, 95*(352), 126–130.

Smyth, E. (2016). *Students' experiences and perspectives on secondary education: Institutions, transitions and policy.* London: Springer.

Smyth, E., Banks, J., & Calvert, E. (2011). *From leaving certificate to leaving school: A longitudinal study of sixth year students.* Economic and Social Research Institute (ESRI) Research Series. Dublin: ESRI.

So, K., & Kang, J. (2014). Curriculum reform in Korea: Issues and challenges for twenty-first century learning. *The Asia-Pacific Education Researcher, 23*(4), 795–803.

Stobart, G., & Eggen, T. (2012). High-stakes testing – Value, fairness and consequences. *Assessment in Education: Principles, Policy & Practice, 19*(1), 1–6.

Tan, K. (2011). Assessment for learning reform in Singapore – Quality, sustainable or threshold? In R. Berry & B. Adamson (Eds.), *Assessment reform in Education. Policy and practice* (pp. 75–87). London: Springer.

Tan, A. L., & Leong, W. F. (2014). Mapping curriculum innovation in STEM schools to assessment requirements: Tensions and dilemmas. *Theory Into Practice, 53*(1), 11–17.

Tindal, G. A., & Marston, D. B. (1990). *Classroom-based assessment: Evaluating instructional outcomes.* Columbus, OH: Charles Merrill.

TUI and ASTI. (2014). Retrieved from http://www.asti.ie/news/latest-news/news-article/article/second-level-teachers-vote-for-industrial-action-over-ministers-plan-to-abolish-junior-cert/

TUI and ASTI. (2015). Retrieved form https://www.education.ie/en/Schools-Colleges/Information/Curriculum-and-Syllabus/Junior-Cycle-/Junior-Cycle-Reform-Appendix-to-Joint-Statement-on-Principles-and-Implementation.pdf

Tveit, S. (2014). Educational assessment in Norway. *Assessment in Education: Principles, Policy & Practice, 21*(2), 221–237.

Waldron, F., & A. McCully. (2016). Republic of Ireland and Northern Ireland: Eroded certainties and New Possibilities. In R. Guyver (Ed.), *Teaching history and the changing nation state: Transnational and intranational perspectives* (pp. 53–73). Bloomsbury.

West, A. (2010). High stakes testing, accountability, incentives and consequences in English schools. *Policy and Politics, 38*(1), 23–39.

Wiggins, G. (1998). *Educative assessment.* San Francisco: Jossey-Bass.

Willis, J., Adie, L., & Klenowski, V. (2013). Conceptualising teachers' assessment literacies in an era of curriculum and assessment reform. *The Australian Educational Researcher, 40*(2), 241–256.

Xu, Y., & Brown, G. (2016). Teacher assessment literacy in practice: A reconceptualization. *Teaching and Teacher Education, 58*, 149–162.

Yan, C. (2015). 'We can't change much unless the exams change': Teachers' dilemmas in the curriculum reform in China. *Improving Schools, 18*(1), 5–19.

Ambitious and ambiguous: shifting purposes of national testing in the legitimation of assessment policies in Norway and Sweden (2000–2017)

Sverre Tveit ⓘD

ABSTRACT

This article promulgates a conceptual framework for researching various roles of educational assessment emphasised in governments' assessment policies as a basis for comparing policy-making related to national testing in primary and lower secondary education in Norway and Sweden from 2000–2017. The study analyses policy documents and expert interviews with politicians from the Ministry of Education and Research as well as government officials from the associated executive agency in each country. The official policies gave shifting emphases towards the use of national tests to (a) certify, (b) govern and/or (c) support learning and instruction. Both countries struggled to integrate formative assessment into their national testing programmes. The study illuminates (over)ambitious political demands for integrating multiple purposes into single national testing programmes, and raises questions as to whether national states' Assessment for Learning efforts can be well served in national testing programmes primarily designed for conventional governing or certification purposes.

The article promulgates a conceptual framework for researching the various *roles of educational assessment* emphasised in governments' assessment policies as a basis for comparing policy-making related to national testing in primary and lower secondary education in Norway and Sweden from 2000–2017. The study illuminates that the official policies gave shifting emphases towards the use of national tests to (a) certify, (b) govern and/or (c) support learning and instruction. The article identifies principal problems associated with the integration of multiple purposes of assessments into one testing programme: for Sweden, the integration of certification and governing roles; and for Norway, the integration of governing and support roles. For both countries, the study reveals (over)ambitious political demands for the formative use of national tests, which are primarily designed to serve a conventional role in the governing or certification of education.

The comparison is motivated by the inconsistency – and at times, radical shifts – in the countries' emphasis on the purposes of the national testing. Further, by the countries'

ⓑ Supplemental data for this article can be accessed at https://doi.org/10.1080/0969594X.2017.1421522.

different traditions and contemporary approaches to utilise national assessment instruments in the governing and certification of education. Finally, the study is motivated by the Swedish government's ongoing evaluation and reconceptualisation of the purposes of its national testing programme.

For each country, the study analyses policy-making undertaken by the Ministry of Education and Research (onwards called *Ministry* or *education ministry,* interchangeably) and the associated executive agency responsible for implementing and administrating the national tests: in Norway 'Utdanningsdirektoratet', the Directorate for Education and Training (DET); and in Sweden, 'Skolverket', the National Agency for Education (NAE). The analysed policy documents include the Norwegian and Swedish education ministries' commission letters to government commissions, the reports of these commissions (green papers), the governments' associated propositions to their parliament (white papers) and the Ministries' commission letters to its executive agencies (DET and NAE, respectively). Furthermore, the paper analyses the executive agencies' reporting on these commission letters and on the overall administration of, and reforms to, the national testing programmes. The paper also reports on expert interviews undertaken in 2013 with representatives from the political leadership of the education ministries in Norway and Sweden and the general director and assessment division director of the DET and NAE, who oversaw the implementation and reforms that shaped the countries' contemporary national testing policies.

The first section establishes Norway and Sweden's different traditions and contemporary approaches to utilise national assessment instruments in the governing and certification of education and thus envisions the different contexts of the two national testing programmes that are compared. The second section addresses the limitations of the binary distinction between formative and summative assessment and promulgates a threefold theoretical framework for undertaking comparative analyses of national states' educational assessment policies. The third section outlines the study's data, methods and approach to sampling, coding, data generation and reduction. The fourth and fifth sections analyse how the emphasis on the purposes of the national testing programme changed during the policy-making from 2000–2017 in Norway and Sweden, respectively (Research Question 1 and 2). The sixth section discusses the similarities and differences that can be identified in the countries' national testing policies with respect to the (conflicting) roles of educational assessment (Research Question 3). The article concludes by addressing principal problems that apply to Scandinavian education and beyond with respect to the legitimacy of assessment policies which (attempt to) integrate multiple purposes into single national testing programmes.

The Scandinavian context of educational assessment

National states are largely reliant upon the use of national assessment instruments to certify and govern education. For centuries, primary and secondary education in the Scandinavian countries sustained a (largely Germany influenced) continental European tradition of certifying and governing learning and instruction based on exit examinations along with teachers' grading. During the expansion of the education system after WWII, however, Sweden formed its own approach to educational assessment. National tests, based on psychometric principles, incrementally replaced the traditional examinations (ultimately terminated in 1968) as the national assessment instrument used for both certification and governing (Tveit, 2018).

Norway (and Denmark), on the other hand, resisted the increased emphasis on psychometric testing during the second half of the twentieth century, both the transnational emphasis on utilising standardised testing for certification in the 1950s and 1960s and during the global push for increased accountability measures in the 1980s and 1990s.[1] It was not until the new millennium, as a response to the 'PISA shock', that these transnational trends were manifested in a new national testing programme (Tveit, 2014, 2018).

Thus, the official purposes of the contemporary national testing programmes in the two countries are significantly different. Norway has national examinations that are used for certification and undertaken by all students in either Norwegian, English or mathematics subjects at the completion of lower secondary education (Year 10), along with national tests undertaken by all students for reading and numeracy in Years 5, 8 and 9 and for English in Years 5 and 8.[2] In Sweden, the national testing programme is the only national assessment instrument, undertaken by all students for the subjects mathematics, Swedish, and Swedish as a second language in Years 3, 6 and 9; for English in Years 6 and 9; and for one natural science subject and one social science subject in Year 9.

Despite these differences, the two countries' national testing programmes are the key national assessment instruments used to monitor the quality of the education provisioned and, thus, to govern the education system. Table 1 summarises the main features of the two countries' national assessment instruments.[3]

Theoretical perspectives: three roles of educational assessment

The distinction between formative and summative assessment is commonly used to distinguish between the various uses of educational assessment. After it was coined by Scriven (1967) in the American context of educational programme evaluation five decades ago, the distinction was soon used by other American scholars focusing on the processes of individual assessment (rather than curriculum programmes), pioneered by Bloom, Hasting, and Madaus (1971). In the past two decades, the concept of formative assessment was used extensively in educational research and in policy-making in Scandinavia, largely influenced by Black and Wiliam (1998) and the Assessment Reform Group (2002), among others (see, e.g. Tveit, 2014, 2018; Burner, 2016; Gamlem, 2015; Hopfenbeck, Flórez Petour, & Tolo, 2015; Jonsson, Lundahl, & Holmgren, 2015).

Black and Wiliam's definition of formative assessment has been a fruitful framework for coming to terms with how assessment can be used to improve learning and instruction (e.g. Burner, 2014; Gamlem & Smith, 2013). However, their conceptualisation of formative assessment was not explicitly related to summative assessment, which may explain researchers and policy-makers' struggles to come to terms with the meaning of the distinction (Bennett, 2011). A review of the use of the formative and summative assessment distinction in research literature (Tveit, 2017, August) suggests that if we use this binary distinction, we risk undermining rather than facilitating a comparative analysis of countries' assessment policies because the various uses of so-called summative assessments are obscured.

Herman and Baker (2009) wrote that 'articulating the specifics of how assessment can be orchestrated to serve these various policy goals is a matter of understanding an array of potential purposes of assessment' (p. 177). An important premise of my conceptual approach is that I follow Newton's (2007) lead and recognise each role as relying on summative

Table 1. Contemporary national assessment instruments in primary and lower secondary education in Norway and Sweden.

Country	Norway		Sweden
Assessment instrument	National examinations[a]	National tests	National tests
Year and subject/skill	Year 10: One examination in either Norwegian, English or mathematics	Year 5: English, reading, and numeracy Year 8: English, reading, and numeracy Year 9: Reading and numeracy	Year 3: Mathematics, Swedish, and Swedish as a second language Year 6: Mathematics, Swedish, Swedish as a second language, and English Year 9: Mathematics, Swedish, Swedish as a second language, and English. Additionally, one natural science-oriented test (biology, physics or chemistry) and one social science-oriented test (geography, history, religion or social science)
Instrument developer	Developed by expert groups of teachers and scholars, commissioned by the Directorate for Education and Training	Developed by expert groups at universities, commissioned by the Norwegian Directorate for Education and Training	Developed by expert groups at universities commissioned by the Swedish National Agency for Education
Marking procedures	Two external and trained examiners mark the responses based on guidelines from the Norwegian Directorate for Education and Training	Auto-computerised marking of most items. For open questions in the reading tests, teachers assign scores, based on guidelines from the Norwegian Directorate for Education and Training	The teachers mark the responses themselves, based on guidelines from the Swedish National Agency for Education
Subject or skill orientation	The instruments are constructed based on disciplinary goals (competence aims) stated in the curricula for the respective subjects	The instruments are constructed based on the basic skills, which are integrated in the competence aims for all subjects' curriculum	The instruments are constructed based on disciplinary goals stated in the curriculum for the respective subjects

[a]The table includes the national examinations in Norway to inform about this important context; however, the empirical investigation is limited to the national tests in both countries.

judgements.[4] I draw on Stobart (2008), who used a threefold classification of the purposes of educational assessment:

(1) Selection and certification;
(2) Determining and raising standards; and
(3) Formative assessment – Assessment For Learning (p. 16).

Paul Black (1998) also outlined three overall purposes of educational assessment that largely correspond to Stobart's (2008) classification, although listed in a different order:

(1) Formative, to aid learning;
(2) Summative, for review, transfer and certification; and
(3) Summative, for accountability to the public (p. 35).

Drawing on Scriven's (1967) foundational paper, Newton's (2007) critique of the application of the formative and summative distinction, and the classification of purposes proposed by Black (1998) and Stobart (2008), I have promulgated a theoretical framework for researching purposes of educational assessment. I define educational assessment as *the processes of determining educational goal (or standard) attainment* and distinguish between *three roles of educational assessment*. Using Scriven's 'role' concept, I acknowledge that assessments may have (unintended) implications beyond defined policy purposes. As shown in Table 2, I distinguish between assessments used to *certify*, *govern* and *support* learning and instruction. The next section outlines the use of this theoretical framework to analyse the policy-making that shaped the contemporary national testing programmes of Norway and Sweden.

Data and methods

The analysis of policy documents starts with the policy-making that prepared the national testing programme implementation in Norway and the reforms that expanded the national testing programme in Sweden.[5] I identified policy documents for both Norway and Sweden through searches on the education ministries and executive agencies' official websites, first by searching for *national tests* ('*nasjonale prøver*' and '*nationella prov*', respectively). Within these reports, I searched for the *purpose* ('*formål*' and '*syfte*', respectively). Through a second read of the documents, I gave attention to texts that may refer to or be related to the roles of the test without explicitly addressing its purpose(s). Third, I used a snowball sampling approach (Krippendorff, 2004) to identify other potential relevant policy documents that were referred to in the already generated and analysed policy documents. Documents identified as relevant through the snowball sampling, but could not be accessed online, were obtained from the respective government body's archives.

All the generated documents were stored in the NVivo 11 software, and the relevant paragraphs were coded. The coded text was transferred to MS Word documents, where the most relevant texts were highlighted and, in turn, translated into English.[6] The investigation generated a comprehensive set of policy document data, especially for the Swedish case, which included 31 policy documents as compared to 13 for Norway[7] (see Supplementary material). All quotes in the analysis sections are translations to English that I have undertaken from the native languages (Norwegian and Swedish) of the respective policy document. A certain limitation to the scope of the analysis of the Swedish case was necessary due to the vast data material.[8] To ensure that all relevant policy documents were included

Table 2. Classification of roles of educational assessment.

Process	To determine educational goal (or standard) attainment		
Purpose	To *certify* learning and instruction	To *govern* learning and instruction	To *support* learning and instruction
Level	Student and teacher level (teachers' grading, exit examinations)	Organisational level (schools, municipalities, national states)	Student and teacher level (classroom assessment)
Institutional practice	To identify and report the final level of attainment (a grade/mark, examination); used for certification or selection for further education and professional life	To evaluate (aggregated) student attainment data; used to (a) inform decision-makers' quality development efforts; and (b) to control application of curricula and regulations	To identify and communicate gaps between the current and desired attainment levels used to support learning and instruction strategies
Associated with	Summative assessment	Summative assessment	Formative assessment

in the analysis, and that each country's history of policy implementation was well accounted for, two researchers with expertise in educational measurement and educational assessment policy, respectively, were consulted in each country.[9] These experts' comments did not bring about significant changes to the analysis but improved its precision and helped reassure a defendable outcome of the undertaken data generation and reduction.

Analyses of expert interviews undertaken in 2013 with politicians and government officials in the two countries' education ministries and their associated executive agencies were included at the end of each policy document analysis (see Table 3). Interviews with policy-makers can be particularly important to identify tacit knowledge, silences and inconsistencies in official written policies (Dexter, 1970/2006). Interviews with the state secretary[10] to the Norwegian education minister (who was part of a socialist coalition government) and the political advisor to the Swedish education minister (who was part of a conservative coalition government) captured the political views of these governments, which held office from 2005–2013 and from 2006–2014, respectively.

Interviews with the general director and the assessment division director convey the views of lead policy-makers in the executive agencies. The interviewees consented to be referred to by their formal role, even knowing that this made it possible to indirectly identify them. This was a premise of the interviews, as the validity of expert interview data relies on the interviewees' expertise and formal responsibility.

Stobart (2008) stressed that it is common that assessments have multiple purposes. Perceiving several purposes as being present, but that there may be shifts that 'bring one into the foreground while another fades into the background' (p. 15), can be a helpful perspective. I looked for what was *most in focus*, *most thoroughly deliberated*, and whether the emphasis on purposes expressed a *priority or ranking*. Thus, rather than merely *identifying* roles of educational assessment, the next sections analyse how these roles were *emphasised* in the policy documents and by the policy-makers, using the framework outlined in Table 2.

The implementation of contemporary national testing policies in Norway (2000–2017)

Figure 1 summarises the emphasis on roles of educational assessment in the 13 analysed policy documents underpinning the national testing policies in Norway from 2001 to 2017. The next sections report on the document analysis and expert interviews, focusing on the major shifts and reforms.

Table 3. Policy levels investigated and expert interviews undertaken in the study.

Country	Norway	Sweden
Ministry of Education and Research	State secretary to the minister of education (quoted: Norwegian education ministry politician)	Political adviser to the minister of education (quoted: Swedish education ministry politician)
Executive agency	General director, Norwegian Directorate for Education and Training (quoted: DET general director)	General director, Swedish National Agency for Education (quoted: NAE general director)
	Assessment division director, Norwegian Directorate for Education and Training (quoted: DET assessment division director)	Assessment Unit director, Swedish National Agency for Education (quoted: NAE assessment division director)

Year	Norwegian National Testing Policy Documents (2000 -2017)	SUPPORT	CERTIFY	GOVERN
2002	NOU2002:10		/	X
2003	Report to the Parliament 1, Annex 3 [2003–2004]	/		X
2003	NOU2003:16	X		X
2004	Report to the Parliament 30, 2003–2004		X	
2006	Report to the Parliament 16 (2006–2007)	X		X
2007	Report to the Parliament 31 (2007–2008)	X		X
2009	Report to the Parliament 19 (2009–2010)	X		X
2010	DET (2010). The National Testing Framework	/		X
2011	Report to the Parliament 22 (2010–2011)	X		X
2012	Report to the Parliament 20 (2012–2013)	/		X
2015	Report to the Parliament 28 (2015–2016)			
2016	DET (2016): Methodological basis for the national tests			X
2017	DET (2017). The National Testing Framework.	X		X

Figure 1. Emphasis on roles of educational assessment in the Norwegian national testing policy documents (2000–2017).

Purposes of assessment emphasised in Norwegian policy documents (2000–2017)

Following the 'Pisa chock' in December 2001, the newly elected conservative coalition government, and its education minister from the Conservative Party, nominated eight additional members and expanded the mandate of a government commission that was already established to evaluate and propose reforms to the primary and secondary education system.

The commission's first report (*NOU2002:10*) proposed a new national testing programme and emphasised that the main intention was that 'all users and participants get information about the development in central areas' (p. 27). The commission also indicated that the tests may serve a certification role. In its second report *NOU2003:16*, the commission emphasised both the *governing* and *support* roles, stating that the tests were to 'both serve as a basis for school evaluation and to give the student feedback on subject attainment and learning outcomes' (p. 226).

Report to the Parliament 30 (2003–2004) was foundational to the Ministry's preparation of the 2006 primary and secondary education reform. After considering the commission's proposals, the Ministry decided that the basic skills were to be assessed through new national tests in Year 4 and Year 7 and in the first year of upper secondary education. This policy document stands out by only giving emphasis to the certification role of the national tests, which were then already about to be undertaken for the first time (spring 2004). The Ministry referred to the national tests as 'important tools' for ensuring that teachers' final assessments ('standpunktvurdering') were '*standard-based*' (p. 40).

These initial policy deliberations demonstrate the ambitious and ambiguous character of the implementation phase of the new testing programme. The assessment purposes were not consistently addressed at the time of implementation; emphasis was given to all three roles of educational assessment.

Following the 2005 elections, a new socialist coalition government was formed with an education minister from the Socialist Party. The government soon decided to have a one-year moratorium in 2006, to terminate national testing in upper secondary education, and to move the Year 4 and Year 7 exit tests to the beginnings of Year 5 and Year 8. This change reflected a shift in the emphasis on roles of educational assessment, which can be observed in *Report to Parliament 16 (2006–2007)*:

> The tests should give information to students, teachers, school leaders, parents, municipalities regional authorities and the national level as basis for targeted development measures. The tests will be held early in the fall in Year 5 and Year 8. The Ministry expects that schools and municipalities use the results of the national tests for follow-up work. (p. 78)

This purpose description reflects an emphasis on the governing role and the support role, at the expense of the prospective certification role. This is also reflected in *Report to Parliament 31 (2007–2008)*.

Report to Parliament 19 (2009–2010) is the first report that refers to the purposes as 'set by the Ministry and incorporated in the National Testing Framework' (p. 21). In the 2010 version of the National Testing Framework, DET stated that:

> The national tests should assess the extent to which the students' skills are in accordance with the curriculum's aims for the basic skills of numeracy and reading in Norwegian and English, as they are integrated into the competence aims for LK06 after the 4th and 7th year. The samples shall provide information to students, teachers, school leaders, guardians, municipalities, regional authorities and the national level as the basis for improvement and development. (DET, 2010, p. 5)

The executive agency's official framework focuses on the tests' governing role, and it does not specify how the tests should be used on the individual or classroom (student and teacher) level.

Report to Parliament 20 (2012–2013) is the first report to the Parliament that explicitly emphasises the support role, focusing on the individual level (students, teachers and parents) as well as (the conventional) organisational level (school leaders, municipalities, and regional and national authorities). In this report, the government retrospectively summarised the challenges of the first implementation of the national testing programme that was undertaken by the previous government:

> Rapid pace without proper grounding and dialogue with those who would use this tool led to poor test quality and a lot of uneasiness about how to use these tools. It was also criticized that there were too many tests, and that the workload for teachers in schools was too large overall. Comprehensive publication of results led to ranking of schools and presentation of results that did not meet scientific standards. National tests were therefore primarily regarded as a control system, and worked poorly as a quality development system for teachers, schools, and municipalities. (p. 150)

After 2013, the national testing policies have not been discussed in the analysed ministry documents. DET (2016) reported that, since 2014, the national testing programme has been 'based on the use of IRT ("Item Response Theory") calibration and scaling methods', which makes it 'possible to integrate an anchor test that (…) allows us to say something about changes from one year to the next' (DET, 2016, p. 3). Thus, this important aspect of the tests' governing role was achieved 10 years after the first implementation of the national testing programme.

When the Conservative Party, which was in charge of the first implementation of the national tests, won the election and once again became in charge of the education ministry in 2014, it did not bring about changes to the official definitions of the purposes of the national tests. To date, the *Report to the Parliament 20* (2012–2013) of the previous government quoted above is the last official policy document from the Ministry that discusses the purposes of the national testing programme.

Thus, the increased emphasis on the national tests' support role appears to be the official national testing policy to date. The current official National Testing Framework, available on the DET website, provides a more elaborated description of the purposes of the national tests:

> The purpose of national tests is to provide the school with knowledge about the students' skills in reading, numeracy and English. The information from the tests should form the basis for formative assessment and quality development at all levels in the school system. (DET, 2017, p. 2)

It adds that 'National tests provide information about individual students, groups, stages and schools that teachers and school leaders need to undertake quality development' and that

> for the student, the results of national tests, in accordance with the provisions in Chapter 3 [of the Regulations to the Education Act], should be a tool in the learning process as a basis for adapted education and help the student increase his/her competence in subjects (DET, 2017, p. 2)

The strong emphasis on formative assessment[11] in the contemporary National Testing Framework (DET, 2017) can be understood in view of the socialist coalition government's (2005–2013) increased emphasis on formative assessment, including a comprehensive revision of the Regulations to the Education Act in 2009, and a comprehensive Assessment for Learning programme (DET, 2014).

Purposes of assessment emphasised by Norwegian policy-makers (2013)

The expert interviews further substantiate the increased emphasis on the support role during the socialists' rule from 2005–2013:

> The way I think it worked at first, with the scope of the tests, the quality of the tests, not to mention how results were published, I believe that it served, too primarily, as a control system or a governing instrument for the authorities, and to a lesser extent was suitable as a pedagogical tool. (Norwegian education ministry politician)

The state secretary gave emphasis to both the governing and support roles but called for more emphasis on the latter.

When asked about the purposes of the contemporary policies of national testing, the DET director emphasised the governing role first before acknowledging support as another purpose of the national tests.

> What has been there all the time, and which was a little awakening after PISA … is that we should have a national system that could give us the information that PISA did. That we should not be dependent on an international test to get information about how we were doing with the basic skills. So that was there as a purpose. And another purpose, which relates to the discussion of which Year they should take place, is that it should be undertaken at important stages in the training so that it is possible to do something about it, both at school level and at individual level. (DET general director)

The assessment division director also perceived the national tests' role in providing 'steering information' (governing) as the most important, especially when the tests were first implemented. The assessment division director further observed that the transition from exit tests to entrance tests following the 2006 moratorium reflected an increased emphasis on the support role: 'Although national tests continue to serve two purposes, and the primary purpose is steering information, much more emphasis has been put on the pedagogical value after the tests are undertaken' (DET assessment division director). The assessment division director elaborated on the challenges with respect to the initial implementation of the tests, its purposes, and associated discussions about the timing:

> There was a lot of discussion about it, the time in relation to the purpose. Initially it was governing information that was most strongly emphasised, and that too related to the time of the year the tests were. In 2005 it was a lot of boycotts; the data were not sufficiently good to be published – they were not reliable enough because of the boycott actions and low turnouts in many places. And then it was decided to have that break. And after that the tests were moved to the fall on the subsequent Year. And that was to facilitate a pedagogical value (DET assessment division director).

The expert interviews envision the governments' dilemmas when deciding what purposes of educational assessment to prioritise.

The reform of the contemporary national testing policies in Sweden (2000–2017)

Figure 2 summarises the emergence of the emphasis on roles of educational assessment in the 31 analysed policy documents underpinning the national testing policies in Sweden from 2000–2017. The next sections report on the document analysis and expert interviews, focusing on the major shifts and reforms.

Purposes of assessment emphasised in Swedish policy documents (2000–2017)

Based on an evaluation of 20 municipalities' grading practices, NAE's *National Quality Audit 2000* expressed a sharp critique of Swedish municipalities' grading practices. The report addressed both the certification and governing roles of the national tests and became important for reform deliberations in subsequent years. The report's overall conclusion was that 'there are significant shortcomings in terms of fair and equal grading' (NAE, 2000, p. 175).

In the following years, NAE reports addressed either the governing and certification roles (NAE, 2001, 2002) or only the certification role (NAE, 2004). In 2004, the Ministry of Education and Research started to elaborate on new purposes of the national testing programme, listing five purposes of the national tests:

- Contribute to increased goal achievement for the students
- Clarify the goals and identify the strengths and weaknesses of students (diagnostic function)
- Specify course objectives and grading criteria
- Support an equal and fair assessment and grading
- Provide the basis for an analysis of the extent to which the knowledge objectives are reached at the school, municipality and the national level. (p. 1)

This was the first time the national tests' support role was emphasised and marked the beginning of a phase in which this was a key focus of the policy-making. This development was also reflected when the Ministry of Education and Research (2005) comissioned the NAE to produce diagnostic support material to accompany the national tests.

Year	Swedish National Testing Policy Documents (2000 -2017)	SUPPORT	CERTIFY	GOVERN
2000	NAE (2000). National quality audits.		X	X
2001	NAE (2001). Assessment and grading. Comments with questions and answers.		X	X
2002	NAE (2002) Grading practices in 18 independent schools.		X	X
2004	NAE (2004). Action plan for fair and equal grading.		X	
2004	Ministry of Education and Research (2004). Commission to the National Agency for Education regarding the national testing system.	X	X	X
2005	Ministry of Education and Research (2005). Commission to the National Agency for Education regarding National Tests and Diagnostic Support Materials.	X		
2006	Swedish Parliament (2006:19). Committee Directive. Review of primary and secondary schools' goal and monitoring systems, etc.	/	/	X
2007	SOU2007:28. Clear goals and knowledge requirements in primary and lower secondary schools. Proposal for a new system for goal monitoring and follow-up.		X	X
2007	NAE (2007). Test grades – Final grades – Equality. A statistical analysis of the relationship between national test grades and final grades in Year 9, 1998–2006.		X	
2008	Bill 2008-09: 87. Clearer goals and knowledge requirements.		X	X
2008	Ministry of Education and Research (2008). Regulation letter for the 2008 fiscal year regarding the National Agency for Education. Change decision 2008-09-25.		X	X
2008	Ministry of Education and Research (2008). Ministry memorandum. More compulsory national tests in primary and lower secondary school.	X	X	X
2008	NAE (2008). Goals and national tests in Year 3.	X		X
2009	NAE (2009). Proposal for how the national testing system should be developed and designed.	X	X	X
2009	NAE (2009). National tests for Year 3.	X		X
2009	Ministry of Education and Research (2009). Commission to the Swedish School Inspectorate on certain re-marking of national tests.		X	X
2010	Bill 2009-10:219. Grades from Year 6	X		
2011	NAE (2011). Knowledge Assessment in School.	/	X	X
2011	Bill 2011-12:1. Budget bill for 2012.		X	
2011	Ministry of Education (2011). Commission regarding national tests.			X
2012	NAE (2012). Commissoned quality assurance of the national tests.		X	X
2013	NAE (2013). National tests in basic school spring 2012.	/	X	X
2014	SOU2014:12. Evaluate for development -on evaluation of school policy reforms.			X
2014	NAE (2014). Commissioned quality assurance of the national tests.		X	X
2015	NAE (2015). Test grades' stability. On national tests – Year 9 1998-2012.		X	X
2015	NAE (2015b). National test credit reliability. On national testing. NAE's current analyses 2015.		X	X
2015	NAE (2015c). School reforms in practice. How the reforms were implemented in everyday school life.	X		
2016	SOU2016:25. Equal, legal, and effective – a new national knowledge assessment system.		X	X
2016	SOU 2016:38. Gathering for the school. National objectives and development areas for knowledge and equivalence. Interim report.		X	X
2017	SOU2017:35. Gathering for the school – National strategy for knowledge and equivalence.		X	X
2017	NAE (2017). National tests	/	X	X

Figure 2. Classification of emphasis on roles of educational assessment in the Swedish national testing policy documents (2000–2017).

In 2006, the Swedish Parliament's education committee issued a directive that mandated a 'review of primary and secondary schools' goal and monitoring systems' (p. 1). The committee addressed concerns that 'schools and principals do not make sufficient use of the results of the national tests to analyse the schools' goal attainment' (p. 8). The review, *SOU2007:28*, criticised the national testing programme for having too many purposes. It proposed a new system for goal monitoring and follow-up, of which the purpose of the national testing system should primarily be to:

- support an equal assessment of pupils' knowledge development and a fair grading, as well as
- provide an analysis of the extent to which knowledge requirements are reached at school level, at municipality level and at national level. (p. 281)

In Bill *2008-09:87*, the government outlined its policy for expanding the national testing programme to include tests in Year 3 and to transfer the tests in Year 5 to Year 6. The bill was the first step in major curriculum and assessment reforms of Swedish primary and secondary education, which were fully implemented as of 2011. It followed up on the green paper's critique of the national testing programme having too many purposes, suggesting that 'the test system should primarily aim at supporting an equal assessment and fair grading, and provide a basis for analysing the extent to which knowledge requirements are reached at school level, at municipality level and at national level' (p. 19). Year 3 tests, however, were to 'provide support in the teacher's work with the students' learning' and were perceived as 'an important tool for teachers, schools and school principals in assessing the need for support efforts when it comes to developing activities in the direction of national goals' (Ministry of Education and Research, 2008b, pp. 4–5).

In the reform document *Knowledge Assessment in School* (NAE, 2011), the executive agency provided guidance material for the 2011 reform. Here, two sets of purposes were identified for the national tests, which relates to the certification and governing roles, while it was added that national tests can also contribute to 'specify the curriculum' and 'an improved goal attainment for students' (p. 54). These additional prospects of the tests can be related to the support role; however, it is unclear what is implied by the support role not being listed as a 'main' purpose. This way of addressing the tests' purposes has been sustained (in almost identical phrases) on the NAE website since then (NAE, 2017).

Bill *2011-12:1* presented the priorities for the new reform in the national budget for 2012, addressing concerns over the comparability of teachers' grading. Later in 2011, the Ministry of Education and Research commissioned the NAE to 'quality assure national tests so that they can be better used than today to assess the development of knowledge over time' (p. 1). Thus, the government further strengthened the emphasis on the governing role of the national tests. In its report on the commissioned quality assurance of the national tests, NAE (2012) addressed its concerns over conflicting purposes of the national tests that would arise if one continued to strengthen the emphasis on the tests' governing role.

SOU2014:12 criticised the national tests for having many different purposes and suggested that an 'investigation should focus on clarifying the purposes that can and should be linked to the system, which instruments should be linked to the respective purposes and what actors' need for information the different instruments should respond to' (p. 19).

Reporting on yet another commissioned quality assurance of the national tests, NAE (2014) discussed the tests' incapacity to serve as a trend measure instrument, due to the importance of 'wideness' in form and content required for serving a role in (content) steering and grading. As such, the NAE report identified a principal conflict between the two main roles (see Discussion).

National testing and grading policies were disputed political issues in the election campaign of 2014. Following the change of government in October 2014, the new Minister of Education and Research from the Green Party announced that the national tests in social science-oriented subjects and natural science-oriented subjects in Year 6 would become voluntary starting in spring 2015. This reduction of the national testing programme reflected the new governments' greater scepticism of national testing.

The previous government had commissioned a thorough review of the national testing programme, and the outcome of the review, *SOU2016:25*, outlined a new knowledge assessment system for the new government to consider. The proposal suggested that national tests would be only *one* component of the knowledge assessment system and have only *one* purpose:

> To strengthen an equal grading and the legal rights of students, we propose that the national tests' purposes shall be to support the grading. Equality and legal rights are important because grades are so important for the individual, especially in Year 9 and upper secondary school, where admission to different courses often takes place based on the grades. (p. 233)

The report suggested further reducing the number of national tests by terminating the tests in social science-oriented subjects and natural science-oriented subjects in Year 9 and replacing these with a voluntarily 'grade supporting national assessment support' (*betygsstödjande nationella bedömningsstöd*). Furthermore, the report suggested that in primary education, there should be a mandatory 'diagnostic national assessment support' (*diagnostiska nationella bedömningsstöd*), the purpose of which should be 'to provide support, diagnostic or formative' (Ibid). It is not clarified, however, how the governing role would be associated with the respective components of the new knowledge assessment system.

In the reports *SOU2016:38* and *SOU2017:35*, a school commission, established by the newly elected government, provided comprehensive recommendations for policy changes following the critique addressed in an OECD (2015) report. The commission emphasised the critique from the OECD, which called for a coherent monitoring and evaluation system:

> Results on national tests and grades are reported at national level, municipality level and school level, but these are not appropriate instruments to monitor results development over time … There is also, as the OECD points out, generally insufficient habits in many schools' work with quality development to systematically use data that reflects students' knowledge development. (SOU2016:28, p. 129)

The commission followed the recommendations of the green paper *SOU2016:25* and proposed that 'the purpose of the national tests should be streamlined to support a fair and equal grading' (SOU 2016:28, p. 24). This was also stressed in the conclusive report, *SOU2017:35*, where the commission emphasised that there was a need for 'a coherent monitoring and evaluation system' (p. 30) based on outcome information beyond what grades and the national tests provide. Although these new reform deliberations are currently undertaken, to date, the NAE still operates with the definition of purposes of the national tests that was formulated in the preparations of the 2011 reform (NAE, 2017).

Purposes of assessment emphasised by Swedish policy-makers (2013)

When interviewed, the political adviser to the Swedish Minister of Education and Research from the Liberal Party, who was responsible for the expansion of the national testing programme, stated that 'the most important subjects should have support in grading to ensure equivalence or at least improve the chances of ensuring equivalence' (Swedish education ministry politician). The political adviser was concerned with the need for stronger control of the market-based education system:

> One is tempted to demonstrate that one is a good school, to market oneself, and then it is a certain help to have higher grades, unfortunately ... However, we think the advantages of free choice are greater than the disadvantages. (Swedish education ministry politician)

The political adviser continued advocating for 'free choice' despite certain disadvantages related to grade inflation, emphasising 'the need to get at that tendency', pointing out that the ministry had given the national agencies 'the task of keeping track of grade inflation and investigating how we can terminate it' (Swedish education ministry politician). While the problems of grade inflation concern the *certification* role, they also prompt a challenge for *governing* related to the market-based education system.

The general director of the NAE pointed to the recent increase in the number of national tests and the number of subjects that are tested, which the Parliament and government had decided:

> How do we ensure that the tests become useful for students' gathering of knowledge and learning? How do we ensure that they are as useful for the teachers as possible? (NAE general director)

Following up on these rhetorical questions, the general director emphasised the importance of supporting teachers in taking responsibility for professional practices. Thus, by emphasising teachers' instruction, the general director first strongly advocated for the instruments' support role. The general director continued to emphasise two official purposes of the national tests that corresponded to Swedish legislation and the website's defined purposes:

> One purpose is to contribute to students' increased knowledge. Another purpose is to ensure equal grading. It is sometimes hard to achieve both, and our ambition is obviously to find the right balance so that the governments and Parliament's intentions are achieved. (NAE general director)

Thus, referring to the official legislative purposes, the director emphasised the governing and certification roles. The director observed that a change in emphasis between these purposes occurred over the past decade:

> If one can see a shift in the legislation and regulations that the government and Parliament state, there has been more focus on equivalent grading compared to earlier, but one has consistently balanced between these two. And the government and Parliament have consistently intended to achieve both at the same time, and this is difficult. (NAE general director)

The assessment division director of the NAE observed an increased emphasis on publishing the results of national tests in recent years. Furthermore, the assessment division director experienced increased emphasis on the comparability of the tests from one year to another:

> There is a political demand for the tests to be equally difficult from one year to another, so that it is possible to measure the outcomes. (NAE assessment division director)

This reflects increased emphasis on the tests' role in governing education. The assessment division director expressed concerns that it is difficult to meet these expectations due to the way in which the national tests are constructed.

Discussion: the accumulation of assessment purposes in the legitimation of national testing

The study identified substantial similarities and differences in the countries' national testing policies during the investigated period. Both in Norway and Sweden, the national tests were motivated by a need for better information about students' outcomes to be used to *govern* education. Furthermore, both countries increased the emphasis on the use of the tests to *support* learning and instruction. This can be related to a transnational emphasis on formative assessment and to national Assessment *for* Learning efforts in both countries (Tveit, 2018). What separates the countries is that, in Sweden, the tests also have an important role in the *certification* of learning and instruction, which Norway 'flirted' with yet abandoned. In the next sections, I discuss how the emphasis on multiple and conflicting roles of educational assessment posed substantial challenges to Norwegian and Swedish policy-makers, respectively.

The integration of governing and support roles in Norway

The analysis of the Norwegian case illuminates that policy-makers had not thoroughly discussed potential uses of the national testing programme beyond the governing role. While not ultimately implemented, both the government commission and the Ministry of Education outlined the national tests' potential to be used for certification purposes. Other studies have also observed uncertainty as to the potential use of the tests and the purposes they should have (Skedsmo, 2010).

The changes undertaken for the national testing programme during the one-year moratorium in 2006 were related to the strong critique of the initial testing programme, both from researchers and stakeholders. Between 36 and 45% of the students boycotted the tests in upper secondary education in spring 2005, jeopardising the validity of the assessment data (Tveit, 2014; Hølleland, 2007). The scientific quality of the 2004 and 2005 tests were scrutinised (Lie, 2007; Lie, Hopfenbeck, Ibsen, & Turmo, 2005). While the teachers' union did not officially back the boycott, many teachers did, and the union advocated strongly for discontinuing the publication of results (Hølleland, 2007). Elstad (2009) observed that this first implementation led to 'shaming and blaming' league tables in Norwegian newspapers which put pressure on teachers and school leaders.

Following the 2005 parliamentary election, the new government and the Socialist Party was given a mandate from the electorate to change the testing programme. As the state secretary addressed in the interview, the new government wanted the tests to be 'suitable as a pedagogical tool' (see Analysis section). This is not straightforward, however. It implies that the tests should be available to teachers and students after they have been taken so that teachers can obtain information about what types of tasks the students have and have not succeeded in, thereby forming a basis for follow-up. This implies that the items cannot be reused, which in turn imperils the monitoring of students' attainment over time. The latter was a key intention with the testing programme's role in governing the education system at the national, municipality and school level. This dilemma of integrating governing and support roles was finally settled in 2014, by the inclusion of anchor items (a set of items not made available to teachers afterwards and which can thus be repeated each year), more than 10 years after this key purpose was raised. This delay can be explained by the strengthened emphasis on the tests' support role from 2006 onwards, which – in the policy-making – somewhat overshadowed the governing role.

Evaluations show that although municipalities and school leaders found the tests useful for decision-making, many teachers reported that the national tests were not helpful for their instruction and provision of feedback on students' learning (Aasen et al., 2012; Allerup, Kovac, Kvåle, Langfeldt, & Skov, 2009; Seland, Vibe, & Hovdhaugen, 2013). Skedsmo (2010) noted that improving individual outcomes 'requires other tools and sources of information, not at least processes of feedback and support by the teachers' (p. 18). Nevertheless, Norwegian authorities continue to emphasise the formative use of national tests.

Based on interviews with key experts associated with implementing the accountability policies in Norway, Hatch (2013) noted that some scholars may describe the policies as "half-way accountability". He perceived the struggles to implement the national testing programme as demonstrating

> the difficulties of navigating the tensions between promoting two key aspects of accountability—answerability for the achievement of short-term goals and responsibility for the fulfilment of broader purposes—and the challenges of building capacity for both. (Hatch (2013), p. 113)

Hatch (2013) argued that the policy interventions undertaken in 2005–2006 express a compromise between responsibility and answerability: 'Moving the tests suggested instead that the tests should be used in a monitoring capacity to provide teachers and schools with information to guide their instruction of students' (p. 126).

It can be argued that, if a pure governing role was prioritised, the tests should have been sustained as exit tests because this would provide more direct information to teachers, schools and municipalities regarding the attainment levels of the students and thus hold both educators and municipalities accountable for their own students' outcomes. The transition from exit tests to entrance tests instead implied a shift from emphasis on educational outcomes to the (student) input that forms the basis for teachers' instruction and schools' educational provision.

The Swedish case demonstrates substantial challenges associated with the integration of certification and governing roles in a single instrument (discussed below). Norway's shift to include a support role effectively terminated the tests' capacity to be assigned a certification role. This may have spared the national testing programme in Norway from purpose conflicts associated with the integration of certification and governing roles that continue to pose challenges to Swedish policy-makers.

The integration of governing and certification roles in Sweden

Lundahl (2009) noted that the official purposes of national testing in Sweden emerged in an ambiguous fashion. The conservative coalition government implemented comprehensive assessment reforms that expanded both the national testing programme and its purposes. The focus on the comparability of assessments, in relation to both the certification and governing roles, significantly increased.

The general director's reference to the formal purposes is consistent with the NAE's official expression of the purpose of the national tests on its website, which primarily emphasised the certification and governing roles. The third purpose, addressed on the executive agency's website and in the first remark by its general director, indicates that more emphasis on the support role became important for NAE in response to the expansion of the testing programme. Thus, it can be alleged that emphasis was put on the support role (formative use of summative tests) to legitimise the expansion of conventional tests that primarily serve certification and governing roles.

Grade inflation was a major public concern in Sweden (Gustafsson & Erickson, 2013; Wikström, 2005; Wikström & Wikström, 2005). The political adviser to the Minister of Education was concerned with the grade inflation critique. The Ministry's commissioning of the Swedish School Inspectorate (SSI) to supervise and remark national tests (Novak & Carlbaum, 2017) can be interpreted in view of the tests' role in the certification of individual students because the tests form a significant part of the evidence that is the basis for teachers' determination of students' overall subject grades.

The certification role also received increased attention due to the emergence of a market-based school system (Rönnberg, 2011) in which independent schools were observed to be more lenient in their grading than public schools (Wikström & Wikström, 2005). In a marked-based education system, grades work as a currency (Baird, 2013) that needs strong regulations.

When national tests have both governing and certification roles, it puts a stronger pressure on teachers' grading practices. Teachers are not only evaluated with respect to their teaching; they are also held accountable for their capacity to meet *the standard for holding students accountable* (comparability of grading). Not only are the students' outcomes high stakes for the students (the certification role) and for the schools (the governing role), but the process of determining levels of attainment itself is a high-stakes procedure for teachers and schools. This synergy between the certification and governing roles associated with national testing undermines the public trust in teachers and threatens the teaching profession's credibility and autonomy.

Despite the critique of the emphasis on too many purposes in *SOU2007:28*, the former government emphasised all three roles of educational assessment when motivating the expansion of the national testing programme (Bill *2008-09:87*). Following the change of government in 2014, and in response to policy reviews which criticised the excessive range of purposes, government commissions proposed to restrict the purposes of the national tests to one designated purpose. Gustafsson, Cliffordson, and Erickson (2014) proposed implementing new sample-based approaches to better serve the governing demands, while designing the national tests solely to improve the comparability of teachers' grading. According to Erickson (2017), procedures for developing a common framework for test development are currently undertaken to better ensure that the national tests and overall knowledge assessment system serve their purposes. It is yet to be seen, however, whether and how the government ultimately proposes to reconfigure the purposes of the national testing programme.

Conclusion: (over)ambitious emphasis on support causing ambiguous policies

The empirical investigation of 17 years of policy-making in Norway and Sweden demonstrates how politicians and government officials have pushed the official purposes of the national tests in all directions: to certify, govern and support learning and instruction. It can be questioned whether the increased transnational emphasis on formative assessment, manifested through national Assessment *for* Learning efforts in both countries, can be well served in national testing programmes that primarily have a conventional certification and/or governing purpose. Furthermore, the study illuminates a need for more critical investigation into how the roles of educational assessment can be integrated and balanced in national states' overall assessment policies, of which national tests are only one element.

The distinction between assessments used to *govern*, *certify* and *support* learning and instruction captured country differences that could not have been well accounted for using the conventional binary summative and formative assessment distinction. The framework's classification of three roles of educational assessment has the potential to be useful for researching assessment policies in countries and contexts beyond the Scandinavian region.

Notes

1. For a more elaborated overview of the Norwegian and Swedish examination and testing traditions, see Tveit (2018).
2. The DET also provides quality assured 'grade-supporting tests' that can be used as basis for grading students' overall achievement ('standpunkt'). These are however voluntarily, as opposed to the national tests. National examination grades are reported separately on the students' transcripts. Norwegian teachers thus have full autonomy with respect to the evidence produced to determine students' overall achievement grades (standpunkt), which form more than 80% of the students' transcripts.
3. Note also that in both countries, the executive agency provides schools with mapping tests to be used to identify students with special needs using an intervention limit. This analysis is however restricted to the national testing programmes that all students are required to sit.
4. For a comprehensive theoretical discussion, including a more elaborated analysis of Scriven's (1967) distinction between formative and summate evaluation that forms the basis of the analytical framework, cf. Tveit (2017), August.
5. For Norway, the study starts with the government's nomination of a committee in 2001, which was commissioned to evaluate and propose a new framework for a comprehensive approach to quality assessment in primary and secondary education. For Sweden, the study starts with the NAE's Quality Investigation of 2000, which identified several weaknesses of the national testing programme.
6. 'Formål nasjonale prøver' [Purpose national tests] and 'Syfte nationella prov' [Purpose national tests] were the only codes used, upon which a qualitative analysis of the established content was undertaken. Thus, the coding was not part of a quantitative content analysis. As the coding was not intended used in a quantitative analysis upon which classification of concepts is pivotal for the ultimate outcome, co-coding (with other scholars) was not undertaken. It would also have been beyond the research study's scope and financial premises to involve more researchers in the coding.
7. The Norwegian case analysis includes quotes from the 13 policy documents in Norway, which were translated into English, counting (merely) 950 words. The Swedish case analysis includes quotes from the 31 Swedish policy documents, which were translated into English, counting 7340 words. For each case, a comprehensive narrative describing the 'elaborated story' of the policy-making was developed in interaction with empirical case documents. The full Norwegian narrative spanned 2968 words, while the full Swedish narrative spanned 6100 words. These narratives were ultimately reduced to about 1200 and 1400 words, respectively—the analysis sections of the present paper—to meet the requirements of the journal. Both the initial rich data-set for both cases, and the reduced policy texts determined to be relevant, can be obtained from the author upon request.

8. In 2008 the Swedish Ministry of Education and Research commissioned its executive agency (NAE) and inspection agency (SSI) to control schools' grading practices (Bill, *2008-09:87*). Since 2009, the SSI has supervised and remarked selected schools' grading practices, while annual reports from the NAE have reported on the comparability of national test scores and final subject grades. To meet the journals length requirements, the analysis of these commissioning letters and reports are not reported.
9. Cf. Acknowledgements.
10. State secretary, in the Scandinavian context, is the Minister's closest associate (a deputy Minister) and part of the political leadership of the Ministry. Typically the political leadership of a Ministry includes two state secretaries and a political adviser, all of whom appointed to support the Minister.
11. DET's official translation of the concept of '*underveisvurdering*' is 'formative assessment'; however, this translation may confuse both the legal and practical interpretations of this concept.

Acknowledgements

The article reports on the PhD project Assessment and Selection in the Scandinavian Education Systems (ASSESS), undertaken at the Department of Education, University of Oslo. The author is indebted to members of the university's research group Curriculum Studies, Leadership and Educational Governance (CLEG) and to members of the research group Studies in Educational Policy and Educational Philosophy (STEP) at Uppsala University, for their comments on an early version of the manuscript. Furthermore, the author is indebted to the Department of Education, University of Agder, particularly its research group Didactics, for providing research facilities and comments on the manuscript during the completion of the PhD project. Further, the author expresses his appreciation to Professor Rolf Vegar Olsen and Associate Professor Tine S. Prøitz for their comments on the raw analysis of the Norwegian case, to Associate Professor Christina Wikström and Professor Christian Lundahl for their comments on the Swedish case, and to the special issue editors and reviewers for their valuable suggestions for improving the accuracy of the analysis and the overall quality of the manuscript.

Disclosure statement

No potential conflict of interest was reported by the author.

ORCID

Sverre Tveit (iD) http://orcid.org/0000-0002-8789-1322

References

Aasen, P., Møller, J., Rye, E., Ottesen, E., Prøitz, T. S., & Hertzberg, F. (2012). *Kunnskapsløftet som styringsform – et løft eller et løfte?* [The knowledge promotion as governance – a lift or a promise?] (Report No. 20/2012). Oslo: NIFU.

Allerup, P. V., Kovac, G., Kvåle, G., Langfeldt, G., & Skov, P. (2009). *Evaluering av det Nasjonale Kvalitetsvurderingssystemet for grunnopplæringen* [Evaluation of the national system for quality assessment in primary and secondary education]. Kristiansand: Agderforskning.

Assessment Reform Group (2002). *Assessment for learning: 10 principles: Research-based principles to guide classroom practice.* London: Assessment Reform Group.

Baird, J.-A. (2013). The currency of assessments. *Assessment in Education: Principles, Policy & Practice, 20*(2), 147–149. doi:10.1080/0969594X.2013.787782

Bennett, R. E. (2011). Formative assessment: A critical review. *Assessment in Education: Principles, Policy & Practice, 18*(1), 5–25. doi:10.1080/0969594X.2010.513678

Bill (2008-09:87). *Tydligare mål och kunskapskrav – nya läroplaner för skolan* [Clearer goals and knowledge requirements].

Bill (2009-10:219). *Betyg från årskurs 6 i grundskolan* [Grades from Year 6].

Bill (2011/12:1). *Budgetpropositionen för 2012. Utbildning och universitetsforskning* [Budget bill for 2012. Education and university research].

Black, P. (1998). *Testing: Friend or foe?* London, England: Falmer Press.

Black, P., & Wiliam, D. (1998). Assessment and classroom learning. *Assessment in Education: Principles, Policy & Practice, 5*(1), 7–74. doi:10.1080/0969595980050102

Bloom, B. S., Hasting, J. T., & Madaus, G. F. (1971). *Handbook on formative and summative evaluation of student learning.* New York, NY: McGraw-Hill.

Burner, T. (2014). The potential formative benefits of portfolio assessment in second and foreign language writing contexts: A review of the literature. *Studies in Educational Evaluation, 43*(4), 139–149. doi:10.1016/j.stueduc.2014.03.002

Burner, T. (2016). Formative assessment of writing in English as a foreign language. *Scandinavian Journal of Educational Research, 60*(6), 626–648. doi:10.1080/00313831.2015.1066430

DET. (2010). *Rammeverk for nasjonale prøver* [The national testing framework]. Oslo: Directorate for Education and Training.

DET. (2014). *Vurdering for Læring* [Assessment for learning]. Oslo: The Directorate for Education and Training.

DET. (2016). *Metodisk grunnlag for de nasjonale prøvene* [Methodological basis for the national tests]. Oslo: Directorate for Education and Training.

DET. (2017). *Rammeverk for nasjonale prøver* [The national testing framework]. Oslo: Directorate for Education and Training.

Dexter, L. A. (2006). *Elite and specialized interviewing.* Colchester: ECPR Press. (Original work published 1970).

Elstad, E. (2009). Schools which are named, shamed and blamed by the media: School accountability in Norway. *Educational Assessment, Evaluation and Accountability, 21*(2), 173–189.

Erickson, G. (2017). Experiences with standards and criteria in Sweden. In S. Blömeke & J.-E. Gustafsson (Eds.), *Standard setting in education. The Nordic countries in an international perspective* (pp. 123–142). Cham: Springer.

Gamlem, S. M. (2015). Feedback to support learning: Changes in teachers' practice and beliefs. *Teacher Development, 19*(4), 461–482. doi:10.1080/13664530.2015.1060254

Gamlem, S. M., & Smith, K. (2013). Student perceptions of classroom feedback. *Assessment in Education: Principles, Policy & Practice, 20*(2), 150–169. doi:10.1080/0969594X.2012.749212

Gustafsson, J.-E., Cliffordson, C., & Erickson, G. (2014). *Likvärdig kunskapsbedömning i och av den svenska skolan – problem och möjligheter* [Equal assessment in and of the Swedish school system: Problems and potentials]. Stockholm: SNS Utbildningskommission.

Gustafsson, J.-E., & Erickson, G. (2013). To trust or not to trust? – teacher marking versus external marking of national tests. *Educational Assessment, Evaluation and Accountability, 25*(1), 69–87.

Hatch, T. (2013). Beneath the surface of accountability: Answerability, responsibility and capacity-building in recent education reforms in Norway. *Journal of Educational Change, 14*(2), 113–138.

Herman, J. L., & Baker, E. L. (2009). Assessment policy: Making sense of the babel. In G. Sykes, B. Schneider, & D. Plank (Eds.), *AERA handbook on education policy.* Newbury Park, London: Sage.

Hølleland, H. (2007). Nasjonale prøver og kvalitetsutvikling i skolen [National tests and quality development in school]. In S. Tveit (Ed.), *Elevvurdering i skolen – grunnlag for kulturendring* [Student assessment in school: A basis for change of culture] (pp. 22–43). Oslo, Norway: Universitetsforlaget.

Hopfenbeck, T. N., Flórez Petour, M. T., & Tolo, A. (2015). Balancing tensions in educational policy reforms: Large-scale implementation of Assessment for Learning in Norway. *Assessment in Education: Principles, Policy & Practice, 22*(1), 44–60. doi:10.1080/0969594X.2014.996524

Jonsson, A., Lundahl, C., & Holmgren, A. (2015). Evaluating a large-scale implementation of assessment for learning in Sweden. *Assessment in Education: Principles, Policy & Practice, 22*(1), 104–121. doi:10.1080/0969594X.2014.970612

Krippendorff, K. (2004). *Content analysis: An introduction to its methodology.* Thousand Oaks, CA: Sage.

Lie, S. (2007). Evalueringen av nasjonale prøver og hva vi kan lære av dem [The evaluation of national tests and what we can learn from them]. In S. Tveit (Ed.), *Elevvurdering i skolen – grunnlag for kulturendring* [Student assessment in school: A basis for change of culture] (pp. 74–84). Oslo, Norway: Universitetsforlaget.

Lie, S., Hopfenbeck, T. N., Ibsen, E., & Turmo, A. (2005). *Nasjonale prøver på ny prøve* [National tests retested]. Oslo: Department of Teacher Education and School Research, University of Oslo.

Lundahl, C. (2009). *Varför nationella prov? – framväxt, dilemma, utmaningar* [Why the national test? History, dilemma, challenges]. Lund: Studentlitteratur AB.

Ministry of Education and Research. (2004). *Uppdrag til Statens Skolverk avseende det nationella provsystemet* [Commission to the national agency for education regarding the national testing system]. Stockholm.

Ministry of Education and Research. (2005). *Uppdrag til Statens Skolverk om nationella prov och diagnostisk stödmaterial* [Commission to the national agency for education regarding national tests and diagnostic support materials]. Stockholm.

Ministry of Education and Research. (2008a). *Regleringsbrev för budgetåret 2008 avseende Statens skolverk* [Regulation letter for the 2008 fiscal year regarding the National Agency for Education]. Stockholm.

Ministry of Education and Research. (2008b). *Departementspromemoria. En individuell utvecklingsplan med skriftliga omdömen* [Ministry memorandum. More compulsory national tests in primary and lower secondary school]. Stockholm.

Ministry of Education. (2011). *Uppdrag om nationella prov* [Commission regarding national tests]. Stockholm.

NAE. (2000). *Nationella kvalitetsgranskningar* [National quality audits]. Stockholm: National Agency for Education.

NAE. (2001). *Bedömning och betygssätnning. Kommentarar med frågor och svar* [Assessment and grading. Comments with questions and answers]. Stockholm: National Agency for Education.

NAE. (2002). *Betygssättning vid 18 fristående skolor* [Grading practices in 18 independent schools]. Stockholm: National Agency for Education.

NAE. (2004). *Handlingsplan för en rättssäker och likvärdig betygssättning* [Action plan for fair and equal grading]. Stockholm: National Agency for Education.

NAE. (2007). *Provbetyg – Slutbetyg – Likvärdig bedömning? En statistisk analys av sambandet mellan nationella prov och slutbetyg i grundskolans årskurs 9, 1998-2006* [Test grades – Final grades – Equality. A statistical analysis of the relationship between national test grades and final grades in year 9, 1998–2006]. Stockholm: National Agency for Education.

NAE. (2008). *Mål och nationella prov i årskurs 3* [Goals and national tests in year 3]. Stockholm: National Agency for Education.

NAE (2009a). *Förslag på hur det nationella provsystemet bör utvecklas och utformas* [Proposal for how the national testing system should be developed and designed]. Stockholm: National Agency for Education.

NAE (2009b). *Nationella prov årskurs 3* [Nationel tests for year 3]. Stockholm: National Agency for Education.

NAE. (2011). *Kunnskapsbedömning i skolan* [Knowledge assessment in school]. Stockholm: National Agency for Education.

NAE. (2012). *Uppdrag om kvalitetssäkring av nationella prov* [Commissoned quality assurance of the national tests]. Stockholm: National Agency for Education.

NAE. (2014). *Uppdrag om kvalitetssäkring av nationella prov* [Commissoned quality assurance of the national tests]. Stockholm: National Agency for Education.

NAE. (2017). *Nationella prov* [Nationella prov]. Stockholm: National Agency for Education. Retrieved from https://www.skolverket.se/bedomning/nationella-prov

Newton, P. (2007). Clarifying the purposes of educational assessment. *Assessment in Education: Principles, Policy & Practice, 14*(2), 149–170.

NOU (Government Official Report). (2002:10). *Første klasses fra første klasse. Forslag til rammeverk for et nasjonalt kvalitetsvurderingssystem av norsk grunnopplæring* [Proposed national quality assessment framework for primary and secondary education]. Oslo: Ministry of Education and Research.

NOU (Government Official Report). (2003:16). *I første rekke. Forsterket kvalitet i grunnopplæringen for alle* [A better education for all]. Oslo: Ministry of Education and Research.

Novak, J., & Carlbaum, S. (2017). Juridification of examination systems: Extending state level authority over teacher assessments through regrading of national tests. *Journal of Educational Policy, 32*(5), 673–693. doi:10.1080/02680939.2017.1318454

Organisation for Economic Co-operation and Development (2015). *Improving schools in Sweden: An OECD perspective*. Paris: Author.

Report to the Parliament 30. (2003–2004). (2004-04-02). *Kultur for læring* [Culture for learning]. Oslo: Ministry of Education and Research.

Report to the Parliament 16. (2006–2007). *... og ingen stod igjen. Tidlig innsats for livslang læring* [Early efforts for lifelong learning]. Oslo: Ministry of Education and Research.

Report to the Parliament 31. (2007–2008). *Kvalitet i skolen* [Quality in schools]. Oslo: Ministry of Education and Research.

Report to the Parliament 19. (2009–2010). *Tid til læring* [Time for learning]. Oslo: Ministry of Education and Research.

Report to the Parliament 22. (2010–2011) (2011-04-29). *Motivasjon – mestring – muligheter* [Motivation, mastery – Opportunities]. Oslo: Ministry of Education and Research.

Report to the Parliament 20. (2012–2013). *På rett vei* [On the right track]. Oslo: Norwegian Ministry of Education and Research.

Report to the Parliament 28. (2015–2016). *Fag – fordypning – forståelse - en fornyelse av kunnskapsløftet* [A renewal of the knowledge promotion]. Oslo: Norwegian Ministry of Education and Research.

Rönnberg, L. (2011). Exploring the intersection of Marketisation and Central State control through Swedish national school inspection. *Education Inquiry, 2*(4), 689–707.

Scriven, M. (1967). The methodology of evaluation. In R. W. Tyler, R. M. Gagne, & M. Scriven (Eds.), *Perspectives of curriculum evaluation* (Vol. 1, pp. 39–83). Chicago, IL: Rand McNally, American Educational Research Association Monograph Series on Curriculum Evaluation.

Seland, I., Vibe, N., & Hovdhaugen, E. (2013). *Evaluering av nasjonale prøver som system* [Evaluation of the national tests as a system]. Oslo: NIFU.

Skedsmo, G. (2010). Formulation and realisation of evaluation policy: 'Inconsistencies and problematic issues'. *Educational Assessment, Evaluation and Accountability, 23*(1), 5–20. doi:10.1007/s11092-010-9110-2

SOU (Official Government Report). (2007:28). *Tydliga mål och kunskapskrav i grundskolan. Förslag till nytt mål- och uppföljningssystem* [Clear goals and knowledge requirements in primary and lower secondary schools. Proposal for a new system for goal monitoring and follow-up]. Stockholm: Fritzes.

SOU (Official Government Report). (2014:12). *Utvärdera för utveckling – om utvärdering av skolpolitiska reformer* [Evaluate for development – On evaluation of school policy reforms]. Stockholm: Fritzes.

SOU (Official Government Report). (2016:25). *Likvärdigt, rättssäkert och effektivt – ett nytt nationellt system för kunskapsbedömning* [Equal, legal, and effective – A new national knowledge assessment system]. Stockholm: Fritzes.

SOU (Official Government Report). (2016:38). *Samling för skolan. Nationella målsättningar och utvecklingsområden för kunskap och likvärdighet. Delbetänkande* [Gathering for the school. National objectives and development areas for knowledge and equivalence. Interim report]. Stockholm: Fritzes.

SOU (Official Government Report). (2017:35). *Samling för skolan. Nationella målsättningar och utvecklingsområden för kunskap och likvärdighet. Slutbetänkande* [Gathering for the school – National strategy for knowledge and equivalence]. Stockholm: Fritzes.

Stobart, G. (2008). *Testing times: The uses and abuses of assessment.* London: Routledge.

Swedish Parliament. (2006:19). *Översyn av grundskolans mål- och uppföljningssystem m.m. Kommittédirektiv* [Review of primary and secondary schools' goal and monitoring systems, etc. Committee Directive]. Stockholm.

Tveit, S. (2014). Educational assessment in Norway. *Assessment in Education: Principles, Policy & Practice, 21*(2), 221–237. doi:10.1080/0969594X.2013.830079

Tveit, S. (2017, August). *50 years' legacy of formative and summative evaluation and assessment: A critical theoretical review of education policy and research.* Paper presented at the European Conference on Educational Research, Copenhagen, Denmark. Abstract retrieved from http://www.eera-ecer.de/ecer-programmes/conference/22/contribution/41939/

Tveit, S. (2018). (Trans)national trends and cultures of educational assessment: Reception and resistance of national testing in Sweden and Norway during the twentieth century. In C. Alarcon, & M. Lawn (Eds.), *Assessment Cultures.* Bern: Peter Lang.

Wikström, C. (2005). Grade stability in a criterion-referenced grading system: The Swedish example. *Assessment in Education: Principles, Policy & Practice, 12*(2), 125–144. doi:10.1080/09695940500143811

Wikström, C., & Wikström, M. (2005). Grade inflation and school competition: An empirical analysis based on the Swedish upper secondary schools. *Economics of Education Review, 24*(3), 309–322. doi:10.1016/j.econedurev.2004.04.01

Index